HEEDING THE CALL

WILLIAM JOLLIFF

Heeding the Call

A Study of Denise Giardina's Novels

West Virginia University Press / Morgantown

Copyright © 2020 by West Virginia University Press
All rights reserved
First edition published 2020 by West Virginia University Press
Printed in the United States of America

ISBN
Cloth 978-1-949199-42-0
Paper 978-1-949199-43-7
Ebook 978-1-949199-44-4

Library of Congress Cataloging-in-Publication Data
Names: Jolliff, William, author.
Title: Heeding the call : a study of Denise Giardina's novels / William Jolliff.
Description: First edition. | Morgantown : West Virginia University Press, 2020. | Includes bibliographical references and index.
Identifiers: LCCN 2019039062 | ISBN 9781949199420 (cloth) | ISBN 9781949199437 (paperback) | ISBN 9781949199444 (ebook)
Subjects: LCSH: Giardina, Denise, 1951—Criticism and interpretation.
Classification: LCC PS3557.I136 Z66 2020 | DDC 813/.54—dc23
LC record available at https://lccn.loc.gov/2019039062

Book and cover design by Than Saffel / WVU Press
Cover portrait of Denise Giardina by Robert Shetterly, 2007, for inclusion in his Americans Who Tell the Truth portrait project (www.americanswhotellthetruth.org).

For Brenda, Jacob Henry, Rebecca Peace, and Anna Fulton

For we wrestle not against flesh and blood, but against principalities, against powers, against the rulers of the darkness of this world, against spiritual wickedness in high places.

Ephesians 6:12

Contents

Preface xi

1. Called to Mystery: Place, Politics, and a Life of Faith 1
2. *Good King Harry*: The Formation and Paradox of a Christian King 21
3. *Storming Heaven*: Colonization and the Roots of Resistance 50
4. *The Unquiet Earth*: Confronting the Coalfield Apocalypse 84
5. *Saints and Villains*: Conscience, Doubt, and the Call to Action 112
6. *Fallam's Secret*: One True Sermon 139
7. *Emily's Ghost*: The Making of a Giardina Hero 160
8. Conclusion: Facing the Questions, Living with Mystery 185

Notes 191
Bibliography 201
Index 209

Preface

For nearly a decade now, I have been teaching the novels of Denise Giardina in my literature courses at George Fox University. Preparing to discuss her work with determined and motivated students has been a joy, and their insights have invariably enhanced my own. The pages that follow reflect much of what our conversations have taught me.

Discussing the books with concerned, thoughtful readers has naturally directed my focus to facets of the texts that create challenging questions. Although such questions are seldom simple, I have often found that just a bit more consideration of some matter of interpretation, whether historical, formal, or thematic, leads fairly quickly to greater understanding. And with greater understanding comes greater pleasure in reading. The primary purpose of the present book, then, is to explore on the page some of the topics that have arisen in the classroom. In doing so, I will concentrate on Giardina's literary craft while at the same time addressing—not as an expert but as an engaged reader—pertinent aspects of history, culture, politics, and economics.

Just as importantly, classroom discussions have alerted me to significant dimensions of Giardina's fiction that are commonly overlooked. This problem is especially apparent regarding the religious grounding that informs all six of her novels. Many readers who are adept at literary analysis—even those with a background in the social disciplines—may fail to discern the theological force that drives the author's work. Indeed, Giardina has often referred to herself as a theological novelist, but that claim has at times been neglected or ignored. The longer I study and teach Giardina, however, the more I am convinced that her achievement cannot be fully understood, appreciated, and taken to heart without some knowledge of the religious convictions and influences central to her thought. So more than may be usual in a book of literary criticism, theological questions will be part of my exploration.

A secondary purpose of this study is to encourage my fellow critics to give Giardina's books the close attention they deserve. Of the thousands of novels published every year, only a handful will be read by future generations. Giardina's, I believe, should be among them. Even a study like this one, which strives to keep theoretical apparatus to a minimum, will suggest that her oeuvre, though slim by some standards, offers much to admire, much to discuss, and much to critique with care. Though she is well known as an important

Appalachian regionalist, future critical discussion of her contribution will necessarily pay greater attention to the universal themes that pervade her work, themes she handles with a level of craft and gravitas easily overlooked when we are blinded by her sometimes disarming clarity. Her breadth of reading, political acuity, psychological insight, and theological sophistication—along with her storytelling imagination—will repay serious study.

My first chapter presents a brief biographical overview of the author, primarily to underscore her identification with Appalachia. In addition, it offers three categories in which her work may be rightfully considered: regional, political, and theological. A full chapter is then dedicated to each of the novels, addressing historical, formal, and thematic elements. With occasional exceptions, the discussions are more expositional than argumentative, and that has meant including sections on background I believe to be essential to a full understanding. Because I imagine many readers will turn to a given chapter just after finishing the novel considered, I have attempted to write each in such a way that, if necessary, it may be read as a stand-alone piece. Some repetition is therefore inevitable, but I hope it will be tolerated for the sake of making the book more immediately and broadly useful.

I am indebted to many scholars and critics whose work informs my own, and these pages will demonstrate that debt. Several current and former students, too, have given their support by reading parts of the manuscript, among them Jade Becker, Brendan Comiskey, Heather Harney, Ryan Lackey, and Alicia Wolverton. My daughters, both accomplished writers, have been especially helpful. Rebecca Peace read early drafts of several chapters and kindly told me when I was missing the mark. And Anna Fulton turned her critical razor toward excising at least some of the bad habits a professor picks up from talking too long about something he loves. In addition, her background as a therapist was crucial in the completion of chapter 7.

But my deepest debt is to Brenda, my wife of thirty-five years. By doing work I should have been doing, she gave me the space and grace to do this instead.

William Jolliff
March 15, 2019

CHAPTER 1

Called to Mystery: Place, Politics, and a Life of Faith

No contemporary writer has lived a life more closely woven into the complex fabric of West Virginia.

Denise Giardina was born into a mining family whose heritage suggests the many and varied cultural threads of Appalachia. Her paternal grandfather, Sam Giardina, was a Sicilian immigrant who landed in West Virginia searching for economic opportunity, hoping to make a quick fortune and return to Italy. Though he made no fortune, he did find work in the coal mines, married Sara Peduzzi (another Sicilian immigrant), and had five children. But he longed for home. So he moved his wife and family back to Sicily when Denise's father, Dennis, was still a toddler. Times remained difficult there too, however, and Sam could not make a living on the family farm. After eight years of trying, desperate for work, the family returned to settle in McDowell County.[1]

Giardina's maternal forbears were Appalachian natives with deep roots in the mountains of eastern Kentucky. Some had followed the migration through the Appalachians after the Revolutionary War. Others came a half-century later: Quakers fleeing North Carolina during the Civil War, they were seeking freedom to live out their beliefs in a place with abolitionist sympathies. Once in Kentucky they assimilated into the local culture and customs, carving out a life of comfortable self-sufficiency.[2] They logged, farmed, taught school, and made a little liquor; and in time, their lives would inevitably intersect with the coal industry. Giardina's mother, Leona, was born into the fortunes of this large family in the community of Grapevine in Pike County.[3]

So Appalachian culture runs deep in the novelist's blood, and part of that culture is coal. Her grandfather Sam was an underground miner, and one of his sons joined him in the mines. The fate of Giardina's father took a different turn.[4] Through the beneficence of one of his schoolteachers, he was given the chance to leave home and earn a two-year degree in business. With that completed, he returned to the coalfields and became a bookkeeper and later a personnel manager at Page Coal and Coke. On her mother's side, her grandfather worked for a time as a manager at a company store and as a mine guard, among other jobs.[5] One of his sons became a miner and another a mining engineer. Giardina's mother had the opportunity to earn a nursing degree and practiced in several capacities.[6] When the children were small, she worked the night shift in a local hospital so that she could care for Denise and her brother during the day. Eventually she took a job with the Public Health Department and worked as a school nurse.

That Giardina's family came from both native and more recent immigrant stock, and that the two lineages would come together in the coalfields, is a good representation of the nature of Appalachian mining culture. Reflecting on the diversity of her childhood, Giardina notes that in McDowell County "there were probably people from a hundred nationalities. So I was always conscious that this thing we call Appalachia is much more complex than was being presented. And yet these were all mountain people; they were all Appalachian."[7]

Her parents' professions gave the Giardina household some financial advantage over most of their fellow residents in the ten-house coal camp of Black Wolf. Though not affluent by contemporary middle-class standards, in their context they were more comfortable than most of their neighbors. They lived in a standard four-room, company-owned house, but a fifth room was added on; and they were not bound to worry about the next meal like many of their friends and kin who worked underground. Even as a child, Giardina was aware of this slight privilege: "We were just really lucky," she notes, "and I was always a little guilty about that."[8] But she was also aware that their daily life was far from that of the coal company executives, like the superintendent whose big house sat up on the hill. She learned early of class distinctions and of the tenuous existence of mining families.

Though coal camp life was hard, even poor, Black Wolf proved to be a rich place for a writer to grow up. Giardina's first thirteen years would provide the tenor and details of her eventual portrayals of life in mining country: the threads that ran through the company town, the textures that would later weave their way through the coal camp communities of her novels, were lasting and strong. Giardina remembers Black Wolf as a place where "people's lives in all their quirky variety were lived in full view of their neighbors, where stark good and evil showed their face with some frequency, and at the same time moral ambiguity could be readily noticeable even by a small child."[9] It was a childhood that instilled good and bad memories, many of them related to the mines. She recalls her uncle, like thousands of other miners, dying of black lung, "literally drowning in his hospital bed."[10] Her next-door neighbor was crushed to death in a mining machine. Another neighbor was a sometimes violent alcoholic, self-medicating for the chronic back pain caused by a mining injury. Many of her schoolmates lost their fathers in the mines.[11]

Yet Black Wolf was also a place where an imaginative little girl could listen to wonderful stories "while perched upon the bony knees of old men"; or she could idle on her neighbor's porch, listening to the frogs and watching lightning bugs, hearing that same alcoholic spin the traditional tales of the booger man.[12] It was a place where children could run out-of-doors, play with their critters, and ramble among the hills and along the creek. But it was also a place where parents warned them not to wade into the creek: the water was toxic, poisoned by the chemicals seeping from mining refuse piles.[13] For good and for ill, these were her people, and this was her place, and Giardina writes affectionately of life in a company town: "No matter where or when," she noted in an interview with Thomas Douglass, "if you grew up in a coal camp, people looked after each other; you usually had close friends that you could trust; there was a sense of community. But," she added, "there was absolutely no freedom. . . . You can't measure human dignity without freedom."[14] That statement suggests an ethical tension that persists in one form or another throughout Giardina's work, a social consciousness that drives her novels regardless of the particular setting. The seed of her sensitivity was planted early. She remembers her classmates with their blackened teeth, the result of poor nutrition and dental care. She remembers, as a fourth grader, seeing the younger children at school wearing her hand-me-down clothes.[15] She even remembers arguing with her father, whose job included working on behalf of his company to keep miners from compensation to which they were entitled.[16]

Along with her sense of community, her sense of justice, and the sense that her community was being denied something essential, Giardina's literary sensibilities were also developing in Black Wolf. Her Methodist upbringing made the Bible her "basic literary influence,"[17] and its language pervades her work. Significantly too, as an eighth grader she discovered Shakespeare, to whom she refers as "my first love."[18] That was her beginning in McDowell County. But coal mining has never been a stable industry, and there were hard times in the 1960s. When Giardina was thirteen, the camp at Black Wolf closed and her father lost his position. His next job moved the family a hundred miles north.[19] The family's new home was in Kanawha County, near Malden, now part of the Charleston metropolitan area. As might be expected, Giardina was a good student. She read avidly and even had premonitions of becoming a writer, though for her that exotic profession seemed far outside the realm of possibility. Still, she remembers, as a part of an eighth-grade writing assignment, crafting a sentence praised by her teacher—a sentence that later appeared in revised form in *Good King Harry*.[20] Even more prophetically, she recalls in high school reading George Orwell's *Animal Farm* and after that "a lot of Orwell."[21] It is telling that already as a high school student, she was drawn to a novelist who is politically weighty and broadly accessible, traits that would come to characterize Giardina's own work.

After graduating from DuPont High School as a National Merit Scholar finalist, Giardina attended West Virginia Wesleyan College, her attendance made possible in part by a scholarship from the United Methodist Church. But hers was not the typical academic training for a novelist—she studied history and political science. "In college," she notes, "I hardly read fiction. I didn't take a lot of literature classes. I took a class in Shakespeare, but I was reading mostly history, books about the Russian Revolution and Trotsky, and books by John Stuart Mill and Hegel. Most of them I disagreed with, Rousseau and Locke for instance, but the ideas were interesting to me."[22]

By the end of her undergraduate experience, Giardina had also transitioned from the Methodism of her childhood to the Episcopal Church.[23] During a semester of studying abroad in England, she became more interested in the founder of Methodism, John Wesley, and discovered that he always considered himself an Anglican.[24] And even more importantly, she fell in love with the liturgy and theology of the Anglican Church. So once home, she started to worship in a nearby Episcopal congregation.

She had thoughts of attending law school and even took the Law School Admission Test during her senior year, but realized "there was no way I wanted to spend three years studying that stuff."[25] After a variety of clerical jobs her first three years after graduation, she did choose graduate school, but not to study law. Through attending the Episcopal Church, she gained a friend and mentor in the Rev. Jim Lewis, an Episcopal priest whom she places alongside her mother as one of the two most important people in her life."[26] In part due to his influence, she decided to attend Virginia Theological Seminary, sensing a call toward ordination. She was in fact ordained in 1979 but would later realize that writing was her primary life's work, her true vocation, and that her theological education had trained her to consider the important questions that would become the stuff of her fiction.[27]

During her final year at seminary, Giardina lived off campus in Washington, DC, with a group of radical young Christians.[28] This group, Sojourners Fellowship, would later become one of the more high-profile progressive Christian organizations, gaining considerable notoriety by publishing the magazine *Sojourners*. Giardina's association with these politically engaged believers would prove to be important for her faith and for her political understanding. After seminary and a period of activism in Washington, she returned to serve in a church in southern West Virginia. There, however, she found that her engagement in social issues, particularly her criticism of the coal industry, was not welcome. Some parishioners complained to her superiors, and, according to Lewis, "The church double-crossed her. . . . The bishop didn't give her the support he should have."[29] From there she moved back to Washington, where she worked on a peace campaign and lived once again as part of the Sojourners Fellowship. Concerning her time in that community, Giardina reflects, "We were kind of young and self-righteous, but we were really trying to live our faith."[30] And Giardina was also living the life of the writer, drafting her first novel, *Good King Harry*, during lunch breaks from her job at the National Cathedral.[31]

After this period in Washington and spending some time in rural West Virginia, Giardina worked at secretarial jobs in the Charleston offices of various Democratic politicians. It was then that she completed *Good King Harry*. Having already finished a draft of the book, she took a writing class with the poet and novelist George Garrett, who helped her place the novel with a publisher through an agent.[32] With one major piece of historical fiction completed, she turned her attention to the coalfield novels for which she is best known. In fact, even while writing *Good King Harry* she already had the idea simmering for her second novel, *Storming Heaven*. She suspected, however, that a book set in the West Virginia coalfields might be hard to place with a publisher. Indeed, when she pitched the idea to the publishers of *Good King Harry*, her judgment proved to be correct: they weren't interested.[33]

But that did not deter her from writing the novel. It speaks to Giardina's commitment, to the authentic integration of her life and work, that after publishing a first novel she chose to immerse herself once again in a coal camp, this time David, Kentucky. As she explained it, "While writing *Storming Heaven*, I thought it would be beneficial to actually live in a coal camp again."[34] During her time there, she worked with the activist group Kentuckians for the Commonwealth, serving as its secretary-treasurer. The organization managed to get an amendment on the ballot to forbid coal companies from strip mining land they did not own, and their amendment passed with 80 percent of the vote. Giardina refers to that work as "one of the few examples where the people actually stood up to the coal companies. It was a very proud moment."[35] In maintaining her pattern of keeping at least two fires burning, one literary and one political, it was also during her time in David that she was formulating *The Unquiet Earth*.[36]

In 1988 Giardina left the coal camp to see more of the world, this time moving to Durham, North Carolina. In addition, she says that she "wanted to feel homesick."[37] There she worked in a bookstore ("the best job I ever had"[38]) and also took a class at Duke University with Laurel Goldman. The course proved important in her completion of the third novel, and it gave her the confidence to believe she could teach writing.[39] She enjoyed life in Durham, but after three years she felt like she needed to get closer to home again, believing it was there that she could make an impact. She moved to a writer-in-residence position at Appalshop in Whitesburg, Kentucky,[40] then returned to Charleston to teach at West Virginia State College. "I started getting homesick," she states, "and my parents were getting up in years. I felt I could make more of a difference here than in North Carolina."[41]

While the first twenty years of Giardina's adult life may seem to have been somewhat unsettled, a closer consideration reveals that they were a focused interweaving of the continuous threads that are the writer's life. Always, it seems, she was working on a novel, always investing time and energy in progressive causes, and always working out her love for Appalachia. She never lived more than a few hours away from West Virginia, and both in her fiction and her political work, her attention was on concerns relevant to her home state. As she confesses, "I've tried to live other places, but it never works out for very long."[42] In many ways, her situation is typical of many West Virginia natives: dealing with displacement is as much a part of the identity as staying put. Perhaps it is an Appalachian characteristic always to long for home but always to be leaving and returning.

After moving back to Charleston and a position at West Virginia State College in 1991, Giardina finally began a long tenure of teaching and writing. With a third well-published novel on her résumé by 1992 and a place on faculty, one might think that this is when she would become a more typical academic novelist, teaching her courses and then retreating to the office to shut her door and write. But instead, she continued to maintain the public profile of an engaged intellectual. In other words, Giardina kept working hard at being a good citizen who does not mind getting blood on her knuckles. Her love for her home state led her to continue her political action work alongside other activists, and to write about the concerns of the state in high-profile newspapers and magazines. The political aspect of her life's work reached its pinnacle when friends convinced her to run for governor in 2000.

Knowing that she would be overlooked as one more Democratic primary contender, she ran as the Mountain Party candidate. Her realistic purpose was not to get elected—a near-impossibility for any third-party candidate—but to gather public support to combat mountaintop removal, the method of mining she has termed "the environmental counterpoint to the Holocaust."[43] Though a victory was out of the question, her campaign helped call state, national, and international attention to that most disastrous and irreversible of mining practices.[44] Her candidacy made the newspapers in this country and even abroad,[45] and at least a few people started talking about this destructive form of mining. She posed enough of a threat, in fact, that two officials from the Democratic Party, fearing she would draw votes from their candidate, offered her a seat in the legislature if she would quit her campaign, an exchange she recalls as particularly repulsive.[46] Running for governor, overall, was not a good experience. Even for a longtime activist and lover of lost causes, it was disillusioning and draining, physically and emotionally. She did not enjoy public speaking before large crowds, and she did not like chatting at receptions. "Twice on statewide television I got to get up and talk for two minutes on mountaintop removal," she told an interviewer. "A year and a half of work to get to speak for two minutes."[47]

Although she was burned out by the race and demoralized by the process, she has nevertheless maintained her engagement with the concerns of Appalachians, as any search on the internet will indicate. Throughout her twenty-one-year tenure at West Virginia State and since, she has continued as an opinion writer in both local and national newspapers, taking a prophetic stance on issues that concern Appalachia and particularly West Virginia. And her political engagement did not derail her literary work. During her time as a teaching professor, she published her three most recent novels, *Saints and Villains* (1998), *Fallam's Secret* (2003), and *Emily's Ghost* (2009). Retired from the university, she now lives in Charleston, where she continues to write and to remain engaged in political causes.

The Appalachian Novelist

Given her literary and political service to West Virginia, her passionate arguments on behalf of the common good, and the public pulpit that rewards distinguished publication, it is little wonder that Giardina is so closely associated with her region. Even aside from her fiction, she bears an Appalachian identity, and hers has become one of the voices most closely and publicly associated with progressive thinking in coal country. But for readers and critics, what recommends to her the title *regionalist* is more particularly literary: Giardina's two most acclaimed novels are inextricably grounded in and generated from the coalfields of southern West Virginia. They feature so prominently the politics, economics, and community structures of their settings that they might well be considered her own kind of social realism. Certainly they could not exist without the particular landscapes, the cultural complexities, and the microcultures of their particular places and times.

The majority of *Storming Heaven* takes place in a fictional version of the McDowell County of the author's childhood, and the rest of it in counties and regions close by—just across the Kentucky border, briefly up in Charleston, and most climactically on the slopes of Blair Mountain. The book is a carefully articulated window into the place, and a rare one, since everyday life in that misrepresented region has often been hidden in the ignorance of popular culture or caricatured by ethnocentric inaccuracies. *The Unquiet Earth* continues the saga of the region, in some of the same coal camps and even the same houses, following the descendants of the previous novel's characters. It traces their lives through the changes of post–World War II America all the way up to her rendering of the 1972 Buffalo Creek flood (moved a few years later to better fit the narrative). The place itself, no less than the people who live in it, is a focus of the fiction: it becomes a character, a force, an evolving factor in the narrative. Whether we choose to honor or disdain the title *regionalist*, it would be impossible for Giardina not to be considered one.

Two of her books not centered in the coalfields make important use of Appalachian settings. One brief but important sequence in *Saints and Villains*, Giardina's fictional biography of the life of Dietrich Bonhoeffer, imaginatively portrays the German theologian and martyr taking a trip through the Mountain State. He visits a fellow Union Seminary student in Charleston, and that relationship leads him to his own experience of the Hawks Nest Tunnel disaster. But the placement is not simply one of convenience. What Bonhoeffer experiences in West Virginia—abuses by the economically powerful, environmental desecration, and especially racism—drives the plot by prefiguring the heinous crimes that Germany would commit against the Jews and, finally, against Bonhoeffer himself. *Fallam's Secret*, the author's winsome and imaginative time-travel fantasy, also uses West Virginia as one of its settings. It begins and speculatively ends in the New River Gorge and makes several forays through the region in between. On the comic, brighter side, it addresses the campiness of American freeway tourist culture: Uncle John's Mystery Hole in all its tackiness is at once appealing and repulsive. But on the darker side, this novel portrays the tragedy of mountaintop removal, pairing it metaphorically with historical desecrations of the holy in a seventeenth-century English chapel.

A realistic chronology denies Giardina's first and most recent novels, *Good King Harry* and *Emily's Ghost*, the opportunity to mention West Virginia, but in both cases attentive readers will find echoes of the author's Appalachian passions and connections. In these books it might even be suggested that the depth of her regionalism is more, or at least differently, indicated.

A myriad of subtle but important factors come into play to inform the concerns and textures of an authentically regional fiction. Most accurately considered, regionalism has less to do with local color and more to do with a grounding in the author's psyche: a way of seeing and perceiving the world that is only gained by an author's formative identification with a place. For example, a child who lives where the sun does not rise above the ridge until the middle of the morning gains a different understanding of morning. A child who lives in a town that can be shuttered and dissolved, even bulldozed, by the decision of a corporate interest a thousand miles away has a different idea of community. A child who lives half a mile from a mine, who subconsciously listens for its warning whistle to blow and dreads what the sound might mean, grows up with a particular set of ideas about the vagaries of providence.

Such factors and thousands more, both overt and subtle, create a grounding in a place and become what I am calling the *deep regionalism* of Giardina. Taken together, the factors create a particular lens—a way of attending to the world and processing what is perceived. And when a person with her vision thus formed looks at another mountain, another region, another cultural slice of the world, that lens does not change. So in *Good King Harry*, the protagonist is portrayed as feeling his deepest kinship with the Welsh, and especially with those on the borders who suffer the unjust treatment of an outside power. Class concerns receive close attention, as do the motivations of those who defy them. And religion is shown as at times a boon, at times a curse—at times appropriately in the service of the downtrodden and at times in the service of the powerful. Such considerations create an appropriate historical setting for Henry V, but they are also clearly grounded in Giardina's Appalachia. They are the kinds of things her deep regionalism necessarily makes her see.

A similar deep regionalism may be discerned in Giardina's most recent novel, *Emily's Ghost*. Allusions to the Brontës find their way into most of Giardina's books, and we assume the writer feels a certain affinity with her protagonist. But more directly in keeping with Giardina's Appalachian vision, several foci return from earlier works. Socioeconomic class plays a key role, as the poor of Haworth, like the Appalachian miners, suffer under the conditions of a brutally imposed poverty. A mining disaster wipes out an entire Sunday school. Religious institutions often support the malevolent agenda of money and power. And the countryside—here the moors—is the protagonist's greatest passion: she cannot be away from her place and still maintain her sense of self. None of these details is untrue to 1840 England; they fit Emily's story perfectly. But the details Giardina sees and chooses to portray most clearly are precisely the ones to which her deep regionalism would most readily and consistently attend.

In a panel discussion entitled "The Perils of Regionalism: Labels and Their Limitations," Giardina stated,

> If you look at my novels, I've written two set in West Virginia, one set in medieval England, one set in Nazi Germany, and now one set in Victorian England. So I'm a majority non-Appalachian at this point. Yet in every book I've written the mountains are central, and I couldn't have written any of those books without the mountains, and every single one of those books has been written by an Appalachian writer who brings that sense of place to her writing.[48]

Giardina's regionalism is a sense of place, to be sure, but what she presents is far more than mountains. Hers is a way of seeing the world that is unique to a particular place and time: a psychological topography, a grounded set of questions most worth asking, generated through an essential knowledge of a particular landscape and microculture. It is only by knowing one place so intimately that one may work through the narrowest particulars toward the broadest truths. Ron Rash, another deep regionalist who has gained international fame, puts it well: "The most intensely regional literature is often the most universal. The best regional writers are like farmers drilling for water; if they bore deep and true enough into that particular place, beyond the surface of local color, they tap into universal correspondences."[49]

It is through her deep regionalism that Giardina's fiction gains its particular psychic weight. Whether she examines King Harry's Wales, Emily Brontë's Haworth, or Dietrich Bonhoeffer's Berlin, she does so through Appalachian eyes. She is suited and attuned to pay attention to particular aspects, none of which individually might appear different from those of any person whose region shares one of her concerns. But taken not individually but in her unique confluence, the sum of the parts creates a uniquely Appalachian perspective. McDowell County, it seems, is never far away.

As the term has been used above, many novelists might welcome the label *regionalist*. But the usage is not always seen in such a positive light. Assuming a definition less benign, W. Dale Brown writes, "It would be careless and reductive to refer to Denise Giardina as a regionalist."[50] Given the tacit definition implied, he is certainly correct: Often *regionalist* is used in a diminishing manner, even dismissively. It implies that considered in a broader context, the writer is not worthy of extended attention; but because she wrote of an otherwise little-considered place, her work might hold some interest. Sloppy criticism may even confuse the term with "local color" writing—writing that is valuable not so much because of its literary excellence but because it presents, often in a picturesque manner, the folkways, the speech patterns, or customs of a particular time and place. As such, local color works can be congenially considered, then dismissed. Such has no doubt been the fate of much Appalachian writing, and sometimes that treatment has probably been appropriate. The works of Mary Noailles Murfree or John Fox Jr., for example, are interesting today as period pieces, but they are unlikely to find a place in a typical American literature survey.

Yet there is a history of writers once considered regionalists who have become so firmly established in the literary canon that they are no longer referred to by that term: the examples of James Joyce, Flannery O'Connor, and William Faulkner come to mind. And it is not coincidental that those writers, all now considered among the finest of their time, focused on regions that have often been belittled or ignored, socially as well as artistically. One particularly appropriate historical comparison with Giardina is Sarah Orne Jewett. A half-century ago she was considered a New England local colorist, a minor talent easily left off the course syllabus. But in more recent years and with more appropriately focused critical attention, she has found her way toward the center of the canon. No longer is her *Country of the Pointed Firs* read as an example of local color but as a minor masterpiece that conveys a progressive vision of the world too long ignored. Few scholars today would argue against her place at the table, but it took years of rereading and renewed critical attention for the weight of her work to be recognized. It is true that she often limited her view to a village in Maine, but her insight into human relationships is all the deeper for it. Like Giardina, she was a deep regionalist.

Recently in an interview with the online journal *Still*, Giardina was asked, "Do you think being identified as an 'Appalachian writer' has hindered your writing career in any way?" Her answer is worth repeating:

> To be honest, I think it has. Perhaps not so much the identity, as the fact that I continue to live in the region. I think the most successful in terms of gaining some national attention—Barbara Kingsolver, Lee Smith, Jayne Anne Phillips—spent major portions of their lives outside the region. I lived outside for only a brief time and then I came back to West Virginia. I'm not known in writerly circles. I don't know that there's any literary critic on a national level who knows I exist. So yes, it has been a hindrance.[51]

Giardina's response is telling because she suggests that it is not the regional particularities that have been a hindrance but the fact that she has not lived the typical literary life or situated herself in the centers of literary culture that offer a higher profile and improved professional networking. Instead, she stayed in Appalachia, living out her allegiance to her place. So her strength and her lack of recognition may have grown from the same seed. As she told Tim Boudreau in a 1998 interview, "Growing up [in Appalachia] is what made me a writer. Staying here is what keeps me the kind of writer I want to be."[52] She made her choice.

The Political Novelist

Next to *regionalism*, Giardina's work has most often been characterized as *political fiction*. In light of the discussion thus far, it should be no surprise that her novels would inevitably portray the political aspects of life, in ways both overt and subtle. This focus has been lauded by those for whom she advocates (the working people of Appalachia) and noticed by those who oppose her. Tellingly, novelist Lee Smith once joked that "Denise is the only person I know who has her publication parties given by the United Mine Workers. . . . I'm serious. And she's really flying in the face of a lot of different kinds of conservative pressure to stop her."[53]

Throughout her career, Giardina has deliberately embraced both her call to write and her call to be a politically active citizen. While some writers might see direct political involvement as one more time-consuming distraction from their literary work, she makes no such complaint. As she stated in *The Progressive*, "The writing fed the activism, and the activism fed the writing."[54] Neither does she apologize or make excuses for the political aspect of her writing: "My work has political content because it has to be there. In a sense that is a part of me, part of my interest, part of the way I see the world. I have to tell stories that way, like some people have to tell mysteries."[55]

Because of her public status as an Appalachian writer and because of her activism on behalf of causes affecting the region, the most weighty critical attention given to Giardina's work has focused on the political aspects, primarily of the coalfield novels and especially *Storming Heaven*. For example, the critic and folklorist Cecelia Conway, drawing on the work of Russian political theorist Peter Kropotkin and her own extensive knowledge of Appalachian culture, has demonstrated how the novel successfully portrays the social and political changes that took place in the region with the coming of the coal industry.[56] A community once centered on custom, egalitarianism, cooperation, and mutual aid is disrupted and destabilized by the competitive values of consumer capitalism. The novel details the destructive shift in relationships that comes with that colonizing influence, as well as the resistance of the community, particularly the women in the community, to this outside force.

Terry Easton takes a different angle, but still grounds his reading in political theory. Building on the work of Antonio Gramsci and Raymond Williams, he argues that Giardina's fiction demonstrates the power of absentee corporate ownership to wield a repressive force that exploits both the natural resources and the people of the region. Easton's work demonstrates how *Storming Heaven* reveals the class situation produced with the coming of the coal industry; and by doing so, the novel provides a way of seeing and better understanding the socioeconomic history of the region. The families portrayed experience "pain and loss from the openly repressive and covertly ideological forms of power created during the industrialization of central Appalachia."[57] Significantly, not only was the mountain economy transformed, but with it the very nature of how families and communities functioned, usually for the worse. It is a troubled and troubling history: the transition to industrial capitalism disrupted the culture and defiled the landscape of the region. But such a story is fertile for compelling, politically important fiction—fiction that engages readers while drawing them into a clearer historical understanding. As Laurie Lindberg has stated, *Storming Heaven* is "a subversive book, Giardina's challenge to the bullies who have tried to rule Appalachia."[58] In an era when deception is the rule, to tell the truth plainly, even in fiction, is a political and sometimes a dangerous action.

Giardina's other novels have received less attention from critics, but any careful study demonstrates that a strong political element is present as an essential strain of each narrative. And like the coalfield novels, each might appropriately be called *subversive*. *Good King Harry* is both an accomplished and nuanced historical novel and a deftly constructed psychological portrait. But it is worth noting that the most essential problem over which Harry is agonizing—the struggle that makes his suffering so engaging—is a timeless political question: What is the right function of power? And more directly, what are the potentialities and the limitations of responsible political power? *Saints and Villains* is certainly a biographical study, but more to the point, it is the story of one responsible man's struggle to act in a context of unprecedented political evil. *Fallam's Secret*, though a fantasy, deals cogently with the abuses of power in Cromwellian England and details one man's attempt to do the right thing in that setting. Finally William Weightman, the protagonist's love interest in *Emily's Ghost*, is engaged in subversive political action on behalf of the poor. Emily loves him for it, and as the story progresses, she assists him.

These struggles between political power and individual conscience demonstrate that Giardina's fiction is at core engaged in the most profound ethical questions; and ethical questions inevitably lead to political questions, whether in a romance or a region, a village or a nation. In her closely articulated social realism, the way political and economic power disrupts and redefines the most basic human relationships is starkly portrayed. And in a region that has been as exploited as Appalachia, the question for a novelist is not *whether* to incorporate a political strain in the writing but *how*. So if a weighty political element is not always crafted to be the most immediate focus of readers' attention, that is not because of its absence but due to a clear rhetorical choice. Giardina's first intention is not to present her agenda but to be an accessible and engaging story-teller who reaches a popular audience. "I write for people around here," she told Boudreau, "not for academics."[59] What has drawn thousands of readers to her work is not her political weight but the factors that might make any novel a good read: her skill at creating characters, her ability to bring historical scenes to life, her expert depiction of what is still for many Americans an unknown region, and her deft and sensitive delineation of relationships. But scratch the surface, and it becomes clear that her novels have a political motivation. All of her plots are constructed around a regional or national sociopolitical crisis, and every one of her heroes is created and judged in the light of his or her active response to political power.

The persistent message in Giardina's work is that individuals are ethically responsible for their own action or lack of action, and this includes their relationship to the state. In following such a trajectory, she takes her place in the tradition of those thinkers who ground their ethical decisions in something deeper, something more essential, than the laws of any land at a particular point in history. Each individual must consider and define his or her own relationship to power, and in this moral mandate she joins those writers who, like Henry David Thoreau, believe that "any man more right than his neighbors constitutes a majority of one already."[60] Such a lofty position is always open for critique. And, as Thoreau knew, after making such a subversive claim, one must give some explanation to justify possession of the moral high road. For Giardina, part of that explanation is in her radical understanding of Christian faith.

The Theological Novelist

Giardina's constancy in the Christian faith has formed the center of her identity. From her upbringing in the fundamentalist Methodist Church in Black Wolf, through falling in love with Anglican music and liturgy, through embracing a socially engaged Episcopal expression and graduate education at Virginia Theological Seminary, through her work with the radical, progressive

Sojourners Fellowship in the late 1970s and '80s, and throughout her career as an award-winning writer, she has followed an intentional religious trek. As an activist, an intellectual, and an artist, she has been forthright about the central role of Christianity in her thinking. And just as there is a certain risk in being labeled a *regionalist* or a *political novelist*, there is an equal or greater risk for a serious writer welcoming the label *Christian*. To make Christianity not simply one's private practice but a central aspect of one's public identity is a choice with consequences.

The last several decades have seen the rise of various types of religious fundamentalism, and that phenomenon has not enhanced the respectability of religious identification among people in many literary and academic communities. In the United States, this is especially true as it relates to the media-driven version of Christianity that has become dominant. Since the Reagan years, this version of religion has become identified with a specific political, social, and economic outlook; and as a belief system, it is quite distinct from what once was considered mainstream Christianity. As Giardina states, one result of this phenomenon is that religion, "Christianity, especially, has gotten a bad name. I think in some ways you can wrestle with the other faiths, but when you have a character who says, 'I am a Christian,' you have a problem."[61] This problem is certainly present among many progressives and intellectuals in Appalachia, and their reservations are not without historical reason.

The economic colonizers who invaded Appalachia were soon accompanied by ideological colonizers—including Christian missionaries. As Giardina has stated, "It is hard to say who came to the mountains first, the mine owners or the missionaries. As in Africa and Asia, they seem to have arrived simultaneously, the twin harbingers of empire."[62] The population was already dominantly Christian, but that fact was overlooked or held in convenient disregard, since it would not benefit the interests of extractive industries. If the natives could be portrayed as primitives, and if the mountaineers could be shown as people in need of conversion, it would be far easier to see them as Other and treat them accordingly. Giardina quotes Loyal Jones's ironic appraisal: "No group in the country . . . has aroused more suspicion and alarm among mainstream Christians than have Appalachian Christians, and never have so many Christian missionaries been sent to save so many Christians than is the case in this region."[63] Appraising the cultural and religious damage is made more complicated by the fact that, as Giardina has noted, some genuine good was done, "especially in eastern Kentucky."[64] Still, for many historically educated Appalachians today, the sordid aspect of the history of Christianity in the region often remains dominant. Especially when coupled with the political conservatism of today's nationalistic media image, it is easy to see why the term *Christian* is often held in a negative light. To be an Appalachian intellectual *and* a Christian may be perceived as aligning oneself with the oppressor.

In spite of this atmosphere, Giardina has spoken plainly and publicly about the place of her Christian faith. Her brief essay "Allegiances" is telling:

> At the risk of sounding like a denizen of the religious right, I must say that my primary allegiance is to God. I hope I do not mean this in a self-righteous, holier-than-thou sense. But that which is greater than we comprehend, "in whom we live, and move, and have our being," must come first. Everything else is subsumed in God: all understanding, all emotion, all allegiances.
>
> Such a God, of course, must be far larger than the God of the religious right.[65]

This statement makes two important moves: first, it clearly suggests the complexity of Giardina's faith; and second, it distances her faith from any media-driven version, a distinction that must be understood and maintained if critics are going to understand the religious foundation of her work. In direct contrast to a religious faith that functions to encourage compliance in oppressed cultures, Giardina's vision of Christianity labors toward the contrary outcome. Describing to an interviewer how she sees herself "both as a social activist and servant minister," she states, "The Church radicalized me. . . . The phrase in the prayer book is 'Interpret the world to the church and the church to the world.' It's a totally different way to advocate, with a spiritual point of view."[66] In an exchange with the online journal *Still*, she elucidates the point further:

> **STILL:** You've always been vocal about your strong Christian identity but in the past few years the word "Christian" has become synonymous—for many people—with words like "conservative," "traditional," and "right-wing." Does this trouble you? Does it have an impact on your own faith?
>
> **DG:** The word has indeed been hijacked, but that is nothing new. It's been going on at least since the early days of Pat Robertson and Jerry Falwell and the Moral Majority in the 1970s. Before that, being a Christian meant walking with Martin Luther King and speaking out against the Vietnam War like the Berrigans and William Sloane Coffin. Then liberal Christians grew quiet and the media looked elsewhere. Unfortunately

now, both the media and liberal secularists seem to equate Christians and fundamentalists. They don't see a distinction. And that's partly our [Christians'] fault. We need to be more outspoken about who we are.[67]

Giardina's deep familiarity with religious history in Appalachia has given her a particularly nuanced perspective, and this perspective comes through in her novels. She admits that there has "always been a strain of religion in the mountains that has been bought off by the company. But there has also always been a strain of real active religious groups, like during the early union days, when Holiness preachers would lead the strikes. But that seems to have disappeared for the most part."[68] If that strain has disappeared, so nearly has the public memory of it.

So it is not surprising that some contemporary readers—whose understanding of Christian thinking is formulated by popular stereotypes—may misunderstand Giardina's progressive, radical vision of Christianity as something outside the Christian tradition, or on the fringes at best. But, as she implies, it is the disingenuous co-opting of Christian language for coercive political purposes that is the more heterodox phenomenon. It is ironic that the *radical*, even *liberal* Christianity of people like Giardina or groups like the Sojourners Fellowship is in truth a more *conservative* reading of Christian tradition and even a more straightforward reading of the Bible than that of many right-wing conservatives. Such difficult theological and historical complexities find their way into much of the novelist's work.

Indeed, what sets Giardina apart from most contemporary writers, in addition to her lived familiarity with various Christian traditions, is her unassuming but persistent theological sophistication. That she sometimes embodies that sophistication in her plainest, apparently least sophisticated characters can at times allow otherwise careful critics to overlook the weight of what is being put forth. We expect theological sophistication in the thoughts and actions of Dietrich Bonhoeffer in *Saints and Villains*; he is, after all, a distinguished academic. But we are prone to overlook the realistic, equally complex theology of *Storming Heaven*'s Albion Freeman, a farmer and coal miner. To do so, however, is to miss much of the best Giardina has to offer. Like Flannery O'Connor, a writer she much admires, Giardina often places the weightiest thoughts in the humblest dialects. It behooves readers and critics to look hard, and to know what they are looking for.

Though Giardina's Christianity informs her work foundationally, one can read the books without seeing them as particularly religious. Some of her characters, both good and evil, are Christians, but that fact, and the role of religion in life, is appropriate to their time and place. And there is nothing pious about the tone and content of her novels that would suggest that they are *Christian* fiction. For good reason, Giardina has reservations about being called a *Christian* writer; indeed, to call her that may be misleading. On several occasions she has, however, referred to herself as a theological writer. "I've been labeled an Appalachian writer, a political writer," she states, but

> if I have to have a label on my writing, I'm a theological writer. It's not so much any one specific place that I keep being drawn back to, but it's the same questions over and over again and the people who are exploring those questions of existence and the meaning of existence, which seems to me a central mystery of life. For me, that word *mystery* is a very important word.[69]

Giardina does not explain the difference between being a Christian writer and a theological writer, but it may serve our purposes to offer a stipulative distinction here. A Christian writer, as the term is typically used today, writes the kinds of books published by evangelical publishers and sold through Christian bookstores. If the books are novels, the worlds portrayed are readily consistent with evangelical Christian assumptions, and the narratives center around faith-related questions engaged by the characters. The answers to any questions, readers may be sure, are equally and easily consistent with the beliefs of popular evangelicalism, and both questions and answers are straightforward and transparent. Readers may also be assured that there will be no foul language and that only the most heavily veiled or doctrinally compliant sexual behavior will be affirmed. Overall, good is rewarded and evil punished, and ultimately the former wins out or shows promise of doing so.

This description does not, of course, represent Giardina's work. When asked by W. Dale Brown whether Christian bookstores sell her books, she simply responded, "No. I don't think they would consider me a Christian writer."[70] Her answer was neither cynical nor discourteous; it was a simple statement of fact. In another interview she pressed her concern further: "If I'm called a Christian writer and that means I can't explore spiritual issues that seem in opposition to Christianity, that attitude would cause me problems. I certainly am a Christian, and I don't mind any label as long as it is not used in a restrictive way. Once it begins to chafe, it bothers me."[71]

In contrast to that of a Christian novelist, the trajectory of a theological novelist, or of a novelist whose work is theologically informed, is something quite different, something much weightier and much less comfortably affirming in a context of popular Christian thought. And most of all, Giardina's task is something far more psychologically complex. While the doctrinally simple may be desirable for the Christian novelist, the challenges of paradox better concern the theological novelist. In reference to her own classroom work, Giardina once described it this way:

> In almost everything I'm teaching right now in my course on Theology and Literature, I keep running into the issue of paradox. You've got one truth over here, and you've got this totally opposite idea over here that you also think is true. They can't both be true, and yet they are. If you can live with such paradox, then you can live with complexity, you can live with mystery, and you can live with ongoing exploration of all the questions that we have as human beings."[72]

The theological novelist necessarily engages in a dialectic, an argument, that addresses some element of Christian theology; and readers who enter into the philosophical depth of the narrative will necessarily have to rethink, clarify, and maybe even revise the way they perceive the world. For one who thinks theologically, every question of life has theological implications. Yet at the same time, it is possible to read Giardina with any theological element remaining essentially tacit. She never casts her questions in technical theological terms. They are simply presented as the lived philosophical questions that all great art asks, the great thematic problems, the pervasive moral dilemmas. What makes Giardina a theological novelist is the fact that the questions chosen will be informed by, and may lead the readers toward, her most foundational philosophical and theological quandaries. The novelist's perspective introduces and shapes the considerations, but conclusions are never foreclosed, nor do they fall into the pale of easy Christian orthodoxy. And invariably more questions are raised than answered.

It is pertinent here to recall that Giardina's vocation as a novelist came about through her formal study of theology. In her own words,

> I went to seminary, and at some point in the middle of seminary I realized that I hadn't been able to write because I really needed to come to seminary first to explore the things I was interested in, to explore the kinds of questions I was interested in. I knew that experience would help me to focus and would give me something to write. And that's what happened.

> As soon as I got out of seminary, I began working on my first novel, *Good King Harry*. Theological issues are at the heart of my own work, although I'm not sure I like the term *religion*.[73]

In the chapters that follow, the realization to which Giardina refers will direct our study of the novels. What were the questions that would give her "something to write"? We can only enter the discussion by reading closely enough to see, forty years after she experienced this epiphany, what she has written about.

CHAPTER 2

Good King Harry: The Formation and Paradox of a Christian King

Most scholars who study Denise Giardina's fiction focus primarily on her two novels grounded in the coalfields of West Virginia, *Storming Heaven* (1987) and *The Unquiet Earth* (1992). Those books secured her critical reputation and established her position in the canon of the finest Appalachian literature. But before she embodied the voice that would earn such status, she was already making her name with a novel of a very different kind, a work that portrays the complex machinations of a world far from the mountains of her home state.

Good King Harry (1984) is easily overlooked in the shadows cast by her later work, but it too received positive if limited attention from reviewers. Lydia Burruel in *Library Journal* noted that with "a strong and accurate grasp of history, first novelist Giardina conjures up a medieval England with just the right touch of earthiness and pageantry."[1] The *Los Angeles Times*' Sharon Dirlam agreed: "Giardina tapped the same vein Shakespeare found so rich. She found the mother lode; out came more treasure."[2] And *New York Times* critic Barbara Tritel described the work as a "richly imagined historical novel" and praised the author's "unusual skill . . . in making psychological sense out of the dynamics of a complicated family situation in which a false move can cost one's life."[3]

As suggested by the reviews, the novel may rightly be read as an engaging historical romance. It is that, to be sure, but the fuller critical perspective that comes with time has allowed us to understand more of the work's gravitas. W. Dale Brown rightly concludes that the novel "established Giardina as a writer of considerable insight into the psychological and spiritual forces that motivate human action."[4] Similarly, Sandra Ballard and Patricia Hudson note the book's success in "introducing moral dilemmas that are a hallmark of Giardina's fiction."[5] In fact the closer we study *Good King Harry*, the more clearly we see how thoroughly it establishes the themes and lays bare the obsessions that characterize all her best work: the struggle for justice, the nuanced presentation of religious belief, and, most of all, the intricate battleground of conscience.

From History to Fiction

Good King Harry is a historical novel set in the late Middle Ages, spanning the years 1398–1422. The fourteenth century in Europe was a time of political and social upheaval precipitated by a catalog of tumultuous events, the results of which stretch into the time frame of the story, among them the Black Death, widespread famine due to climate changes, the Hundred Years' War, the Great Schism of the Catholic Church, and the threat of Islamic advance. In addition, feudalism was finishing its course, and the seeds of capitalism were being sown in a growing merchant class. And Henry V, Giardina's Harry, was born just a decade after the Peasants' Revolt. It was, to say the least, a difficult time to be a king.

But bad times make good stories, as confirmed by Shakespeare's histories of the period. In choosing to retell the tale of Henry V, Giardina wrote with an awareness that her hero would inevitably be colored by Shakespeare's version, Prince Hal. But she wisely takes another tack, basing her character more closely on contemporary historical understandings of the man himself. She calls her portrayal a "reversal of Shakespeare," noting, "I especially wanted to dig beneath the plays to the actual historical figure."[6] She was attempting to create a protagonist who is neither the "model Christian king" nor the "monstrous figure" as Shakespeare's Hal is sometimes interpreted. "I was angling for somewhere in between," she states, "looking for the human, the insecure, the person trying to do what was right but failing miserably. And asking where the redemption is in that."[7] With some exceptions, Giardina stays true to a reading of history, both in her characters and the most important events. She takes a free hand, however, with those things that history can never fully recover; most significantly, she portrays Harry's interior life, his motivations. And it is that interior life that makes the novel. As she states with humor tinged with ironic truth: "The fiction writer jumps in where historians fear to tread!"[8]

One of her achievements is not only creating a psychologically relevant fifteenth-century context but doing so in a literary style that maintains the feeling of a long-ago time. Her diction and syntax faintly echo late Middle English while remaining completely transparent to modern readers. It is not surprising that one reviewer termed the book "anachronistic in tone"[9]; but it is hard to discern a perfect imaginary language, and her imperfect one works well for most readers. As Tritel noted, "It is no mean feat to invent a diction in modern English that is perfectly readable while capturing the flavor of an older language."[10] Giardina's construction of a fantastical idiom that maintains its strangeness without distracting speaks to the caliber and maturity of her craft.

Good King Harry may be considered genre fiction, but sometimes the difference between popular *genre* fiction and *literary* fiction is the quality of attention critics give it. Close reading reveals that while this book is certainly a page-turner, it carries weight and should be analyzed as painstakingly as it was constructed. To give the book its due, two critical angles will be used here to focus our attention and allow us to understand more fully its achievement. Most broadly, it will be considered a novel of ideas, but before exploring it as such, we will examine the book in light of a somewhat more defined set of conventions.

A Novel of Development

Good King Harry divides roughly but usefully into two halves. The first, sections 1–3, may be read as a *novel of development*, or *bildungsroman*. Jerome Hamilton Buckley summarizes the key elements of the bildungsroman as "childhood, the conflict of generations, provinciality, the larger society, self-education, alienation, ordeal by love, the search for a vocation and a working philosophy."[11] His description of the typical plot goes briefly like this: A sensitive child grows up in a provincial area, where he finds his relationship with his father constraining. He goes off to the city, where he gains a broader education, has multiple love affairs, and must reconsider his values. Moving from adolescence to youth, he decides how he must accommodate the ideals of his youth to the ways of the world. Marianne Hirsch's discussion of the form supplements that model, listing seven characteristics of what she terms the "novel of formation"[12]: focus on a single character; consideration of both biographical and social concerns; a protagonist who goes on a quest for a meaningful existence within society, "for the authentic values which will facilitate the unfolding of inner capacities"[13]; attention to "the development of selfhood"[14] and not the full biography; a narrator who takes an ironic stance "toward the inexperienced protagonist"[15]; other characters who fulfill roles as educators, companions, and lovers; and a didactic function—it "educates the reader by portraying the education of the protagonist."[16] Our study will demonstrate that the first half of *Good King Harry* holds fairly closely to most of these characteristics.

Giardina's prologue situates the first-person protagonist, Harry, on his deathbed—a choice that establishes the way the next four hundred pages must be understood. We know how the story will end: Harry will be king, and he will spend his final days contemplating his failed life. In addition, this prologue reveals the key traits that will be developed throughout the story: Harry's love for Wales, his appreciation for the common man, his disrespect for the office of king, his disdain for chivalry and the nobles who profess it, his cunning tactical sense, his powerful gifts of leadership, his devout Christian faith, and his unrelenting guilt. But the most important aspect of the prologue is that it creates the book's ironic tone. Harry prefaces his story by voicing his contempt for coronations, and he sees one of the compensations for his coming death as not being forced to "suffer through" another one. His gallows humor continues: "The King is England. Here then lies God's servant with the blood of thousands upon his hands. Here lies England, emaciated and staining his bedclothes with the foulness of the bloody flux."[17] The rest of the text must be understood through the filter of this worldly-wise but disillusioned perspective.

With this tone established, the sequential story begins. From the first line of section 1, Harry's alienation from his father is clear: "I had been nine years in this world when my father put an end to his *knightly ramblings*" (11, italics mine). His dismissive diction characterizes all the narrator's reflections on the chivalrous undertakings of his father, the dashing and courtly Henry Bolingbroke. Harry states that when his father first returned to his family, he was "a gallant and exotic figure to us [Harry and his three brothers]. . . . It was not long, though, ere I tired of him" (11). The temper of the opening may strike readers as prematurely knowing, since Harry is only nine years old. But these are the perceptive reflections of an adult: memories seasoned by the wisdom of experience and wizened ruminations. Such alienation is an appropriate beginning for a bildungsroman. Buckley places the "loss of father, either by death or alienation" as a central tenet of the form and states that the "defection of the father becomes accordingly the principal motive force in the assertion of the youth's independence."[18]

Harry's alienation results not only from his father's neglect but from his overt rejection. Bolingbroke values chivalry above all things, and the young Harry has not only been a sickly baby, bad enough, but he has proven himself unchivalrous. Having been unhorsed in a joust—the most phallic of contests—he has developed a neurotic aversion to the tradition his father considers the essence of his culture and class. Worse yet, the boy asserts his contempt with a strength of will that belies his age: "I shall not joust again. Ever" (13). His father responds, "You are my great shame. You disgrace the name of Lancaster." With this dismissal Bolingbroke sends Harry's younger brother Tom off to receive the training befitting a knight—an education that should rightfully have fallen first to the eldest son—and condemns Harry to Oxford to study under the charge of his young uncle, Henry Beaufort. Bolingbroke states, "You shall . . . say your prayers and study your lessons like a good boy. If you should find any manhood in you, come to me. Until then, I do not want you in my sight" (14).

What Harry's father intends as a curse becomes a blessing. Beaufort becomes Harry's first initiator into a social awareness that will motivate his life and heighten his contempt for his father's world. Beaufort perceives in Harry what his father has failed to value or even recognize: he is a boy of cunning and passionate intellectual gifts. Oxford is the rich intellectual environment where his development can happen, and it is also a context in which Beaufort can speak freely to his charge "as a man, sometimes of theology but more often of statecraft" (15). Harry relates, "These discussions I considered another element of my education, for Beaufort held to ideas which I knew instinctively my father . . . would find revolting"—a fact that makes his uncle's diatribes all the more attractive. Beaufort teaches Harry that the nobles' way of life, especially chivalry, is dead, comparing their culture to a rotting corpse. The future, he asserts, lies in the merchants, the nascent capitalist class that is rising in the early fifteenth century. "They are our destiny," he teaches Harry. "Their code is not chivalry but power" (16). And he offers this advice regarding Harry's relationship to his father and the nobles:

> "You must play their game, Harry, but never believe in it. Pretend the corpse is still alive, clasp its hand, clap it upon the back. But take heed how it stinks and get no closer. Damn chivalry! You've a fine sharp mind, Harry Monmouth. Rely upon that alone."
> "And upon God, surely?" [Harry replies.]
> He smiled. "To be sure. Upon God." (16–17)

Beaufort's insights find a ready audience in Harry. Though he only partially understands them, they confirm what he has already intuited and affirm his conflict with his father: something is intrinsically wrong with Bolingbroke's worldview and the society that created it.

A second mentoring figure Harry encounters at Oxford is the young cleric Richard Courtenay. Harry suffers from a painful social reticence, and despite his uncle's presence at the college, he feels isolated by his personality and his youth. One night his loneliness drives him to a tavern where he drinks too much, then leaps into a brawl to defend the reputation of his beloved Wales. He takes a bad thump on the head but is rescued from further abuse by Courtenay, who carries him back to his rooms and tends his wounds. Courtenay listens sympathetically to Harry's woes, and the two discover their shared passion for books. He gives Harry *Piers Plowman*, copied by his own hand. Harry is puzzled by a book about a mere plowman, and Courtenay rightly discerns, "Your father would not approve, nor even your uncle of Beaufort, I should think. . . . It is not of knights and ladies. It is the cry of the poor people of England who ne'er were known to have a voice" (21).

Giardina's choice of *Piers Plowman* offers multiple layers of significance regarding Harry's development. The poem's rustic subject matter recalls to Harry his peasant friends at Monmouth, boys his father wanted him to avoid. And the fact that the book is given by Courtenay, a new friend of both rank and Christian devotion, awakens Harry to the possibility that a devout, well-educated young churchman can share the sympathy he feels for the poor. His uncle Beaufort—a priest, but not devout—has taught him that a new, powerful class is rising, that chivalry and feudalism are dying. Now through Courtenay a complementary seed is planted that, in addition to his own experience with the urchins of Monmouth, confirms his growing egalitarian convictions. And, though for reasons more religious than utilitarian, Courtenay shares Beaufort's judgment of men like Harry's father. "Our nobles are fools," his new friend tells him. "Forgive me if I speak plainly" (21). In Courtenay he has found a guiding friend who confirms an aspect of Harry's worldview beyond his own youthful articulation. Speaking again of *Piers Plowman*, a book he has shared with other, less approving friends, Courtenay applauds Harry's reaction: "None respond as you did. Something alive I saw in your eyes, and my heart leaped at it. You want to do good in this world" (23). Thus Harry's development is advanced by two key mentors: Beaufort has pointed him toward the political changes in England's near future, changes that would be furthered during Harry's reign—and in part *because* of his reign. And Courtenay takes a parallel tack, but grounding and affirming in Christian devotion Harry's respect for the poor, an egalitarian impulse that will characterize his way of viewing the world.

This stay at Oxford, however, is foreshortened. Bolingbroke's exile under suspicion of treason returns Harry briefly to Wales and soon thereafter to King Richard's court, not as an attendant but as a hostage. There he finds a third powerful, if unlikely, mentor in the king. Though his stay in Richard's court is brief, several aspects of his formation are furthered in the company of his father's nemesis. Like Harry's grandfather John of Gaunt, his uncle Beaufort, and his friend Courtenay, the chivalrous but disillusioned King Richard comes to respect and affirm the boy's brilliance. Soon after his arrival, Harry's treacherous cousin York betrays the boy by telling the king that Harry believes he could beat him at chess. Harry plays the fool by admitting his prowess, but he does so in a way that simultaneously humiliates York and ingratiates himself in the king's good favor. Such cunning would never have been possible had Beaufort not initiated Harry's indoctrination into the gospel of power and admonished him to play the nobles' game but never to believe it.

Giardina portrays Richard as an inept politician and warrior, but he nevertheless becomes an alternative father figure for Harry. In contrast to Bolingbroke, who has deemed his son unchivalrous, Richard knights the boy and values his devotion and service. He recognizes Harry's abilities and takes him into his confidence. Most importantly, he shares freely his own disgust with the position of king and with the aristocracy (though for no egalitarian reasons). Through Richard, Giardina introduces Harry to the double bind that makes the idea of a "good king" an apparent impossibility. "The better man a king is," Richard tells Harry, "the more he is abused" (41). His confessions further Harry's suspicions that kings are "creatures of malice" (34). This lesson comes to a head when, provoked by his fear of Bolingbroke, Richard considers executing Harry, despite his affection. Significantly, Richard's child-queen Isabel explains to Harry, "It is not Richard who uses you unjustly, but it is the crown that possesses him" (42). The apparently unavoidable evil that comes with being a king persists as a formative strain in Harry's thinking, even as he finds himself heir to the throne.

While Richard makes an ill-fated trip to put down rebellion in Ireland—a futile attempt to garner the respect of his nobles—Bolingbroke violates his exile and claims the kingdom. His rebellion reconfirms Harry's low view of his traitorous father and reiterates Bolingbroke's rejection of him as well. When Richard warns Bolingbroke that he holds his son hostage, the rebel responds that "he has three other sons, all healthy, promising lads, and these three are now with him," adding that Richard may do whatever he wishes with Harry: "He [Bolingbroke] cares not" (45). Reunited after Bolingbroke's successful usurpation, the angry Harry confronts him: "Richard has been more father to me than have you" (47).

Bolingbroke has not returned alone to England but has brought with him a fellow exile who plays an important role in Harry's formative understanding of the ways of the world: "the despicable Arundel, the unholy Archbishop of Canterbury," who would serve Bolingbroke the rest of his life (111). Arundel and Harry immediately hate each other. Here and throughout the novel, Giardina uses Arundel to represent what Harry detests about the institutional Church; in that role, Arundel serves as a strident counterpoint to the devout Courtenay. Arundel has nothing of Courtenay's devotion but is wholly the politician who has chosen the Church as his most likely pathway to power. His self-serving utilitarianism suggests a darker extension of Beaufort, with the important exception that in Arundel, utilitarian thinking is augmented by malice.

At this point in the story, Giardina has suggested the kind of man Harry will become and the dread he feels for his royal destiny: "Someday I would be King of England. Someday I would suffer the same torments which had plagued Richard—if I lived. It seemed to me then that heavy chains fell across me. No matter how dark the dungeon in which Richard would be cast, my own prison would be more foul" (49). His childhood has thus come to an end. With Bolingbroke in power, Harry at age twelve moves into his own manor of Kennington, and Giardina pushes her protagonist on to the next steps of his formation, both physically and metaphorically: "Nor did I dwell in my father's house ever after" (53).

Harry's next initiator into his father's world is Henry Percy, Shakespeare's Hotspur. Like Harry's father, Percy is a marcher lord, one of those nobles situated on the border between England and Wales to ensure the subjection of the Welsh. Also like Harry's father, Percy loathes the boy's aversion to making war against the Welsh. He is made Harry's guardian to teach him firsthand the duties of a military leader, and he does so by putting down an uprising of the Welsh under Owain Glyndwr, a man Harry, with his sympathy for the Welsh, would rather have accommodated than fought. Percy treats Harry severely, belittling him and beating him. So he furthers Harry's development but not in the direction he intends. Harry admits, "As far as I could, I did his bidding only to keep his lash from my body, all the while priding myself that he had not altered me, nor ever would. I was wrong, of course, for I grew hard and reserved under his tutelage, brooding upon how he wronged me and sharing my hurts with no one" (59). Though the education is a brutal one, Harry does learn something of military negotiation as it was practiced by men like Percy and his own father. At one stage of the Welsh uprising, Percy instructs Harry that a good negotiator must appeal to the self-interest of his enemy, in this case the Welsh nobles. After forcing them to terms, Percy frees the nobles to go back to their castles but makes examples of some of their conscripted peasant followers by having them hanged and disemboweled. When Harry objects Percy responds, "You reason like a peasant" (60). And again, "You cannot escape responsibility [for the executions], nor should you wish to. It is time you learned what it means to be a prince." Harry is sickened, not only because he sees those sacrificed as his countrymen but because his sensibility is quickened yet again to the injustice of class. Throughout, Harry is developing an egalitarian sensibility that stands in stark distinction to feudal stratifications and the chivalric warfare that allows nobles to go free while common people are sacrificed. He does grow wiser under Percy, but the effect is not to adopt the opinions of his class but to affirm his own developing values. He even threatens Percy, and he does so in a way that is the first suggestion that Harry may welcome some aspect of his coming reign. He tells his advisor, "Percy, when I am King you shall ne'er set foot in the realm" (61). After this exchange, "Percy beat me so severely that the skin of my back did split in three places. Yet I sensed fear lay upon him like a cloak." The last sentence is particularly telling: Harry, though a reluctant prince, is beginning to anticipate the power of his position.

Characters like Percy are clearly antagonistic, but Giardina makes it difficult for Harry or her readers to settle into a black-and-white ethical perspective. The first scene of a decimated village that Harry and Percy encounter undercuts any easy moral grounding. The village has been destroyed not by the English Harry has vilified but, as they are informed by the lone surviving priest, by the Welsh under Glyndwr. Percy taunts Harry: "Well, Harry, where shall you take your ideals now? Welshmen! It is a fine joke, indeed. Perhaps you shall now be ready to fight." Harry is taken aback and asks the priest, "How is it that Welshmen did this to their own people?" To which the priest responds, "All men are fallen. All are fallen" (62). Harry's sense of irreconcilable moral conflict grows. Isabel again tries to comfort him by praising his victory in Wales and reminding him, "To fight as a knight is a noble thing," then adding, "You shall soon be used to it, will you not?" Harry responds, "That is what I most fear" (65).

Giardina is portraying Harry as a young man trying desperately to envision a path through life that is true to his developing beliefs and that avoids war's atrocities. But there seems to be none. After one particularly murderous battle, this time under the command of his father, Harry is at the point of suicide (66). He is considering drowning himself when he is interrupted by another character who will serve as a mentor, Jack Oldcastle. Jack, a small-scale landowner conscripted into service, is similarly repulsed by the barbarous injustice of war. Yet as they continue the Welsh campaign, Giardina uses Jack to further complicate Harry's moral understanding. On the one hand, their army devastates defenseless monasteries; but on the other, Jack directs Harry's attention to the vast riches of the monks, amassed despite their vows of poverty and the desperate needs of the people they have vowed to serve. Repeatedly, Jack makes sure Harry sees the unjust wealth of the institutional Church. As much as Harry wants to discover the goodness in his society, he is confronted by personal and systemic evil at every turn: in politics, in class structure, even in religion.

Or especially in religion. Near the end of the campaign, Harry is confronted by his brother Tom, whom Giardina creates as his conventionally chivalrous foil. Tom warns Harry that he is losing the confidence of the other nobles due to his reticence as a warrior. This is a true crisis: to maintain the throne in the future, he will need the goodwill of the peers. Tom assures Harry, "It is the way of the world to fight.... The Church does agree with me, you must admit. It is therefore given to you to strive mightily, to fight hardest and best. God shall bless your efforts if you stand bravely and for the right" (74). Harry has already reasoned beyond Tom's conventionally nationalistic views of war and of Christianity. Yet he is a participant in the destruction and may in fact be more at fault than his chivalrous peers because he knows what they are doing is wrong. With this realization he takes his carved Madonna, a gift from Courtenay, and throws it into the fire with the words, "Harry... you are dead" (75). And he is dead, in a way. He sees the path before him, judges it to be wrong, and knows simultaneously that he can find no better way forward.

In his taxonomy of the bildungsroman, Buckley notes that the protagonist will experience "at least two love affairs or sexual encounters, one debasing, one exalting."[19] The first of these occurs when Jack determines that it is time for Harry to accompany him to a brothel. Joined by Lord Henry Scrope, Harry's steward, Jack leads the prince out among the London lowborn to Chepeside, where they consider options for the evening. Scrope's view of sex is brazen: women "are all the same between the legs" (83). Jack takes a marginally more enlightened view that "there is more to a woman than fucking. I like a woman to talk to when we are done with love" (84). Harry, however, maintains the more youthful ideal of making love, and he is smitten with the thirteen-year-old Alison, the tavern keeper's daughter. Though at first put off by Alison's past sexual experience, he uses her nevertheless and fancies himself in love. After several weeks of visits, he is confronted by Beaufort, who tells him that the girl does not love him for himself but only for his position. "People at bottom are selfish and cruel," Beaufort tells him. "Princes should know this better than any. You shall hear many sweet words of flattery and love. Heed them not. Behind every honeyed word is ever a motive" (90). This assessment proves to be correct in the case of Alison, and Harry is disillusioned in yet another area of life. When he asks Beaufort if such duplicity is true of his friends as well, Beaufort shrugs his tacit affirmation. The Alison sequence prepares the reader for the far different relationship Harry will find with Merryn, but another effect is that his habit of frequenting taverns and brothels itself forms part of his education. He comes to love the Chepeside rabble far more than he likes his fellow nobles. And the common people love him in return, a fact that will pay dividends as he rises to power. Jack's introducing him to life in Chepeside, then, has been important in several areas.

The culminating event of this stage of Harry's formation is the Battle of Shrewsbury. Because of his savvy escape from the duplicitous Worcester, his father wants to reward Harry with greater responsibility, and the treacherous

Arundel advises Bolingbroke to put Harry in command of the most vulnerable force in the battle. Though Bolingbroke may actually have wanted to honor his son, Arundel's suggestion is clearly intended to get Harry killed and put Tom in line to the throne. The tables are turned when Harry leads his men to victory in a complex series of events. He quickly sees that the typical conventions of warfare are not going to work, and he invents a devastatingly effective—and nonchivalrous—use of his archers, foreshadowing his great victory at Agincourt. The battle confirms both Harry's egalitarian sympathies for his common soldiers and his growing desire to succeed. Giardina thus demonstrates that he is learning to play his father's game but doing so in an innovative way that gives him credibility among the nobles and gains him the useful approbation of the common people.

In keeping with the novel of development tradition, Harry is finding his way in a changing world, accommodating himself to it yet maintaining to some degree his own values, his own personhood. Just as important, however, is the fact that he realizes the moral complexity of his victory at Shrewsbury. He has won his father's goodwill and saved many poor soldiers that day. But the salvation has come at the price of a tremendous slaughter of his enemy. "I have bartered lives for lives," he tells Jack and asks, "Who has dared to grant me such power?" (120). But it is power that he must own as a prince, and he works to maintain and expand it. The next several chapters demonstrate how fully he has accommodated himself to the ways of court and how effectively he works to further his position in the way of Beaufort's "new men" (17). He keeps one foot in his father's world, but his tactics of gaining power are not the fading ways of Bolingbroke.

Giardina confirms Harry's transformation with a mix of unseemly and more enlightened actions. An example of the former is his relationship with the Lady Anne Mortimer, reportedly the most beautiful woman in England. The manners of court expect sexual dalliance, and the new Harry is happy to oblige. He sets about to make Anne his sexual partner and does so. Giardina does not present this as abusive, since Lady Anne, too, delights in the infidelities of courtly life. Less ennobling is the fact that Harry wants her not simply for her beauty or even her sexual prowess but because their affair allows him to take further revenge on her husband, Richard of York. Recalling his relationship with Alison, Harry realizes that Lady Anne had been planning his seduction—she gains status by bedding the Prince of Wales—just as he had been planning hers. But he is no longer troubled by the utilitarian aspects of so-called love. As Harry states, "I had outgrown all childish illusions of being loved for Harry alone. No woman could be expected to ignore my rank, to forget that she lay with the future King of England. Best then to shrug and cheerfully accept the favors bestowed upon me, basking in any reputation gained along the way. Would not most men long to be in my place?" (126).

This is a far cry from the romantic Harry of earlier days. As he tells Courtenay, who serves as a moral touchstone, "The boy you knew was slain long ago with other poor wretches at Shrewsbury and in Wales. These other souls have some hope of resurrection. But the boy is dead. He shall never live again" (141). The maturing Harry continues to engage in the intrigues of his father's world, climbing his way into the favor of the London capitalists, battling successfully with Arundel, making himself a brilliant student of statecraft, and, with mixed success, maintaining his tumultuous relationship with the failing Bolingbroke. Most importantly, he earns and enjoys his power. At one point he concludes, "For two years I was the uncrowned King of England" (221).

In her otherwise positive review of the novel, Burruel notes that it would have been strengthened by a "stronger depiction of secondary characters."[20] The novel of development tradition, however, typically has all events turn around one central focus: the character being developed. And through Beaufort, Courtenay, Richard, Jack, and Percy, Giardina maintains our attention on Harry, growing in understanding, questioning his own values and the values of those around him, and earning a place for himself in his world. More so than any thin development of secondary characters, the romantic Merryn subplot is the element of the novel that threatens the book's realism and maybe even the reader's patience. It is hard not to enjoy their story as one might surreptitiously enjoy a pop romance. But the portrayal of Merryn, at times more an old man's fantasy than a character, is only believable if we remember that we are hearing a story recounted on the deathbed, a disillusioned man trying to make sense of an eventful but failed life.

Setting aside the credibility question, however, the relationship with Merryn functions successfully as a bridge between the novel of development and the novel of ideas. As noted above, Buckley suggests that in the bildungsroman form, the protagonist will have an exalting love affair that will affect his values, and the Merryn relationship works well in this regard. Harry has lost the illusions of youthful romance through his affair with Alison, and he has degraded himself with Lady Anne. In the Merryn relationship, the better aspects of his psyche are nurtured. She becomes, like Courtenay, a conscience figure for Harry, reminding him continually of the plight of the poor, of the dangers that accompany power, and of the importance of Christian devotion—all factors that contribute significantly to the book's thematic weight. It is through the Merryn sequence and largely through her influence that the strength and the danger of Harry's call to be a Christian king become clear. Her death in childbirth is not only an emotionally compelling scene but a necessary one. On her deathbed Merryn tells Harry, "You must live for England. You must love her as ardently and truly as you have loved me" (255). With her passing, Harry takes a vow of celibacy that is more significant than sexual continence; it is a symbol of his dedication to his call. As he later confesses to his friend Rhys, "Now England is my only lover" (317).

At this point in the novel, Harry's story considered as a bildungsroman is complete. In keeping with expectations of the form, he has progressed through the stages of alienation and education, and he has discovered his place in society. At the beginning of section 4, Bolingbroke dies, and Harry becomes king of England. The field is now set to see if he can be the kind of king he has been envisioning since Bolingbroke usurped Richard's throne. Were this a traditional novel of development, it could end here.

A Novel of Ideas

But Giardina continues the story. The first three sections portrayed the formation of a man who would be king, and with the beginning of the fourth, he assumes that office. From this point on, it is most helpful to consider the book as a *novel of ideas*: a novel in which a philosophical, religious, or political question is the focus. What might occur if a king happens to be a sincere Christian—a true believer? What if he is utterly devoted to what he perceives as a particular divine call? What if his talents are vastly superior to those of his contemporaries—if he is in fact "the ablest man in Christendom" (346)? What if he has a sincere concern for justice—especially justice for the poor? And what if his true love—the purest joy in his life—has died, admonishing him on her deathbed to "live for England" and "love [England] as ardently and truly as you have loved me" (255)?

In short, the focus of this novel of ideas is whether it is possible to succeed, both politically and spiritually, as a Christian king. And if not, why not?

Two understandable biases need to be set aside in order for contemporary readers to take Giardina's thought experiment seriously. In our day of the nearly universal approbation—if not the practice—of democracy, it is difficult to consider any monarchy as a political context for doing good. Yet Harry's time is not our time, and the position of king would not have held for devout Christians of the fifteenth century the repugnance it holds today. Harry was fluent in French and Latin by the time he was nine; as he states in the prologue, "I daresay no children in England were so well versed in the ancient philosophers or the holy fathers of the Church as were we" (4). He is an expert in the philosophy and theology of his time, and the concept of *king* would not only have been prevalent in his everyday world but affirmed by his studies of great texts. Summarizing, for example, the political thought of Thomas Aquinas—certainly central in Harry's curriculum—R. W. Dyson notes,

> St Thomas holds that the kind of leadership which our condition requires is best provided by a king. Kingship, because it is government by one, is the most natural and therefore the best kind of government. Its archetype is God's government of the universe, and we see it mirrored everywhere in nature.... It is the most efficient kind of government because a king's power is undivided and his freedom of action unlimited. The king has no one to compromise with, dissent from or consult.[21]

This is the reasoning by which Giardina portrays Harry as justifying not only his position in England but his plan to unite Christendom. He judges the greatest peace the Western world had ever experienced as having been under the rule of Rome—"All ruled by one man" (133). So why should he not envision himself as a Christian king, as a new and improved Charlemagne? His political agenda is consistent with the Christian theology of his day.

A second bias to be set aside is our doubt about the very idea of a preternatural call. Granted, the language of *call* is still common in the discourse of many religious people. No churchgoer is shocked to hear a fellow believer proclaim a call to medical research or helping the poor. But even the truest of true believers might have doubts about a friend who says, "I think God is calling me to rule Europe." It is worth noting that in a 1997 interview Giardina was asked, "Do you think of your writing as your calling?" And she responded, "Yes. I think I felt that even as a child, felt that there was something I was supposed to be doing."[22] If only because the author takes the idea of a call seriously for herself, we should leave the option on the table for her protagonist. Yet many readers may understandably find the grandiosity of Harry's call hard to overlook.

In fact, we are tempted to interpret Harry as delusional. Is Giardina presenting the story of a madman or a sane—if misguided or ill-fated—leader? The text itself justifies our question. In a conversation with the visiting Sigismund, Harry plainly tells the debauched and cynical Holy Roman Emperor, "I have sought to know God's will for my life. Everything points to this. Someone must rescue God's people, and to no other has He given the gifts you name for me. If I place myself in God's hands, He shall use me" (346). Taken out of the context, such a claim suggests a doomed megalomania. And so it seems to Sigismund, who responds, "Those whom God uses know little enough of success, it seems to me. *More familiar with madness*, they are" (346, italics mine). Readers may agree. And given the turmoil of his childhood, adolescence, and young manhood, psychological maladaptation does not seem unlikely. His mother died with the birth of his sister; he is rejected and condemned by his father; his life has been under continual threat since boyhood; he has experienced time and again the trauma of war, firsthand, since he was a young teen; and finally the love of his life has died after the stillbirth of their only child. Why would he not suffer mental instability?

Yet aside from the grandeur of his intention, Giardina gives little evidence of Harry being insane. His plan, his claim to a special call, is consistent with the narrative progression. At first he dreads the very idea of the throne. Then, since it seems to be his fate, he begins to see desirable possibilities. The vision increases in scope; the calling grows stronger. Throughout the novel, a very sane Harry has felt a growing sense that he is called by God to a particular task—to be a good king, to reform the Church, and finally to unite Christendom. It seems that in some sense, Giardina is presenting the realistic possibility that a sane king of England might consider himself chosen by God for this purpose. At the least, considering the book as a novel of ideas—an extended narrative thought experiment—we may go along for the fictional ride as a response to a somewhat more restrained foundational philosophical question: Is it possible to successfully merge high political ambitions and Christian devotion?

In following Harry's career as king, Giardina offers, if not an unequivocal answer, a serious consideration of the question. In a novel of ideas, the protagonist struggles to reconcile a particular philosophical theme. And while Harry has many enemies, both at home and abroad, the most complex battles take place in his soul. They center on an intricately interwoven matrix of psychological and ideological factors, developed throughout the novel, that make following his call so challenging. The following pages suggest five factors that complicate and finally render impossible Harry's success as he strives to be both a successful king and a faithful Christian: the institutional Church itself, the oppositional Church, the rise of capitalism, Harry's radical Christian devotion, and, finally, the inescapable limitations of mortality.

THE INSTITUTIONAL CHURCH

It may seem counterintuitive that one of Harry's inner conflicts in succeeding as a *Christian* king is with the theology of the *Christian* Church. Contemporary readers who understand the Church as a corporate expression of a commonly held set of beliefs need to be aware that as represented in *Good King Harry*, the institutional Church has less to do with articulated belief than with political power: it is effectively a sphere of government. So although Harry has determined to be a *Christian* king, he can be supported by the *Christian* Church only to the degree that his actions and beliefs—however true to ideal Christian belief—do not threaten the Church's institutional power. As it happens, Harry has consistently discerned that the beliefs and practices of the Church of his day present a low moral bar. Most significantly, he determines the conventional Just War theology of Augustine and Aquinas to be deeply troubling for his conscience, in practice if not in theory.

Conventional Just War theology sanctions war under particular circumstances; indeed, the conditions under which a war may be justly undertaken have long been and remain in the catechism of the Catholic Church.[23] A historically evident problem, however, has been that these standards seem seldom if ever to have been applied in good faith but instead manipulated to justify actions that nations find to be in their best interest and for which they want the support of the Church's power. A related problem is that once a war is underway, it is essentially impossible to assure that it is carried out consistently with Church teachings. Both of these problems, especially the latter, come into play in *Good King Harry*, and they are a source of Harry's disquietude from the prologue through the epilogue.

Giardina depicts the Church's too-easy acceptance of violence in several sequences, many of which reflect the unjust power structure of the time. For example, when Harry initially meets Jack, the two find common ground in the fact that both are "reluctant warrior[s]" (67), sickened by the way the armies have decimated the peasants. Jack compares what their army has done to the poor of Wales to the work of "the meanest cutpurse in the London stews." But the more devout Jack becomes, the more he embraces the Church's justification of violence. He later tells Harry, "God blesses our striving against the Welsh" (101). Harry disagrees, noting that the Welsh, too, are Christians, but Jack responds, "No. It is a soiled gospel they proclaim, and that is worse than no gospel at all. They cling to the old heathen ways, casting spells and calling upon sorcerers such as Merlyn. It is the Devil, and yet it masquerades as the true faith. Our mission is to defend Christendom against false doctrine" (101). This passage underscores the idea that the institutional Christianity portrayed in the novel justifies the atrocities of war not only as a matter of defense against aggression but for the propagation of the "true faith." Harry can never fully accept these teachings, though to do so would lessen his anxiety. He reflects, "I longed to be as [Jack] was, to go blithely with sword in hand to slay the enemies of God, but I could not. I pondered and wrestled until I thought my soul itself must be a battleground" (101).

In a later conversation with Jack and Courtenay, Harry further rejects the idea that the Church should support war, this time fiscally: "I would not have it. The Church must be above such things"; to which Jack replies, "The Church blesses our warmaking. Why should she not pay for it?" (148). He refers to Harry's tender conscience as "damnable." Even Courtenay, Giardina's most sympathetic model of an institutional cleric, responds, "There are times when force may be necessary, Harry. As a prince you are called to take up the sword if greater good may come of it." As the story progresses, Harry increasingly assumes the conventional theology, and Courtenay begins to see the implications. As Harry uses Just War theory to support his invasion of France, Courtenay confronts him about whether he has lost his ideals. Harry responds, "I have not lost them. I shall rule justly and strive for the good. That I will not compromise. But mark this, Courtenay. I will not trouble with honor when it does defeat good purpose. If I must commit small wrongs to accomplish greater good, I shall do it" (280).

Courtenay's response, "It is a seductive way you choose. Easy it would be to lose yourself," proves to be prophetic. He sees clearly the danger of the Church's—and now Harry's—position, but his reservations are rare among the clergy. The head of the Church, for example, throws his influence behind the drumbeat of war. Once Harry has made public his decision to invade France and regain the French crown, his newly appointed Archbishop of Canterbury, Chichele, gives a speech in which he not only defends the invasion but argues that "according to the teachings of the Holy Church," Harry's war-making is just: "The Church may bless these military enterprises which are undertaken to accomplish a greater good" (281).

Although Harry's actions pragmatically embrace the Just War theology, his heart is not convinced. In one particularly ironic exchange during a French campaign, Harry is refused the absolution he seeks for the desolation he has caused, not because his confession lacks sincerity but because—by the conventional theology of the Church—the murderous actions of his army are *not sin*. The siege of Caen had become a slaughter of women and children under Tom's command, violating all the principles Harry had tried to carry out as a Christian king. In the wake of the atrocities, he entreats his confessor, the scholarly Thomas Netter, for forgiveness: "The blood of hundreds of innocents stains my hands. I crave pardon, though it may not be possible" (350). But the priest responds,

> "There is no need for pardon. There is no sin. You gave the city fair warning, which was not heeded. You have come here for a just cause, a holy mission. The sin is upon the heads of those who stand in your way."
>
> "You will not absolve me?"
>
> "Please, your grace. I pray you put your mind to rest. I shall absolve you, but only for that fallen state into which each of us is born. As for Caen, there is no sin." (350)

This general absolution for original sin does not put Harry's mind at ease. He cannot dismiss what he senses clearly to be true, but the Church does not support his conviction. Neither can it give his soul the relief it needs.

If the conventionally *faithful* practice of the Church creates such spiritual conflict in Harry, it is not surprising that the *corruption* of the institutional Church makes his dissonance more intense. As noted, the Church of Harry's time is a pathway to power and wealth for those who would rise in its ranks. And like any institution, its perpetuation depends on seeing its current systems maintained. As portrayed earlier in the novel, the most important character representing church corruption is Archbishop Arundel. Harry refers to him as "the most powerful man in England next the King. He was hated by clerks and yeomen alike for his arrogance and greed. No poor man's land was safe from his grasping. My father tolerated Arundel's highhandedness because the Archbishop gave generously of this wealth to the Crown" (111). Like a demon on Bolingbroke's shoulder, Arundel persistently works to heighten the tension between the father and son. And on two occasions, once in Shrewsbury as noted above and once in London when the father and son are on better terms, he tries to have Harry killed. Greed, the concomitant of power, is Arundel's dominant trait. Harry reflects, "I detest Arundel and his party. They are vultures who prey on the poor. Aye, I have a care for the reform of the Church, for England's sake and for my own soul's health" (93). When Harry at last forces the archbishop to resign as chancellor, it is through a threat to allow some confiscation of the Church's, and therefore his own, wealth.

The Oppositional Church

A second factor that complicates Harry's pursuit of his call is the oppositional Church, those believers who are devout in their Christian faith but at odds with the theology and practices of the institutional Church. Giardina represents these believers through the Lollards. If the corrupt institutional Church functions as an antagonist in Harry's inner conflict, it might seem intuitive that those who oppose it and hope to reform it would be natural allies of a Christian king who is himself set upon an agenda for reform. Though Harry is occasionally pushed in their direction through his disgust with the institutional Church or pulled there by his friendship with Jack and his love for Merryn (both of whom accept many Lollard beliefs), the oppositional Church ultimately fails him as well. Giardina represents the reformers' failure most clearly through the progression—or regression—of Jack's faith.

The Lollards were a loosely organized group formed around the ideas of John Wycliffe. They believed, among other things, that the Bible should be accessible to individual Christians, that a priest was not needed to mediate a relationship with God, and that the institutionalism of Christianity, particularly due to its privileged association with state power, inevitably leads to corruption. Jack and Harry's first contact with the Lollards is through the limner William Parcheminer. A wholly unlikeable character, he is narrow in his understanding and violent in the implications of his faith. He longs for a king who "shall wield the sword of righteousness, aye, and cut deep with it" (95). When Harry asks how such a ruler would succeed, Parcheminer responds, "He would reject the authority of the pope, that false shepherd who leads men to perdition, and turn out the priests as well. Strip the Church of its wealth and purge it of these unholy monks. Cleanse the churches of their idolatrous images. Aye, and he would stop this veneration of Mary, who was but a woman and so was a weak vessel" (95). He continues to blast many other practices, including those Harry holds dear; most significantly, Parcheminer calls the Church's teaching on holy communion "Sorcery! . . . It is not the Lord's body, but only bread" (95).

The negative results of this kind of teaching are portrayed in Jack. His initial acquaintance with Lollard beliefs seems to strengthen his Christian devotion, but as his contact continues, the new theology makes him more like Parcheminer: narrow in his thinking and willing to rationalize violence, not only against the enemies of England but against any who disagree with his beliefs—including Harry. His convictions lead eventually to attempts to remove his one-time friend and protector from the throne: all who resist the reforms Jack supports "must die as corrupters of the faith who would bear poor men into Hell with them" (267). Close attention to the text reveals that throughout her presentation of the Lollards, Giardina suggestively interweaves the language of theological argument with the language of economics; it becomes evident that Jack's newly found piety may have as much to do with greed as with God. He persistently argues that the Church should be stripped of its wealth and that its holdings should be given "to those with true faith"—which would of course include himself.

The most clearly damning line in the depiction of Jack's corruption is Harry's response to his Lollard agenda: "You sound too much like Arundel for my ears" (268). A commonplace Harry is battling here is the fact that revolutionary groups sometimes tend to recreate the evil they fight against; they can become revised versions of the forces they overthrow in the name of reform. Eventually Jack becomes utterly delusional. By the time he is executed for his second attempt at revolution, he is proclaiming that three days after his death he will rise like Jesus from the dead (352). In Jack, Giardina has created a character far less repulsive than Arundel; indeed, he is Harry's friend, at times as earthy and winsome as Shakespeare's version of the historical John Oldcastle, Falstaff. But his conflation of religious devotion with economic and political ambition keeps Harry from being able to embrace the potential reform offered by the oppositional Church.

The Rise of Capitalism

Related to the economic aspect of oppositional Christian thought is a third force that complicates Harry's striving to be simultaneously a successful king and a faithful Christian: the rise of capitalism. Giardina portrays a changing world, one increasingly willing to embrace power for its own sake, outside the customary institutional sanctions of church and state. In our time many people take it as a given that economic powers, in the form of postnational corporations and economic interests, manipulate nations by determining political elections in their own interest and even influencing countries toward war for their own advantage. But in the world of *Good King Harry*, the articulation of such phenomena was less developed. Because the novel presents these interests as guided by wealth and power, their interest in Harry as a *Christian* king is simply utilitarian. Bracketing any religious factors, these rising capitalists choose to further Harry's purposes based only on whether they are likely to be profitable.

As noted above, Giardina demonstrates this secular force first in Harry's uncle Beaufort, his early tutor, his mentor in the ways of statecraft, and eventually his chancellor. Beaufort is a cleric, but he has become a churchman only as an avenue for advancement, with little veneer of religious sentiment. While at Oxford he tells his young charge, "You are no more fitted for the Church than I. Here I am, of course, but for one in my position it is the only way [to success]"

(16). Beaufort's identification is with the merchant class, the rising capitalists. He pointedly asks Harry,

> What king may rule without them? Indeed, what would your father do? They provide him with goods, aye, and coin. They are our destiny, Harry, and I tell you they care not tuppence for chivalry, though they do acknowledge it from custom. Their code is not chivalry but power. Power governs the King and his nobles as well, yet they give not power its due. They live in their dream world of knights-errant and honor and family name. (17)

And he adds, "I am one of these new men." Such a man Beaufort shows himself to be. Through him Harry has learned how this brave new world will work, and through Harry's position Beaufort continues to rise on a parallel track of increasing political (and ecclesial) power. He chides the adult Harry for his overactive concern with religious convictions. Particularly telling is the exchange in which Beaufort says to Harry, "You are not ignorant of evil, but you seem to think that some are able to avoid it. No one escapes sin, nephew. Some sin more efficiently than others, that is all" (205).

Harry accepts but is slow to understand fully the implications of his uncle's counsel. Through Beaufort's connections and guidance, Harry meets and forms alliances with the capitalists of London, first among them Dick Whittington. Whittington's character is not developed in detail, save that he is portrayed as powerful, personally likeable, and generally bereft of any religious conviction. He is more a force than a man. Like Beaufort, Whittington and his fellow merchants give only formal acknowledgment to church and state. Harry is repulsed by the fact that profit is their final authority, but he needs them. By carefully cultivating associations with the merchants, he gains increasing influence in the realm. And once Harry has taken the throne, it is through his collusion with the merchants that he is empowered—or financed—to pursue his call as a Christian king.

His chivalrous peers tolerate Harry's unconventionality and support his initiatives only because he finds backing in the capitalists. The nobles might desire, for example, to go to war with France for the sake of chivalry. But the merchants will support the war with France only because of the profit in supplying an army: then as now, war creates greater poverty for the poor, but it creates profit for those who keep the business of war going. So ironically, Harry's holy hopes depend on those who care nothing for his holy goals. While the merchants do enable his cause, they do so for reasons that are the antithesis of his own; as such, he gains support only at the expense of his soul.

And he opens Pandora's box. In a masterful stroke, Giardina uses the impeccably chivalrous—and comically sympathetic—Lord Warwick to discern in a prophetic way Harry's mixed accomplishments. After his great victory at Agincourt, he bullies Warwick with one of his many blasts against chivalry, and Warwick's response is both touching and insightful. As much an "old man" as Harry is a "new man," Warwick begs his king, "I pray you mock me no longer, for I have only sought to follow the good as I have been taught it" (335). He then continues in one of the book's most thematically important exchanges:

> "You have spoken of the death of chivalry, and your words are dreadful to me. If chivalry be dead what is left?"
>
> "I know not. I am no seer."
>
> "Then I must hazard a guess. Ever had I thought the world to make sense. If you speak truly, then it does no longer. If knights do not protect the weak, but harry them, and if the weak pick up their bows and slay the knights, what then? Are the weak better off? Or shall they be tyrannized by a new master, who wields power but speaks not of love and honor?"
>
> "What good to speak of love and honor if they are not practiced?"
>
> "Little enough, perhaps. Yet is it not good to hear them spoken of? The speaking of them can conjure them from time to time. When shall we hear of them again, if chivalry be dead?"
>
> He seemed to tower over my bed from a great height. (335)

A "great height" indeed: Warwick sees more clearly into the future than does his king. Harry may have made some progress on his goal of becoming a Christian king and uniting Christendom. But in doing so, he has furthered a change in his world that, despite his meticulous calculations, he seems not to have understood clearly, if at all. And the results of that change, Warwick suggests, may be worse than the chivalrous hypocrisies it has supplanted.

Radical Christian Devotion

Unlikely as it may seem, another factor causing conflict as Harry strives to be a Christian king is his own radical Christian devotion. If the three previous factors have complicated Harry's attempts to realize the *Christian* aspect of being a *Christian* king, his radical devotion would deter him from being a king at all.

Taken literally, the teachings of Christianity (most famously, the Sermon on the Mount) preclude any violent exercise of power. Indeed, nonviolence was the dominant position in Christian thought at least until the conversion of Constantine (AD 312). Since that time most Christians have chosen to understand this position against violence as a too-facile reading of Jesus's admonitions. As through the centuries the institutional Church developed mutually beneficial associations with political power, it was determined that a radical position regarding nonviolence makes governing—or a privileged association with those who govern—impossible. This theological shift led to, among other things, the previously discussed Just War theology that dominated in Harry's era as it does in most churches today. And that strain of thought has inevitably led to the concomitant question of what evil a Christian government (or individual) may commit for the sake of greater good. Still, for some particularly radical strains of Christian thought, the apparent casuistry of Just War theology has never been convincing. The greatest anxiety Harry experiences in pursuing his call occurs as he struggles with the question: Can a devout Christian do evil for the sake of good?

It must be noted that Harry does not seem devout by many standards: he is legendary among the denizens of taverns and brothels. Yet even his activities there are most important because they play a role in his increasing empathy with the poor. Just as his repulsion for the way war abuses common soldiers and peasants develops in part through his participation in these atrocities, his years of frequenting the establishments in Chepeside lead to sincere care for the lowborn of London. He comes to value them, to respect them, and to prefer their company; they in turn see their Harry not as a condescending noble but as a populist hero who is concerned for their welfare. Though not egalitarian in any anachronistic sense, he takes to heart, at the very least, a feudal understanding of the responsibilities of a noble—and a king—to the welfare of those under his care.

Could he, then, even *be* a king, when doing so would by apparent necessity mean wielding his power at their expense? On three occasions this devotion-driven doubt tempts him to trade his call for self-annihilation. As noted above, in one early campaign he contemplates drowning himself as an alternative to destroying his Welsh countrymen. Again at the river crossing before the battle of Agincourt, having helped the others over, he looks longingly at the currents that might sweep him away and keep him from causing the coming slaughter. And the night before his greatest battle, he takes what may be his most dramatic Christian action. A brilliant tactician, he alone sees that his bedraggled army will win a terrible victory and that his greatest success will mean thousands dead. With that dread on his heart, he presents terms to the French, offering his own life in place of those who would be killed the next day. His offer is all the more telling in that his own soldiers are not his only or even primary concern: he knows his army's losses will be relatively few. He is offering to sacrifice himself to save the French, not only the foot soldiers but the very nobles whose decadence he detests and whose chivalrous worldview has plagued his life since he was first injured in a joust as a child. The allusion to the sacrifice of Jesus seems clear: Harry would lay down his life for his friends and even sacrifice himself on behalf of his enemies.[24] Though his offer is refused, it clarifies the conundrum: to succeed as a Christian *king* would be to fail as a *Christian* king.

It is through Merryn, however, that Giardina presents most clearly the enervating complexity of Harry's Christian devotion—and the potential way in which that complexity could keep him from fulfilling his call as a Christian king. Like Courtenay, she serves as a moral touchstone for Harry, and one considerably less yielding than the cleric; unlike Courtenay, she lacks sufficient theological sophistication to distract her conscience. Even readers who question her realism will see, too, that in one way at least she is psychologically vivid: in Merryn, Harry unconsciously recognizes and loves in her a part of himself. In Jungian psychological terms, she functions as one aspect of his anima, his unconscious feminine. And the aspect of himself most clearly portrayed in that anima is a very raw, pure sense of justice that can never be wholly set aside, even for a king assuming the life-and-death functions of state.

Repeatedly, Merryn plagues Harry with the ramifications of his actions. This practice is most conflicting when it seems that Harry is only doing what he must, what his responsibility demands. In one especially telling conversation, she confronts him with the paradox of his office and asks, "Why can you not leave? What would happen if you renounced the crown in Tom's favor and went back to Monmouth to live out your days?" (202). On one level Harry wants to do exactly that. He tells her, "I fear I shall lose my soul. Indeed, I fear it is already lost. There is no good a king may do, none, for when the King raises his little finger, someone is crushed by it. Yet I cannot step back from it, God help me. I fear to die. And I want to rule" (202). This reflection might be read as Harry choosing his will to power over his devotion. But Giardina will not allow that ethical simplicity. If Harry abdicates, the evil will still come to pass; and the evil will be greater with his brother Tom, who lacks Harry's convictions, on the throne. Harry throws the question back at her, that is, at a part of himself: "May I wash my hands of this power and preserve the purity of my soul at the cost of even more lives? I fear not. I think it is wicked to care so much for one's own soul. I must carry this burden myself though it bear me down to perdition" (203). Giardina emphasizes the gravity of this statement by following it with a single-sentence paragraph—"Outside our window a cock crowed"—a richly ambiguous allusion to Saint Peter's denial of Christ.[25]

Merryn is at this point a temptress figure, though an ironically moral one. If we consider Harry's story as a mythic journey, she is the beautiful vision that would lure him away from completing his call to be a Christian king. Part of her power—and her mythical suggestion—is in her identification with Wales, the idyllic, not-quite-real Wales of his boyhood. When he is with Merryn on the marshes, conventional Christianity falls away, and he revels in the bliss of childhood: of his nurse Joan Waryn and her fairies, of the faithful who await the mythical coming of Arthur, of peasants who seek the intervening magic of Merlyn. These are in fact the only times Harry seems anything other than a fairly orthodox, albeit lusty, Christian. Merryn even refers to her influence as having "bewitched" Harry (237). Yet her strongest hold on him has nothing to do with Celtic witchcraft but with his own conscience. She tempts Harry not by calling him to bed—though she does that at times—but by giving voice to a radical understanding of Christianity that is loath to commit smaller evils for the sake of greater good.

As Harry may be perceived as holding the orthodox idea of a Just War in its most ideal sense, Giardina uses Merryn to suggest another conundrum of Christian thought: the fact that a more absolute idea of goodness, though lesser known and seldom heeded, must nevertheless always be a part of any decision to commit violence. The eminent twentieth-century theologian Reinhold Niebuhr, an influential thinker during the years of Giardina's theological formation, addresses the very anxiety confronting Harry in his essay "Why the Christian Church Is Not Pacifist." As the title suggests, Niebuhr does not share Merryn's radicalism but maintains that the evil of war must be accepted as an inevitable result of human sinfulness. He argues, "The good news of the gospel is not the law that we ought to love one another. The good news of the gospel is that there is a resource of divine mercy which is able to overcome a contradiction within our souls, which we cannot ourselves overcome."[26] This is the contradiction that is finally irreconcilable for the Christian king. Yet regarding the kind of temptation Merryn presents, Niebuhr affirms,

> We who allow ourselves to become engaged in war need this testimony of the absolutist [e.g., Merryn] against us, lest we accept the warfare of the world as normative, lest we become callous to the horror of war, and lest we forget the ambiguity of our own actions and motives and the risk we

run of achieving no permanent good from this momentary anarchy [war] in which we are involved.[27]

In fact, Giardina places one of the classic questions of Christian pacifism in Merryn's "absolutist" voice: "Is there not a better way? Can you truly end war with more war?" (224). Niebuhr argues that there is no other way; there is only the possibility of living with the conflict we feel within our souls. Whether Harry ever reconciles himself to the conflict is a more difficult question.

The Limitations of Mortality

The fifth complicating factor as Harry follows his call to be a faithful Christian and a successful king may be the most obvious: regardless of his great gifts, his devotion, and his strength of will, Harry suffers the inescapable weakness of being mortal. In the Second Epistle to the Corinthians, the apostle Paul recounts his many reasons to boast, claiming revelations given to him like no other. Then he writes, "And lest I should be exalted above measure through the abundance of the revelations, there was given to me a thorn in the flesh, the messenger of Satan to buffet me."[28] This phrase "thorn in the flesh" has evolved in idiomatic English as a metaphor for any chronic problem. Most use it today unaware that it comes from a Bible passage.

Giardina, however, uses it with a certain knowledge of its context. In the Bible, the thorn in the flesh functions as a persistent check on Saint Paul's overestimation of his own importance. He prays for its removal but receives only the message of God, "My grace is sufficient for thee: for my strength is made perfect in weakness."[29] The implications of this passage are doubtless in Giardina's mind when she gives Harry a pain in his belly. That he eventually calls it the "bloody flux" is realistically true to the deprivations of warfare, but it is significant that Harry's thorn plagues him even before the war begins, particularly when he is faced with his most perplexing limitations.

The first instance occurs when he receives word that troops he sent to help the Burgundians have succeeded. He has a passing thought that the victory will see "the strife ended" in France (226). But Merryn reminds him of the price paid for such a victory—children orphaned and the seeds of vengeance planted—and she asks the question common to many war resistors: "Where shall it end? It shall not, I fear, until there are none left to slaughter" (226). At this point Harry reports, "A sharp pain tore through my belly so that I wanted to cry out, but I only flinched. Slowly I sat down." And he tells Merryn, "I can defend myself against all save you" (226). Harry's response confirms that the pain is psychological as well as physical. The next occurrence follows Harry's exchange with Courtenay in which he resolves to commit smaller wrong to accomplish greater good. "Soon after our conversation," Harry confesses, "I fell ill and was abed for a fortnight. A fever it was, and some malady of the belly" (280).

The thorn pierces his flesh again after his victorious massacre at Agincourt, which includes the murder of many prisoners:

> I came ill to Calais. My head yet throbbed from the blow I had taken, but it was my belly which griped me most, the pain sucking what little remained of my strength so that I could scarcely sit my horse the remaining forty-five miles to the city. Rhys noted my weakness and stayed by my side.
> "Is it the flux?" he said.
> "I don't know. There is a fever, and my belly burns with fire." (334)

The assault at Caen affects him the same way. He confronts Tom for allowing the horrific atrocities there, then confesses, "Pain shot through my midsection so that I moaned softly and hunched my shoulders" (349). Again at the siege of Meaux, after he matches the French execution for execution, Harry "vomited blood and sent for [his] physician" (386). It is clear that there is a conflict in Harry's soul that worsens after every atrocity. He cannot control the atrocities that war makes necessary. The sins he and his soldiers must commit take a toll on his soul, and his mortal body responds.

Harry sees himself as the most able man in Christendom, and for good reason. But his human limitations cannot be denied. Keeping every aspect of every campaign under his watchful eye, maintaining the loyalty and love of his troops, checking their excesses, and outmaneuvering his enemies is utterly exhausting. Though warned that he is overextending his capabilities, he neither eats nor sleeps. Particularly on later campaigns, he must begin to delegate more authority. When he does so, he wins battles but not in the manner of a Christian king. His lieutenants, like Tom at Caen, lack his commitment. Gradually his illness and exhaustion lead him to fall short of his principles himself.

Harry's mortal weakness takes a different form when he establishes his place in the French monarchical line through marriage with Kathryn. Not only is this marriage a moral compromise—the behavior of the French royalty is even more violent, decadent, and class-centered than the English peers—but the situation is brought about in part by his lust for Kathryn. There is nothing to recommend her save her sensuality and the political alliance marriage brings. But Harry had taken a vow after Merryn's death and made England his only lover. After years of sexual abstinence, he wants Kathryn badly, so much so that his judgment is clouded (365). As he seeks to keep the favor of his licentious bride, he suffers both spiritually and physically.

It is in the context of his conflict with her, after an argument about her lack of faithfulness, that he finally collapses "in a black whirl of senselessness" (388). It becomes clear that he will not recover, and his youngest brother Humphrey tells him he is dying. Though he tries to persuade himself that it is "God's work I have been doing," he is suddenly struck by a new, fuller understanding: his warmaking has been sin. Echoing the Augustinian understanding of original sin, he reflects "that it was ever sin and the same sin from time immemorial. Nothing had come from it save the death of everyone and everything I had loved, and the everlasting fires of Hell would be gentle compared to the knowledge of it" (388). The final factor, then, that stymies Harry's determination to be a Christian king is his mortality: no human is wise enough, shrewd enough, or strong enough to evade this universal complication.

Coming to Terms with Failure

The epilogue returns the story to Harry's deathbed. He narrates once again with the gallows tone of the prologue and reflects upon his wasted life. On his last day, he receives a visitor, a convent servant named Marie, who comes to him because she was ordered by a vision of the Virgin Mary to do so. But she has no message for him; she was only told to come. In essence, she becomes his confessor. Before he knows her full identity, he tells her, reflecting on the dead,

> In heaven they shall live again. But that gives me no comfort. I have robbed them of their earthly time. I have sought power to preserve the good, and even so I have destroyed it. *I think now there is no good unless it also be weakness. I have lacked the courage to be weak.* But then I think, how could I have walked away from my crown? Must not the powerful seek to do good? What shall we do, Marie? Have you no message at all? (391; italics mine)

In this passage, the novel of development and the novel of ideas come together. As noted in relation to Hirsch's model, the novel of formation "educates the reader by portraying the education of the protagonist."[30] And here we see a key idea emphasized for Harry and the reader. Harry's ultimate failure is his failure to accept his mortality, the inevitable weakness that comes with being human: the thorn in his flesh that has haunted his attempts to do good in ways that no mortal could overcome. He has been tragically slow in coming to terms with his weakness, and his hubris has sealed his fate. Like Saint Paul, who also grappled with his mortality and prayed that the thorn would be removed, Harry must finally take to heart the same message from God: "My grace is sufficient for thee: for my strength is made perfect in weakness."

His visitor then confesses that she is the woman in whose cottage he stayed during his first campaign through France. Her children, whom Harry once entertained with legends of Arthur, have all been killed—and she raped—by his own soldiers. She tells him, "I have tried to hate you, but now that I see you here, I cannot" (391). These words echo those of Merryn (169), and it becomes clear that Giardina is here presenting a symbolic conflation of Marie, the woman herself; the Virgin Mary, to whom Harry has prayed all his life and who has given Marie her vision; and Merryn, Harry's idealized true love (and a part of himself). Significantly, he weeps for the first time since Merryn's death: "I weep for Jack and Courtenay, for Rhys and Tom, for my father, for all the nameless ones, for us all" (392). After this he reports, "The dead yet crowd my dreams, but they accuse no more. Their faces are pale and sad, and touched with wisdom." The conflation of *Marys* continues at the moment of death. He can say only "Mer-" and the attendants at his bedside believe he has seen the Queen of Heaven. He has in a way, though in the form of Merryn. She stands across a green river, doubtless in Wales, and he enters the cold water.

This final sequence of events ties the story up neatly, perhaps too neatly. After four hundred pages of inner turmoil, Harry's spiritual resolution comes in the final four pages. Nevertheless, Giardina has succeeded in finding what she was looking for in her protagonist: "the human, the insecure, the person trying to do what was right but failing miserably." And she has led her readers on a careful consideration of "where the redemption" may be found. Maybe, the book suggests, there are truths humans grasp fully only at the moment of death. And if this is the case, Giardina's *Good King Harry* stands squarely, if not comfortably, within the troubling bounds of Christian belief.

CHAPTER 3

Storming Heaven: Colonization and the Roots of Resistance

Long before her publishing success with *Good King Harry* (1984), Denise Giardina was already envisioning a novel that would draw upon her close bond with the West Virginia coalfields. But because she believed New York publishers might be less open to a novel set in her home country, she made a tactical decision: "My idea was that there was a prejudice against Appalachian writers, so if I wrote this other book first, then they would take my coal-mining novels. I wanted to write a novel like *Storming Heaven*."[1] As it turned out, her intuition was correct: "After *Good King Harry*, my publisher asked what I was going to do next. When I told him, he said they weren't interested. My agent found a different publisher."[2]

That "different publisher" must have been pleased with the decision to take a risk. *Storming Heaven* (1987) succeeded with critics and the reading public, earning many glowing reviews and strong sales. Writing for the *Los Angeles Times*, Fred Chappell called it "brilliant diamond hard fiction, heartwrenching, heartwarming, tough and tender," and ranked it alongside John Yount's *Hardcastle* and James Still's *River of Earth* as one of the three great novels about Appalachian coal mining.[3] *Publishers Weekly* called it "one of those rare books that portrays a small world with impeccable clarity" and noted Giardina's "vigorous, elegant prose."[4] The *Tennessean* reviewer Linda Quigley praised it for encompassing "the spirit of humanity, from the heights of greatness to the depths of suffering with a fullness of emotion devoid of sentimentality."[5] And Thomas L. Kilpatrick in *Library Journal* affirmed the author's achievement: "Giardina has taken a little-known event in American history and woven a beautiful and dramatic story into it. Not to be missed."[6] It was named a Discovery Selection by the Book-of-the-Month Club, which certainly helped push the book toward a broad audience outside the region. And most significantly for its enduring importance, it has received persistent scholarly attention: since receiving the Weatherford Award in 1987, *Storming Heaven* has found its place in many discussions of Appalachia's finest creative work.

From History to Fiction

Like *Good King Harry*, *Storming Heaven* is historical fiction. Though it alludes to earlier events, the novel opens in 1890 and continues through the period of the West Virginia Mine Wars (ca. 1912–21). Giardina works carefully within these broad outlines of history while integrating the compelling particularities of the storyteller's imagination. But in contrast to her first novel, the history examined here is comparatively recent. Far more verifiable details are available, thus creating a complex set of opportunities and challenges for the novelist: what to include, what to dismiss, what to modify, and what to create. The result is a mixture of historical specifics, fictionalized composites, and consistently believable invention.

Grounding allusions to historical events of the period abound, among them the Ludlow Massacre, the Haymarket Riot, the Paint Creek–Cabin Creek Strike, and, forming the novel's climax, the march on Blair Mountain. Other events are moved, merged, or made up. Well-known historical figures like Mother Jones and Eugene Debs are briefly mentioned; and lesser-known but important figures like Frank Keeney (the United Mine Workers district president) and Don Chafin (the ruthless boss of Logan County) play roles true to the historical record. Still other characters draw lightly on historical antecedents. For example, C. J. Marcum is the union-sympathizing mayor of Annadel, just as Cabell Testerman was the union-sympathizing mayor of Matewan; and Isom Justice bears some faint relationship to Sheriff Sid Hatfield, whose murder is often considered the flashpoint for the march on Blair. But Giardina makes no historical claim for the characters closest to the center of the drama. They are her creations but creations that clearly find their genesis in the social forces of the time. She develops them in psychological fullness appropriate to the historical situation.

This approach differs from the one Giardina used in *Good King Harry* and would use again in *Saints and Villains* and *Emily's Ghost*. In those novels she began with historical characters and created likely events. But in the coalfield novels, as she has stated, "I chose to create fictional characters based on actual historical events."[7] For as much as *Storming Heaven* is an action story and a love story, it is still more the story of a time and place. Drawing upon her extensive research and on her novelist's—and theologian's—understanding of human nature, she creates characters who, given the historical events, seem necessarily to have lived. For such events to have occurred, such people must, it seems, have made them happen or suffered their happening. Their believability is a measure of Giardina's art. By bringing history into the flesh and blood of fiction, she personalizes it, incarnates it, and places it in a fuller human perspective. As a result, her work has drawn thousands of readers into a more vivid and deeply felt understanding of one of America's untold stories.

While the central characters are fictions, their experiences are all too real. Given the horrific events and soul-crushing conditions the characters live (or do not live) through, readers new to Appalachian history might be tempted to think that Giardina is exaggerating the horrors of the era for the sake of a more exciting story. She insists, however, that the most heinous events in the novel are based on historical precedents just as extreme. In an interview with Tim Boudreau, she noted that she has at least one source for each important incident: "I didn't make anything up. I didn't want to be accused of exaggerating. I even left out some atrocities because I was afraid readers wouldn't believe them."[8] And she told W. Dale Brown, "[Critics] say I exaggerated how bad things were. The truth is that I toned things down."[9] Reading historical accounts such as David Corbin's thoroughly documented *Life, Work, and Rebellion in the Coal Fields* or Lon Savage's *Thunder in the Mountains* (two of several sources Giardina acknowledges) confirms many of the gruesome scenes that stand behind the novel.[10]

THE BATTLE OF BLAIR MOUNTAIN

The climax of the book's action is the historical Battle of Blair Mountain, the largest armed insurrection on continental American soil since the Civil War. This battle was the culminating event of a period known as the West Virginia Mine Wars, starting with the violence at the Paint Creek–Cabin Creek strike (1912–13) and including "the Battle of Matewan (May 1920), the Battle of the Tug (May 1920), and the Miners' March on Logan (August 1921)."[11]

Under United Mine Workers of America leadership, armed miners gathered south of Charleston at Lens Creek to march through Logan County to Mingo County (Giardina's Justice County). There they intended to free miners jailed under martial law for their union activity; to strike out against the oppressive mine-guard system and the abuse of power by local authorities, in particular Sheriff Don Chafin; and to establish at last the right to unionize the southern West Virginia coalfields. By the time the miners reached Blair, there may have been 10,000 to 20,000 in their ranks. Chafin's forces, made up of so-called deputies, private mine guards, civilian volunteers, state police, and state militia, were fewer in number but were already dug in on the high ground. They were armed with full military gear, including machine guns, and were supported by air power with explosive bombs and gas.[12]

The miners made progress throughout the days of fighting and would likely have broken through the lines. But when President Warren G. Harding added 2,500 federal troops and an air squadron, the miners laid down their arms. In part this was due to the additional force, but no less important was the fact that many of these miners were former soldiers who could not feel clear to fire on the flag they had so recently risked their lives defending—regardless of the justice of their cause. And for those who were not veterans, making war on forces that had already proven their gross corruption was one thing, but attacking the United States Army was quite another.

Even after decades of historical study, the Battle of Blair Mountain has not filtered its way into most school history books and certainly not into common knowledge, an absence shared by so many important events in American history—particularly in American *labor* history. It is telling that even though Giardina herself grew up in a coal camp, was educated in West Virginia public schools, and completed her bachelor's degree in history and political science at West Virginia Wesleyan University, she learned of Blair Mountain only as a postcollege adult.[13]

To understand why the mine wars were fought, how desperation sufficient to precipitate a battle like Blair could come about, and how an armed conflict of such magnitude could have been written out of history, it is necessary to understand the cultural changes occurring in the central Appalachian coalfields during the period covered by the novel. As *Storming Heaven* makes clear, the Battle of Blair Mountain was a long time coming, the violent culmination of decades of violence. It was the result of a pattern of injustice that included calculated poverty, the private guard system, the abuses of martial law, and the collusion of industrialists with state and local governments for the repression of basic human rights. Like many international struggles with which readers are far more familiar, it was, foundationally, the result of colonization for the extraction of resources.[14]

THE COLONIZATION OF THE COALFIELDS

Storming Heaven is situated in an era of catastrophic change in the central Appalachians, the period that experienced the coming of industrial capitalism—the onset of economic colonization. Until the late nineteenth century, the region had been to some degree economically isolated from the rest of the United States. The ruggedness of the terrain made large-scale commerce with the nation at large difficult or impossible. But as outsiders became increasingly aware of the abundance of natural resources in the region—timber, coal, and other minerals—and as technologies were developed that made large-scale mining and transportation possible, the forces of capitalism wasted no time in grasping the economic potential and extracting it from the mountains.

Agents and speculators came through the coal regions, buying land or, if not the land, the mineral rights, a purchase that included the right to extract the minerals by whatever means proved convenient.[15] The ramifications of such purchases were as far beyond the ken of the local people as were the legal resources necessary to fight them. At the close of the nineteenth century, legal ownership of most of the region described in *Storming Heaven* and nearly all the mineral rights were held by corporate interests outside the region, and the extraction of natural resources was underway. With that change, the agricultural economy was all but destroyed, and once-independent landowners found themselves servants of their Northeastern masters. Historian Ronald Eller writes, "By the turn of the century, the Appalachian South had become an economic colony of the urban Northeast. . . . As the resources of the mountains flowed wantonly out of the region, so did any hope for the independence and prosperity of the mountain people."[16]

This colonization is reflected in a poignant exchange between protagonists Rondal Lloyd, whose family has lost its land in West Virginia, and Carrie Bishop, whose family land in eastern Kentucky has not yet been—but will eventually be—lost. Rondal begins,

"I was born and raised in Justice County, over in West Virginia. Blackberry Creek. We had some land there oncet. Company took it."

I [Carrie] remembered Albion Freeman, who had spoken of stolen land in West Virginia. I had not thought of him in years.

"They do that a lot? Steal land, I mean."

"Sure. All over. Steal it or put the pressure on to buy it. Same thing, far as I'm concerned. How do you think your brother's company got this here land?"

"I just figured they bought it."

"Oh, they did. Everything legal, but sinful as hell."[17]

By *legal*, Rondal means legal in the sense that the process would hold up in a court system biased toward the coal companies and inaccessible to the mountaineers. And on occasions when legal means failed, illegal means—such as violent intimidation and even murder—were used. Giardina gives an example of this practice when railroad agents murder C. J.'s grandfather and forge his "mark" on a contract. Such actions were taken without any significant legal repercussions.

It was during this time period, too, that persistent stereotypes of the mountaineers as a primitive, inferior race were created. Eller writes that "between 1870 and 1890, over two hundred travel accounts and short stories were published in which the mountain people emerged as a rude, backward, romantic, and sometimes violent race who had quietly lived for generations in isolation from the mainstream of American life."[18] Such portrayals no doubt sold magazines; the public then as now is enticed by the exotic. But more insidiously, such images were a necessary concomitant to colonization, which depends on such a characterization of the Other: if the colonized are understood as inferior, exploitation that might usually be seen as morally reprehensible can be tolerated by the broader culture, or even be transvalued as bringing the Other into the light of civilization.

Readers unfamiliar with Appalachian history understandably struggle to imagine the magnitude and scope, let alone the rapacious, predatory nature, of this colonization. The subsistence-farming economy that had sustained the region—an economy that allowed a level of affluence and independence outside a cash-driven system—declined dramatically.[19] And the social organization of the region, largely based on kinship and community responsibility, was irreparably damaged. Mountaineers were removed from their land and resources were extracted. Even readers familiar with European colonization of Africa or the Americas have difficulty comprehending that similar actions took place just three hundred miles from Washington, DC, and scarcely one hundred years ago. Nevertheless, this is the documented context into which Giardina weaves her story. The very fact that we find it so hard to believe suggests the degree to which the story of the Appalachian Other has been excluded from history.

Aspects of Literary Form

THE CHALLENGE OF THE VERNACULAR

The most immediately apparent literary characteristic of *Storming Heaven* is that it is written completely in local dialects. Far from being incidental or a simple regionalizing factor, the narrative choice to use dialects shapes the novel's effect in intentional ways. Often writers using dialect also use a framing language in more conventional English, providing readers with the sense of an authoritative overarching voice with which they may more readily identify. This was a common practice even among the best local color writers such as Mark Twain, Harriet Beecher Stowe, and Sarah Orne Jewett. But Giardina chooses not to do so. This is a serious commitment, and it challenges the reader in several ways.

The first potential obstacle is that the story can be misunderstood on the most literal level. Because Giardina locks the speech into a specific time and region through particular, idiomatic diction and syntax, readers are forced to bring their best attention to the text simply to follow what is going on. That said, even readers who struggle with the first few dozen pages overcome the distance fairly quickly.

A weightier challenge is that even in twenty-first-century America, when we should know better, there is still a wrongheaded tendency to equate intelligence with the use of more typical mainstream speech. From the book's opening line, "They is many a way to mark a baby while it is still yet in the womb," readers may be confronted with their own unconscious prejudice in this regard. Knowingly or not, they must decide whether they will trust the authority of voices that use a nonstandard idiom. Giardina is, in a way, throwing down a gauntlet, challenging readers' stereotypes, yet opening a way for them to enter fully into a world that may indeed be different from their own, even to develop a relationship with characters who may on some level be the Other. Not surprisingly, Giardina tells of readers who have even complained, "This character seemed too intelligent to talk this way."[20]

Complicating this stylistic risk are the connotations of dialect writing in literary history. Particularly in the local color tradition, dialect was sometimes used with insufficient skill and far too often with the intention of ridicule. In stark contrast, Giardina uses dialect as a matter of realistic specificity, to accurately render speech; in so doing, she is giving fidelity to a speech pattern the same weight that she gives accuracy in other aspects of character and setting. Further, it becomes a way of characterizing particular speakers. Like Twain, her craft goes beyond a simple use of dialect to render nuance that distinguishes *Storming Heaven's* narrators. Stephen Mooney's assessment is sound:

> Giardina possesses a nearly unmatched ability—only James Still and John Yount can compare—to render in literary prose the spoken language of [Appalachian] people. What makes the achievement still more impressive is her capturing the spoken language as it evolved over a hundred-year period. Whether one is reading a section of *Storming Heaven* set in 1895 or a portion of *The Unquiet Earth* set in 1985, the vernacular is delivered with equal ease and with an uncanny sense of the unique rhythms that mark the speech of people in the central Appalachian hills.[21]

Multiple Points of View

Storming Heaven is narrated by four different voices, four distinct viewpoints each positioned to portray an experience of the events not accessible to the others. Through Carrie we understand the supportive, communal nature of everyday life in a traditional mountain community before colonization; her perspective is conditioned by a lived awareness of what is being or has been lost. Through Rondal we see the devastating poverty of the coal camps and how such conditions lead to despair, desperation, and finally to revolt; he has no memory of life before coal, but he understands on the most visceral level the deprivation of the colonized. Through C. J. the assessment of the injustice is broadened because he is able to articulate what the colonized suffer in terms of their basic rights as American citizens; not only is he a native, but he speaks knowledgably about political philosophy. Finally through Rosa Angelelli, Giardina embodies the suffering that comes with the immigrant experience, a vision all the more heart-wrenching for the way Rosa struggles and fails to make sense of her trauma.

This multiplicity of voices not only provides an engaging fullness but, maybe more importantly, allows Giardina to avoid any oversimplification that could easily have characterized the work. Taken in such vivid complexity, what becomes clear—even to readers with little knowledge of the region or its history—is that the novel is not simply addressing the questions of Appalachia. Consistently her work poses the universal questions, psychological and theological, political and environmental, that have motivated and continue to motivate people everywhere. Her achievement is all the more significant because her subjects are people too often and too easily considered the Other (i.e., the *lesser*). What Giardina demands of her readers, then, is a refusal to dismiss the thinking of common people as intrinsically less weighty or complex than that of their fellow citizens who use a more typically articulated discourse. Her treatment of the material is thus an elevation—or more accurately a *recognition*—of the sophistication and complexity of regular people suffering oppression. Together, the four voices create a rich, multilayered description that would be impossible for any single first-person narrator to realistically voice.

Carrie Bishop

Carrie Bishop is the central focus of the romantic plot, first as the lover of Rondal; then as the wife of Albion; then, after Albion's death, as Rondal's lover once again. Though she is not the first narrator, over half the text is related in her voice. She becomes the pedal point of the composition, the character with whom we most closely identify, whom we most deeply trust.

Carrie speaks from a position uniquely privileged to relate the changes of life before and after the onset of the colonizing forces of industrial capitalism. Her story begins on a mountain farm in Kentucky still untouched by the coming of the railroad and coal company scouts. Compared to the other narrators, she experiences throughout her childhood the comparatively idyllic, if not quite Edenic, context of a precapitalist mountain economy. That life is not without challenges: it is filled with hard work, and memories of the Civil War live in the stories of her family. The graves on the hillside are a constant reminder. Her social system is, however, essentially intact. She is part of an extended family and a cooperative community; labor and hardships, along with times of celebration and plenty, are shared in a familial and interfamilial context of holistic commitment and mutual responsibility. The economic culture is small-scale farming and trading: the bottom line is not the bottom line.

Cecelia Conway's study of the novel offers Peter Kropotkin's model of anarchism that focuses on mutual aid as a philosophical touchpoint to characterize the nature of life on Carrie's "Homeplace" and the surrounding community. Kropotkin's central idea is that "within groups, mutual aid precedes competition so that 'sociability is the greatest advantage in the struggle of life.'"[22] Further, Kropotkin's thinking downplays the role of law and central authority, focusing instead on custom and voluntary agreement, ideas that are "indispensable parts of the traditional values and strategies that underpin old-time mountain communities," ideas that make up the warp and woof of Carrie's ethic.[23] Unlike C. J., who is traumatized by the death of his grandfather and the loss of the family farm, and Rondal, who has no memory of life outside the coal camp, Carrie experiences and maintains an abiding sense of what life once was, a fact that shapes her psychological turmoil.

Even as a child, Carrie has a precocious appreciation of the essential goodness of life on the Homeplace and of how awful it would be to lose. At a community corn-shucking, for example, she and her friend Albion take offense at some good-natured teasing and move away from the bonfire. When they return to their place in the gathering, she relates, "I looked around the circle at the smooth faces glowing in the firelight. Then I thought, what agony to truly be cut off from them" (47). What she experiences in this intact community is what none of the other narrators have ever fully known, and it serves as a baseline by which the degradation that comes with colonization may be judged. This community, her ideal of an almost Edenic Homeplace, becomes the standard by which she suffers life in the coal camps: a fallen world of exploitation, poverty, and systemic violence.

Still on the Homeplace, Carrie experiences harbingers of the dramatic disruptions to come. Her brother Miles has attended Berea College and returned home with a very different vision of what the family's—and the community's—future must be. He envisions himself as one of the new men who will lead the mountaineers into a more cosmopolitan future. By persuading their father, Orlando, to cut the timber on the farm to sell to the coal companies, he takes a dramatic step in moving the family away from a self-sufficient mountain economy. Carrie intuitively sees the larger practical and spiritual ramifications of the cutting. As Conway notes, her dream in which Miles pushes a knife through a quilt symbolizes the destruction of the community; and the fact that Miles precipitates the change indicates that the attack from colonizers requires "unwitting, misguided, or silent co-option from within."[24] He acts, albeit unwittingly, as the serpent in the garden. The "ugliness of the cleared mountain" that Carrie hates is more than aesthetic (62): it is a violation of a relationship with the land that has been an essential part of the ordered life of the community. And the only compensation is temporary wealth. Carrie and her closest confidante, Aunt Jane, object but are unable to articulate fully what is so deeply wrong; too, they are powerless as women to stop what the men have decided. Miles encourages them to put up with it with the promise that "this time next year there'll be a big new house" (62).

The trees are cut and the money does come, but the fact that Orlando is killed floating the timber downriver underscores the steep price to be paid. Aunt Becka summarizes the spiritual nature of the loss in the biblical language of Jesus and Judas: "Orlando's gone. Oh, Jesus, he's gone, my poor little brother that I carried in my arms oncet. And all for a handful of silver" (65). The shock of her father's loss causes Carrie's sister Flora to go into premature labor, and she loses her child. These immediate consequences of the shift in values and culture are the first stages of broader, still more devastating losses to come.

It is worth noting that the objections to the shift come from the women in the Bishop family. Through Carrie, Giardina iterates the tradition of the strong, wise mountain woman, a tradition in Appalachian life and literature, as presented in the work of such writers as Harriette Arnow and Wilma Dykeman, and more recently Jeanne Bryner and Ann Pancake. As Mooney has stated, "Without doubt Giardina has created some of the most memorable female characters in twentieth-century Appalachian (and American) fiction."[25] Significantly, Carrie's perspective allows Giardina to embody important concepts about gender and gender complexity in ways that are realistic to the historical time and place. Like many adolescents, Carrie daydreams of a storybook lover to come along (in her case the storybook is *Wuthering Heights*), but she is also very much her own person with a strong sense of self-determination. On the one hand, she worries that she will never find a husband, her doubt precipitated by the fact that she is not as pretty as her sister Flora and by her father's warning that she would never find a husband because she is "too forward" (61). But on the other, Carrie demonstrates and values in herself attributes stereotypically associated with males. Aunt Jane, who has spent most of her life as a widow, helps her to understand and accept her own appearance and also to value in herself an independence of character and strength of will. Carrie recognizes for herself that most of the women in her community find romantic relationships while maintaining their authenticity. She comes to disregard the worst of her father's patriarchal belittling.

An example of her strong sense of self is the agreement Carrie makes with Miles: he teaches her to shoot, and in exchange she does the family hunting—a duty Miles disdains not because of any particular squeamishness but, more likely, because he sees hunting as one more aspect of a traditional mountain culture he does not value. When Orlando discovers the siblings' bargain, he puts an end to it, takes the gun away from Carrie "without a word," and tells her she'll never find a husband because she is

> not "deferrin" enough, my tongue was too sharp and I [Carrie] was too forward in my ways. I didn't believe him. Aunt Jane was not "deferrin" and she had been married. Most of the women I knew on the creeks were strong and feisty and they all had men. Still he hurt my feelings. I held myself distant from him and from other men who might treat me the same. (61)

Carrie suffers from her father's coldness, but she determines to make her own way.

A still more challenging example of gender complexity is the portrayal of Aunt Becka. Aunt Becka, Carrie learns, was married once, but after a month left her husband and made the three-day walk from the next county back to the Homeplace, where she remained unmarried the rest of her life. Neither does Aunt Becka encourage her nieces to wed. When Flora plans to marry Ben Honaker, the elder woman's response is that Flora could do no better for herself "if she must marry." "In other words," Carrie paraphrases, "Ben Honaker was just fine, for a man" (34). Carrie is at first puzzled. She asks Aunt Jane if Aunt Becka's husband had been mean to her, and Aunt Jane responds, "Law, no, child. He was just more man than your Aunt Becka wanted" (35). When Carrie confesses to Aunt Jane her accidental discovery that Aunt Becka has no pubic hair, Aunt Jane simply explains that "hit's just the way she's made" (36). Her explanation continues:

> Your Aunt Becka is funny turned, but she's a good woman. And she's kin. Aunt Becka cant help the way God made her, and she has a right to be the way she is. I should never said things about her to you before, and I wont never say them again. As for you, you just be like your own self. And ifn Aunt Becka dont like it, you and her might not git along. But God help the stranger tries to hurt you, cause Aunt Becka would tear them limb from limb. Whip anybody tried to harm a hair on your head. Dont never forget it. (36–7)

There is a certain obscurity in the response and in the overall characterization, but the implication seems clear. Aunt Becka does not fit easily at either pole of a heteronormative gender binary. That Giardina creates the character ambiguously testifies to the fact that she sees the phenomenon as important; and it has the didactic advantage of reminding readers that gender complexity is not simply a phenomenon of contemporary media and identity rhetoric. The air of secrecy surrounding Aunt Becka as "funny turned" may disappoint twenty-first-century expectations of gender equality, but to have handled it otherwise would have certainly jeopardized the realism of the novel. The degree of advocacy here is significant in that a wise, authoritative voice argues on behalf of Aunt Becka having "a right to be the way she is" and, just as importantly, affirms that ties of kinship and community run far deeper than such differences, even in a category as important as gender. Being "funny turned" does not keep one from having a place in the mountain community. The silence that Aunt Jane recommends for the topic is what David E. Wilson terms "benevolent repression."[26] As presented in the novel, benevolent repression is likely as progressive a stance as could be taken without sacrificing the historical and cultural verisimilitude Giardina strives to maintain. And as we will observe in her characterization of Hassel Day in *The Unquiet Earth* and Lydde Falcon in *Fallam's Secret*, Giardina resists both too-easy conservatism and too-easy progressivism, avoiding the ease of abstractions and persistently confronting readers with the complexity of the particular.

Rondal Lloyd

Giardina's statement noted above, "I chose to create fictional characters based on actual historical events," could find no clearer exemplar than Rondal Lloyd. The massive and violent resistance to the oppression that coal companies executed on native Appalachians must inevitably have created men like Rondal. He offers the perspective of one who has little or no memory of life before colonization. "Earliest thing I recall from when I was a boy," he tells us, "is daddy coming in from the mines and taking his bath. It always scared me when he came in" (12). Rondal is a pure product of the coal camps.

As Terry Easton notes in his insightful class-based analysis of the novel, families in company towns did not only experience the overtly repressive power of the companies (most obviously represented by the company's private police) that sought to control their lives. They also suffered the repression of a civil society that was determined "to alter the habits of miners and their families" with particular kinds of "schools, churches, and recreational activities."[27] In other words, the colonized were manipulated into thinking like the colonizers. Thus "the combined forces of physical repression and ideological manipulation worked in tandem to create a system of lack, loss, and injustice for miners and their families."[28] With economic change, cultural change is inevitable, even including the ways that families function.

We see the results of this process in Rondal's family, where the power of the coal company perpetuates a chilling division. The meager and irregular pay his father, Clabe, receives for his work compels him to follow the company's suggestion that he bring his sons into the mine, ten-year-old Rondal as a loader and eight-year-old Talcott as a slate-picker. Thus the boys are separated from their mother, Vernie—a separation not only physical but psychological. Vernie cannot reckon with the fact that she cannot save them from the danger of the mine or the cruelty of the bosses. After the boys' first day at work, when Rondal can hardly walk home and Talcott cannot stand because of the beatings he has received from his overseer, Rondal hears his mother weeping to Clabe in the kitchen:

> "What am I supposed to do? I'm a-scairt to hug my own babies for fear of hurting them. I seen bruises all over Talcott's back where that boss man hit on him. Aint no mother supposed to let such things happen to her younguns."
>
> "Shut up!" Daddy said. "I can take care of them boys." (24)

Vernie is quite right. No mother should let such things happen to her boys, but her situation has left her powerless. And their father, despite his claims, is equally unable to protect them. The function of the family is utterly disrupted: parents and children lose their identities as they are no longer able to fulfill their roles.

In another telling sequence, Rondal confesses to his mother that he has inadvertently charred her clean newsprint wallpaper. He is expecting, even hoping for, a whipping. But the exchange that follows indicates Vernie's loss of identity as well as the effect that loss has on Rondal:

> I told her what I had done. When she didn't answer, I said, "You going to switch me?"
> "Why should I? . . . You done gone in the mines. Aint no switch going to faze you none. Your daddy done made a man outen you. I cant do nothing with you now."
> I wished she would whip me about the bare legs with a briar switch, like in the old days, then weep at the sight of the scratches, hug me and feed me an apple butter biscuit. But I was left lonesome to chastise myself. (25–6)

This family tragedy must have been repeated thousands of times in the coal camps. Given the cultural shift, there was in fact no good escape. Rondal's mother withdraws from him, remaining distant and cold, and finding her only comfort in an escapist understanding of fundamentalist Christianity, a change that further alienates her from her sons. As Talcott states years later when Vernie refuses to speak to Rondal, "Hell, she's always like that. She dont love nobody but Jesus" (75). Vernie's distress is psychologically understandable, her response maybe even inevitable, but it leaves her an emotional cripple and has an equally crippling effect on Rondal. He bears throughout his short life the results of an inadequate relationship with his mother. He subsequently closes himself off from an emotionally intimate relationship with any woman, including Carrie. To her he confesses, "Now that there is something I understand, needing somebody. But love—they must be something wrong with me, but I just dont know what it is" (243).

The only time we see Rondal break emotionally—with any response other than anger—further highlights his traumatic mother-loss. During one of the battles with the company, the house of coal operator Lytton Davidson is set on fire. Rondal runs in the house to make sure it is empty and discovers the delusional Rosa Angelelli freeing butterflies from their pins on Davidson's collection displays. She thinks Rondal is one of her own dead sons, Francesco; and after he has carried her outside, they sit by the creek and she tenderly washes his face. Still agitated the next day, he relates the incident to Carrie and uncharacteristically adds, "I didnt mind it" (199). Rondal "[d]idnt have the heart" to tell her he was not Francesco, and he confesses, "I'm turned upside down about it." When he later goes to check on the crazed woman, she does not recognize him. Carrie states, "I saw the disappointment on [Rondal's] face" (199). What a delusional Rosa had given him, and just as quickly taken away, is a suggestion of the mother's tenderness he has yearned for since the day he first went into the mines.

The absence of mother-love is just one obvious factor in the development of Rondal's troubled and troubling way of moving through the world. At ten he had witnessed the death of his father's partner in a mine explosion, an event that rendered him mute for days and eventually led to his leaving home to live with C. J.'s family. Add to these crisis factors the continual experience of poverty, hunger, and hopelessness, and we begin to see why Rondal is the man he is and how such a man might be created by this historical situation. More surprising are his many caring and admirable attributes: his compassion for the plight of the miners, his dedication to his cause, the satisfaction he takes in his work, his unflagging courage, and his sophisticated tactical intelligence.[29]

If Rondal proves to be a character more admirable than likable, that is appropriate. It is hard to imagine a well-adjusted man full of the joys of hearth and home doing the desperately dangerous, violent work that his vocation demands. His life is lived under the constant threat of murder by company thugs, he is tremendously outgunned and out-financed, and he is sometimes hated by the people he seeks to serve. He is indeed a troubled man, the product of a troubled time. His own explanation of his personality rings true on a number of levels:

> Coal camps is home to me. Hit's like a baby duck when it's born, it takes the first thing it sees for its mommy. A baby duck spies an old ugly sow first thing, hit thinks, "That there is home." Hit's the same with me. I look for an old rattling coal tipple, or a house covered with the black dust. I look for things to be tore up. I seen so much of death and destruction they feel like home to me. (244)

Rondal is, in the words of Martha Greene Eads, one of the "casualties of the coal-mining industry."[30]

C. J. Marcum

C. J. Marcum is the narrator most politically articulate in his understanding of what has been and is being done to the mountain communities. His perspective provides Giardina an appropriate and realistic vehicle to explore issues of citizenship and unjust practices. In particular, he is positioned to voice how the railroad and coal companies—with the assistance of legal and governmental forces at their disposal—oppress the mountain communities, and to do so in a manner that demonstrates the degree to which their colonizing actions are fundamentally anti-American.

Unlike Rondal, C. J. remembers something of life before the coming of coal, having been present as a child when the colonization began. He is old enough to recall vaguely the world before industrial capitalism. But unlike Carrie, whose early childhood in Kentucky is a homely mountain pastoral, the dominant memory of C. J.'s youth—the loss of his grandfather's farm—yields an unvarying sense of injustice. Because Papaw had refused to follow his neighbors' lead in signing away his mineral rights to the railroad agent, he was murdered and his signature forged. C. J. and his grandmother were then evicted.

His grandfather, however, had schooled C. J. in the foundational American principles of personal rights and liberties. He gave him his name, Cincinnatus Jefferson, to serve as a continual reminder of the highest virtues of political philosophy. The name recalls two great statesmen known to have served their nations. Jefferson's political leadership and agrarian ideals are well known, but readers may be less familiar with the legacy of the Roman statesman Cincinnatus. As legend has it, Cincinnatus led his people selflessly in their time of greatest need. And when he was offered the opportunity to rule Rome, he chose instead to return to his farm, refusing the possibility of greater dictatorial power. Referring to the men who provided him their names, Papaw admonished C. J., "Farmers and freemen. . . . You be just like em, boy" (5).

This naming is all the more significant because, as Giardina portrays throughout the novel, coal companies and the politicians who serve on their behalf often misconstrue union advocacy in a non-patriotic, even an anti-American, light. Those who work for organized labor in the novel are often referred to as radicals and Bolsheviks. The World War I–era *red scare* is very much a part of the later sections of the novel, a fact made clear, for example, when the Annadel Social Club is jailed for sedition, an idea clearly in the air during these World War I years and culminating in the Sedition Act of 1918. Such anti-labor language is less a reflection of reality and more a rhetorical posturing by those in power to sway public opinion in directions that allow the colonizers to use any means, legal or illegal, to obstruct the effective organization of the coalfields. In retrospect it is all but impossible to discern, in the novel and in the historical record, how much of such thinking may have been on some level sincere and how much was a strategic manipulation of the public discourse. What is certain is that the associated language vilified and inhibited the effective organization of the miners. It is all the more important, then, for Giardina to show how those who resisted colonization considered their work fundamentally patriotic.

Because such malicious and inaccurate perceptions persist still today in some popular thought, it is important to remember that unregulated capitalism is not an American value: unbridled free enterprise is not synonymous with Constitutional principles of personal freedom. To elucidate and underscore the miners' legal grievances, Giardina persistently presents the actions of the coal companies as violating the Bill of Rights. C. J.'s presence and voice provide an avenue that allows her to accomplish this in a way that flows realistically within the narrative. The companies, especially through their private guards, repeatedly deny miners and their advocates the freedom of speech. The companies also violate the freedom of the press when they destroy newspaper offices, first at Huntington and later at Annadel. They deny miners the freedom to assemble, making it impossible for them to gather in public or in private. Miners and their families are evicted from their homes, their personal property destroyed, and their mail intercepted. They are frequently arrested and jailed without warrant or cause. Even the right to a trial is denied when guards and state police arrest and then summarily execute miners. The Constitutional emphasis is clear as well when C. J. and the Annadel Social Club take active advantage of the second amendment. After the destruction of the press at Annadel, they start stockpiling Krag-Jorgensen military rifles (126–7). C. J. clearly believes, drawing on the Declaration of Independence, in the "right to overthrow the government when it gits worthless" (20).

The significance of these Constitutional parallels should not be lost on the reader. C. J. is an idealist, a true believer in American principles. Though he dreams of a day when his grandfather's farm might be restored, his emphasis is on justice *now*: he wants justice for his friends and neighbors, and he wants the coal companies to be held accountable for their actions. The depth of C. J.'s patriotism is demonstrated by his attitude toward race as well. Though he lives in a context where racism persists, he takes pride in the fact that "the Jim Crow" has no place in his town of Annadel (54). His closest friend is Doc Booker, the black doctor who mentors him into a more sophisticated political understanding and who guides him in the creation of the *Annadel Free Press* (58). As a result of Doc Booker and C. J.'s influence, Annadel is an example of a town where racial equality approaches realization, and for that reason it draws the ire of the segregationist coal companies and the governmental powers that serve them. Yet Annadel is an integrated town, from the city council to the baseball team.

The memory of his grandfather's ideals, underscored by his having been martyred for defending his principles, becomes the driving force in C. J.'s life and provides his narration with a particular tenor and focus. Like his grandfather, C. J. too is martyred for his principles. This emphasis on foundational American rights opens the text to a larger cultural significance. *Storming Heaven* is one instantiation of ideas that have driven and continue to drive history. The story is inevitably regional but never parochial: Appalachian problems are national—even international—problems.

Rosa Angelelli

Rosa Angelelli, an immigrant from Sicily, presents yet another perspective on the situation of the miners, their families, and the struggle of life in a coal camp. Though her narration comprises fewer than ten pages, her story is essential to an understanding of the period.

Readers unfamiliar with the demographic makeup of Appalachian coal country during this era likely do not imagine the degree of ethnic diversity in the coal camps. Many readers may rightly assume that native Appalachians made up a significant part of the workforce, and they may know that African Americans were often brought in from the deep South. Less well known is the fact that company agents went to Ellis Island and even traveled abroad to recruit thousands of European workers, few of whom had any idea of the situation into which they were being drawn.

As noted in my introduction, Giardina was herself the granddaughter of Sicilian immigrants, and it is likely that her own paternal grandmother provided the author with insight into the lives of immigrant women. In her essay "Coalfield Ancestors," Giardina offers a brief, suggestive portrayal of her "Nona Sara," but their relationship was somewhat distant. "Though I saw them [her grandparents] once a month," Giardina writes, "there was little communication save for mutual observation."[31] She does note, however, that her grandmother never learned more than a few words of English, that every wall of her house was covered with images of religious devotion, and that in memory her house remains shadowy and mystical—all factors that carry over into her development of Rosa.

Although the mysterious impressionism that characterizes her experience of Nona Sara informs Giardina's description of Rosa and her home, it does not serve our intention here to speculate further on the familial connection. It is more important to understand Rosa's character as representing a significant facet of coalfield history and culture. The years 1880 to 1930 witnessed a massive emigration from the south of Italy to the United States,[32] and many immigrants ended up in the mines. Motivating this migration was not so much the appeal of the United States but the widespread hardship in Italy. Not only was poverty rampant for southern Italians especially, but they often faced racial prejudice in the north of their own country.

Given the desperate context, readers are better able to understand why Rosa's father would send his daughter to the United States to marry a man she hardly knows: "I have eight children, he says. How can I feed them all? You are the oldest. You go and send back money. How else can a woman help?" (49–50). That his decision is believable makes it no less traumatic.[33] Such an exile would have been utterly disorienting for anyone, but for a young Sicilian woman, it could be—as indeed, for Rosa it proved to be—unbearable. Helen Barolini writes of the "double alienation" suffered by southern Italians: "The Italian immigration to the United States was preponderantly by people who were not wanted or valued in their land of origin, then found they were not wanted or valued in their new home country when they aspired to more than their exploitation as raw labor."[34] For a young woman, the alienation would have been more dire still: as Barolini has noted, for Italian women even more than for men, "the displacement from one culture to another has represented a real crisis of identity."[35] In Rosa, then, we see someone removed from every source of security—place, culture, and family—she has known.

In the coalfields of West Virginia, she finds herself at the mercy of a spouse who abuses her and their children, of a community that treats her with racist contempt, and, most foundationally, of a brutalizing economic system. In addition, she is taken advantage of sexually by her (and her husband's) employer, the mine owner Lytton Davidson, throughout her employment as his housemaid. Indeed, after the death of all four of her sons in a mine disaster and her subsequent desertion by her husband, events which precipitate a psychotic break, Davidson moves her into his house and assures her daughter-in-law that "all was well" (200). The dark suggestion is that he continues to use her sexually, then, even in her destitution and mental illness.

Readers often comment on the difficulty of the brief Rosa chapters, and they do require close reading. What makes them challenging, however, is clearly intentional, as the difficulty suggests in multiple ways the deep alienation of Rosa's immigrant experience. Most obviously, the broken English in which they are narrated reflects figuratively Rosa's inability to wrap words around her plight. And just as importantly, as Edvige Giunta suggests, the mental illness itself may be used as a metaphor for the phenomenon of an immigrant making her way through a world of which she can never feel a part.[36] Thus in the style of narration as well as in the events related, Rosa's story reveals her intense and ultimately debilitating alienation.

Nevertheless, throughout her two lonely, isolated decades in the coal camps, Rosa has tried to maintain practices and customs that give her life meaning. Even as her psychosis deepens, she strives to express a sense of identity. This is particularly evident in the material culture to which she clings: the way she keeps her household, the food she cooks, and especially the fine cutwork to which she gives her creative attention—the characteristic *punto tagliato* of her Sicilian heritage (68). Even in her climactic psychotic episode, we see an indication of her striving to hold on to her sense of self. When the striking miners set fire to the Davidson mansion in which she works, Rosa tries to free her employer's collection of butterflies from the displays on which they are pinned, doing so even as the house bursts into flames around her. It seems a fitting symbol: on some level, she knows herself to have been a beautiful being, objectified and imprisoned in a cold and alien place. Her psychosis, which may be psychologically protective, prevents her from realizing that she is, in a sense, already dead. She is ultimately rescued from the fire by a figure she believes to be her dead son Francesco but is, as noted above, Rondal Lloyd. When, kneeling by the river, she washes his face and kisses his forehead, she makes herself a mother once again (197).

The aspect of Rosa's life to which she consistently turns for solace is her Catholic faith. Yet even the church she finds in West Virginia is alien to her; it is realistic yet also suggestive that she cannot understand the ceremony that marries her to Mario. The priest is Irish and performs the ceremony in English. But the problem with the priest and the church he represents is not language alone. As Barolini notes, "The Catholicism the [Italian] immigrants found here was a stern, puritanical, inhospitable version of what they had known in their homeland."[37] Rosa's traditional religion is a deeply devotional expression; the faith she maintains is less a particular set of beliefs than a psychological fixation, one that conflates her longing for Sicily, her love for her mother (the church, she states, "is like my mama's scent" [68]), and a devotion to the Madonna; and all this is expressed through a set of devotional practices, artifacts, and icons. The centerpiece of her adoration is the reliquary her mother has sent from Palermo:

> Mama sends the reliquary to me. She saves the money to buy it. I carry it from the wagon. "Now God is in the house," I tell Luigi [her youngest

son]. Mario throws the baseball to Carmello. It skips across the rocks. The pieta is inside the reliquary, behind the purple glass. The holy water is inside, and the candles. The priest gives me Christ's body to live with us. Mario comes in with my babies. We eat pasta and butter. I put on my brocade vest. I light the candles and tell my beads.

Holy Mary, Mother of God, pray for us sinners now and at the hour of our death.

The candlelight dances on the glass. Mario sits in the corner. He says nothing. He holds the baseball, strokes it with his fingers. The candlelight flows over his trousers like water. (69)

It is significant that Rosa describes the reliquary alongside the food and dress of Sicily, in the context of gratitude for her mother and the Madonna. And it is significant, too, that she interweaves the description with her husband's obsession with baseball. The juxtaposition suggests that while Mario is embracing his life in the United States, Rosa's core identity remains deeply Sicilian. In her next brief chapter—after the death of her sons—her mother, a hallucination, looks out at her from behind the reliquary glass; then, after it is smashed by a drunken Mario, the hallucination shows Rosa how to sort the glass (170).

Rosa is clearly created in parallel with Vernie, Rondal's mother. Though the latter is an Appalachian fundamentalist and the former a Sicilian Catholic, both suffer their destitution through psychological struggles expressed religiously. Both have husbands who work in the mines, both husbands brutalize their young sons to force them to the mines as well, and both mothers are helpless to stop them. Vernie loses her husband Clabe and youngest son Kerwin in the Davidson Number Six explosion, and Rosa loses all four of her sons in the same disaster—and her husband deserts her in the aftermath. Though Vernie's ancestral home is the very place the coal camp now stands and Rosa's home is half the world away, both are trapped in a system they do not understand, and the cultures that once guided their lives have been destroyed. Finally, both women take their only comfort in their intense religious devotion, accompanied by psychological disintegration. By creating the parallels, Giardina pushes her meaning beyond the particulars to show the deep systemic evil of the coal economy. She universalizes her portrayal of its effects on women in the coalfields and demonstrates how it could impose the experience of alterity even upon native Appalachians, making them strangers in their own land.

Theology in the Coalfields

In light of religion's importance in Giardina's body of work, the spiritual and ethical issues addressed, and the author's own claim to write theologically—indeed, to "think like a theologian,"[38] it is curious that important early published scholarship on *Storming Heaven* largely avoids the topic.[39] One possible reason for overlooking this particular elephant in the parlor is that many scholars of Appalachian literature consider institutional Christianity to have been an oppressive force in the region's colonization. Given such connotations, it may be disconcerting that Giardina, an outspoken advocate for Appalachia and leading activist for progressive causes, is avowedly Christian. The concern is a significant one. Yet a full understanding of her work can only be gained by studying how her theology informs her writing.

Three fairly typical depictions of Christianity are offered in *Storming Heaven*. Most negative is the version of Christianity that directly serves the purposes of the colonizing forces. The "company churches," those churches financed by the coal companies to do their ideological bidding, are a clear example of this function: to justify oppression and encourage passivity with religious rhetoric. Relatively little is mentioned in *Storming Heaven* about them, possibly because, as Corbin has detailed, company churches were increasingly little attended as the era of the mine wars went on.[40] The most direct reference is to a Catholic priest at Davidson, "a company man who'd threatened [the immigrant miners with] excommunication for joining the union" (215). But Giardina does persistently depict a version of Christianity aligned with social and economic power interests. Miles, for example, works through most of the story to identify himself with the colonizers. So naturally he goes to an Episcopal church to find a wife, since Episcopalians are "good people to socialize with" (92). On another occasion, Episcopal and Presbyterian church women (Miles's wife among them) visit the tent camp during a strike, give paltry charity to the mining families, then report the awful conditions to a newspaper so that it can malign the "monstrous inhumanity" of the strikers that forces "women and children to suffer hunger and cold in order to advance its un-American and, ultimately, doomed goals" (211–12).

A complement to this oppressive version of Christianity is an escapist form of fundamentalism that encourages passivity in the face of oppression. It promises, in the lyric of Industrial Workers of the World organizer Joe Hill, "pie in the sky by and by"—rewards to be gained in the next world for the faithful who tolerate abuse here and now. While rightly recognizing the hardships of the workers' lives and the importance of spiritual comfort, such fundamentalism becomes a de facto ally of the oppressors by discouraging work toward meaningful change. It is reminiscent of that form of Christianity, so painfully and thoroughly detailed in *Narrative of the Life of Frederick Douglass*, that encouraged slaves to submit to their masters and faithfully bear their burden. Rondal's mother Vernie embodies this theological strain. As noted above, after Rondal and his brother Talcott go into the mines, Vernie separates herself from them. Ten-year-old Rondal reflects, "It was Mommy I missed now. I only saw her on Sundays, except for a few moments in the early morning and late at night. Even on Sundays she seemed more distant. She went to church and stayed all morning, or worked in the garden and told me not to come bother her" (25). Vernie offers affection only to Kerwin, her youngest, who "took his religion after her. They went to church together on Sundays and spent all day at it. In the evenings he read the Bible to her" (75). As Conway has stated, Vernie "is driven to madness, then religion, and finally chilling numbness."[41] As noted above, though in the Catholic tradition, Rosa also fits this type. She retreats into her religion even as she slips further into her psychosis. She prays for her boys and leaves a penny—stolen from Mario—in church each day for a votive candle to keep them safe. And at home, her psychological sanctuary centers around the precious reliquary (170).

Finally, a more sympathetic portrait of Christianity is suggested by the recurring character of the lay minister who shares the conditions of the miners because he is one of them: their union is his union too. Corbin refers to these men as "miner-preachers"[42]—often of the Holiness variety—and the type appears briefly in the novel. As the miners' army gathers to march on Blair Mountain, the men hear a church service going on in the camp, and Talcott grumbles, "Damn missionaries followed us out here" (254). But this preacher is not a company man, nor does he preach accommodation: "'Naw, they's a preacher man digs coal at Bull Push that vowed to hold services every night we camped,' someone said. 'He's all right. He's union and he preaches burning hell for the operators'" (254). A few pages later Rondal and Carrie sleep in the barn of another Holiness preacher who has joined the union cause, and Rondal, though no friend of religion, speaks admiringly of him: "They are tough old birds, the Holiness, not scared of a thing" (261).

Into this historically accurate but fairly typical catalogue of fictional depictions, however, Giardina places at the novel's center a fourth, more complicated profile of Christianity that, while grounded in the realities of the period, simultaneously reflects the complexity of her own thinking. What are readers supposed to do, for example, with an enigmatic character like Doc Booker, the black physician who figures prominently in the union's resistance? Mooney has rightly declared Doc "the most fully developed and memorable African American character in any Central Appalachian coal mining novel."[43] One aspect that makes Doc so engaging—and understandably mystifying to some readers—is the fact that he is simultaneously the most doctrinaire Marxist and one of the more devout Christians. He is the primary thinker and writer behind the radical *Annadel Free Press*; and he is the center point, the primary educator, in the Annadel Social Club, where he explains Marxist ideas in the context of current events. But he is also an elder in his fundamentalist church, and he even voices Marxist principles in traditional biblical language: "the man that does the work should own the coal mine. He should receive the fruit of his labor, like the Good Book say" (57).

For many readers, particularly American readers, no two worldviews may seem more oppositional than Christianity and Marxism. But if we have trouble seeing the confluence of these ideological streams, it is likely because we are not accustomed to experiencing the level of theological nuance embodied in *Storming Heaven*. Theology matters to Giardina: she never burdens us with distracting abstractions, but neither does she dumb it down. As she remarked to Jason Howard, "I could not have become a writer if I hadn't gone to seminary and to Washington, DC. The immersion in theology was essential to my writing."[44] While the novel is perfectly accessible to readers with no theological background, attention to the thinking that informs the text is helpful to more fully understand her achievement.

Background: Liberation Theology

During the period of Giardina's formation as a theologian, one profoundly influential strain of Christian thought was liberation theology, and it will repay our effort to sketch out its broader parameters. Liberation theology gained its name and early popularity with the publication of Gustavo Gutiérrez's *Teología de la liberación: perspectivas* in 1971. It reflects, however, the thinking of many theologians, primarily Latin American Catholics, who had been developing their ideas for more than a decade previous to the book's publication. Significantly, liberation theology was the work of thinkers in countries that had been *colonized* by Christian European nations, and it arose in response to the devastating social and economic effects of colonization. Through the 1970s, liberation theology grew increasingly prominent, and its concepts were applied to the conditions of oppressed peoples around the world, including those in South Africa, in Northern Ireland, and in the African American church. Giardina's application to the colonized people of the Appalachian coal-mining region is a fitting extension.

Many characteristics of liberation theology apply readily to the Appalachian situation described in *Storming Heaven*. Unlike more traditional theology that begins with supernatural abstractions—otherworldly thinking—liberation theology takes as its starting point the everyday life, the everyday suffering, of the poor. Using the concept *the preferential option for the poor*, liberation theologians draw upon the tradition of Judeo-Christian prophets who preached that God is on the side of the oppressed, not because they are morally superior but because they are oppressed. In making this move, liberation theologians put forward as well the plainest reading of the actions and teachings of Jesus. He lived among the poor, condemned those who oppressed the poor, and warned, "Inasmuch as ye have done it unto one of the least of these my brethren, ye have done it unto me."[45] Liberation theology holds as foundational the assumption that oppression is flatly against the will of God and takes as self-evident that the plight of colonized peoples falls clearly into that category.

Next, liberation theology understands the Christian faith as *necessarily* embedded in contemporary political situations; that is, to be true to its purpose, Christianity must effectively address the challenges of the situation in which it is lived. The prayer that God's "will be done on earth as it is in heaven" is not a pipe dream or a plea for divine intervention but a call to social and political action on the part of the Church and individual Christians. Through identifying with the poor and committing to action, liberation thinking develops situationally. Hence the concept of *praxis*: action affects reflection and reflection affects action. Put simply, the purpose of theology or, more holistically, of the Christian faith, is to push the world from oppression toward freedom. If for some readers this seems self-evident, it must be remembered that for centuries the Church seems to have sought and usually found a too-peaceful coexistence with whatever political power worked to its best institutional advantage. As noted in our discussion of *Good King Harry*, the Church has sometimes functioned less by principle than by accommodation.

In such a context, liberation theology is potentially disruptive, even revolutionary. It focuses squarely on systemic injustice, and correcting systemic injustice logically mandates correcting systems. Further dramatizing the disruptive potential of liberation theology is the fact that it is often accused of being Marxist, a claim not without some justification. However, as H. M. Conn has carefully noted, liberation theology did not embrace Marxism as "a philosophy or a holistic plan of political action" but "as an instrument of social analysis; the focus was on the economic system as a key factor in oppression and the class struggle as the battleground for that oppression."[46] For readers of *Storming Heaven*, that way of thinking should sound strangely like Doc Booker's own use of Marx.

Anyone studying theology in the 1970s was inevitably influenced by liberation theology, if not by direct study, at least by osmosis. In Giardina's case familiarity came more overtly, likely in theological school and certainly in her association with the Sojourners Fellowship, the Christian community with which she worked and sometimes lived during and after her years at Virginia Theological Seminary. Liberation theology clearly informs the work of Jim Wallis, the most influential and well-known theologian of that group. His book *Agenda for Biblical People*, one might even suggest, is a translation of Latin American liberation concepts into the language of evangelical American Protestants.[47] Such exposure during her days as a developing writer inevitably influenced her understanding of Appalachian colonization. Like their Latin American counterparts, the Sojourners, too, were maligned as Marxists, though they themselves considered their work a prophetic call to biblical Christianity. It should not surprise Giardina's readers that their opponents would pejoratively link the Sojourners to Marxism, just as we see the coal operators characterizing the union organizers as radicals or Bolsheviks.

So is Giardina anachronistically projecting a late twentieth-century theology into an early twentieth-century world? Not necessarily. While liberation theology was articulated under that conceptual framework and nomenclature in the 1960s, many of its ideas were already present in some previous strains of Christian thought. T. Howland Sanks has demonstrated, for example, close similarities between liberation theology and the Social Gospel movement prevalent in the late nineteenth and early twentieth centuries, the period of the mine wars.[48] And that movement gave rise to what Giardina has called the old "Religious Left," the influence of which she personally affirms having "soaked up."[49] Still more profoundly, one could argue that a disruptive approach has been an element of Christianity since its very inception. In fact, most liberation theologians do not see their work as developing a *new* theology but as adhering to a fuller, closer reading of the Bible, one that gives attention to principles obscured by centuries of compromise.

That said, Giardina convincingly portrays a complex, politically engaged Christianity that resonates with much liberation theology while remaining true to the historical period. She accomplishes this feat most explicitly through the character of Albion Freeman.

Albion Freeman: Giardina's Theological Voice

Albion Freeman's significance would not be guessed from the dearth of attention it has received in published criticism. Only recently have scholars begun to see the importance of his role.[50] Yet there is no character who more clearly provides a gateway into the theology of *Storming Heaven* or for that matter, no character who better embodies significant aspects of Giardina's own theology.

Albion's Appalachian Theology of Liberation

Readers will remember that while Carrie is briefly reuniting with Rondal during the dance at the Kingdom Come schoolhouse, Albion is pacing up and down the holler. There he receives a call from God that he can no longer ignore: he must go back to his home county in West Virginia and preach to the miners.[51] "God keeps telling me to do it, too," he tells Carrie. "I'm a preacher, pledged to bring His word to the lost. There's where they are, Carrie, over yonder there. I hear them crying out in my sleep. I got to go" (148). Corbin has noted that such a call was not atypical, and he details the experience of several "miner-preachers" who felt supernaturally called to preach.[52] But Albion's call is more specific. He has already been called to preach, and he is already serving a congregation at Kingdom Come. The call he receives while wandering the holler is a more particular call to a particular place with a particular purpose.

From his first day in the mine, meeting with his fellow workers, it is clear that Albion already has resistance to the coal companies in mind. The men worry about how the guards will react to their gathering. Ironically, the superintendent gives Albion permission to hold his Bible studies. According to Carrie, "The superintendent saw no harm in a daily Bible study and prayer session. He thought it might uplift the men, take their minds off their petty troubles and help them work harder. The company preacher at the Felco Methodist Church was strictly Sundays only and most of the miners didn't attend his services anyway. Albion was a Godsend, the superintendent declared" (164). This passage is significant in the way it grounds the story in history and in the way it relates to liberation theology. According to Corbin, encouraging the miners' religion was "good business" for the companies, in that they believed it would lead to a more stable workforce and instill a work ethic "to create better work habits among the miners."[53] Additionally, Corbin notes that especially after the Paint Creek strike, few miners ever attended the company churches and had little use for company ministers; they realized the distinction between faithful Christianity and the company church. This pattern naturally made a place for

Albion to enter with his ideas of resistance. He is a preacher of the Gospel, to be sure, but in keeping with the ideas of liberation theology, that gospel will not be otherworldly but grounded in the needs of his particular place and time.

The Bible study Albion leads addresses a favorite narrative of liberation theology, God's leading the children of Israel out of Egypt—divine liberation of an oppressed people. In response to Rondal, who is amazed that Albion could organize so many workers "just by preaching," Carrie explains, "Hit aint just preaching. . . . He's preaching God delivering the children of Israel out of Egypt. He's preaching the first shall be last and the last first. You know he goes to folks' houses and speaks the Word? They study the Bible then, too. And they study the United Mineworkers" (173). As Corbin notes, even though miners held many preachers in contempt, they had a very high view of the Scriptures. He quotes one early labor leader as stating that "if the workers had the same faith in the church that they have in the Bible, there would not be half enough churches in the country to hold them."[54] Albion, too, attests to his followers' faith in the Bible's preternatural power. He tells Carrie, "They wont be informers in this bunch. . . . I know them ever man jack. They have been convicted by the scriptures" (165). Albion's preaching of resistance is in this way, too, consonant with the beliefs of liberation theologians and the Sojourners: they set forth their theological understanding not as a departure from orthodoxy but as a close, contextualized adherence to the Bible.

Another similarity between Albion's message and that of liberation theology is in its multifaceted understanding of sin. A conventional understanding, especially in popular Christianity, is that sin is completely personal. Liberation theology, however, highlights the systemic aspects of sin: sin is embedded in political systems that oppress the poor. Thus the Christian faith must engage in the politics of a particular time to work against such systems. Because liberation theology threatens the status quo, it threatens political systems and the institutional forms of Christianity that are privileged by those systems. The traditional preacher's role of confronting sin in the individual believer becomes confronting power—power that oppresses the poor. In fact, a key similarity between Albion's message and that of liberation theologians is the close identification with the poor.

Recalling the conviction of liberation theologians that doing theology must begin in the daily life of the poor, when Albion leaves "such a good life" (148) in Kentucky to minister to the miners at Felco, he does so not in a paid pastoral capacity or even as an itinerant preacher. He takes a job alongside them in the mine and lives sacrificially in the coal camp. Because demand for coal is down and Albion is "not the most efficient miner," he and Carrie often go hungry.

Nevertheless, on days when there is no work (and therefore no pay), he "would come back home and make the rounds of the houses, visiting the families who were hungry and cold, praying over the sick" (165). When Carrie accepts a job as Doc Booker's nurse, Albion insists that they set part of the money aside to aid miners with sick children. And when Albion is let out on bail to await trial for shooting Baldwin-Felts guards—a trumped-up charge since he was not even armed—he and Carrie move back to the tent camp to share the suffering of the striking miners. It is as a participant in the struggle that his theology is formed and practiced.

The troubling question of a Christian use of violence is another issue that complicates our understanding of the novel, and Giardina offers no easy answers. The same may be said of liberation theology. Some liberation theologians follow a Marxist model down the path that violence may sometimes be necessary for people to be liberated. Others do not allow that possibility but point toward Jesus's example of nonviolent resistance. And some, like the Sojourners, go still further, suggesting that liberation theology's condoning of violence demonstrates a thinking that is not as radically biblical as it needs to be.[55] This issue of divinely sanctioned violence arose previously in our discussion of *Good King Harry*, and it will come up again in each remaining novel. It is a question that tasks Giardina's theological understanding and convictions; little wonder it troubles Albion.

Indeed, one of Carrie's concerns with marrying Albion is that she thinks he may be *too* peaceful. She is not comfortable with a man who might "turn the other cheek" when coal companies decide to take land (141). Like many readers, she struggles to understand that Albion is clearly resisting but that his approach is *nonviolent* resistance. He participates in the climactic shootout at Annadel, risking his life and caring for the wounded, but he doesn't carry a gun. He even goes with the other strikers to scare off the scabs; he takes a gun and fires it but intentionally misses, as do his fellow workers, possibly through his influence (202). Albion refuses personally to do violence against other men, yet he will not condemn those who do. This paradox comes to its enigmatic climax when he preaches at C. J.'s funeral:

> "Most of you got your guns there," he said. "Hit's a sin to have them. Hit was a sin to shoot down them gun thugs, even if they was bound to shoot you first. I'll not have a gun with me for the purpose of shooting a man, and I bid you to pledge the same. But I'll not condemn you for carrying those guns. You carry those guns in God's freedom. You make mistakes because you are alive and free. You cant escape your sin, so

sin boldly and know God loves you. Only try to do good for the glory of God." (193)

Rondal correctly reflects that Albion's are "strange sentiments" for a preacher. The remarks are strange, but they are serious. Giardina persistently refuses to downplay her theology; and the paradox Albion presents is in fact a timeless theological tension: the tension between loving one's enemies and restraining evil. Albion's admonitions are intended to direct the men to examine their own consciences and act faithfully within the paradox. We are reminded again of the challenging passage from Reinhold Niebuhr quoted in our *Good King Harry* discussion: "The good news of the gospel is that there is a resource of divine mercy which is able to overcome a contradiction within our souls, which we cannot ourselves overcome."[56]

Possibly the most accessible demonstration of Giardina's theological presence in Albion's character comes with her implied comparison between Albion and Martin Luther King Jr. This similarity becomes clear in Albion's final sermon about entering the Promised Land. Giardina is alluding to Moses, to be sure, but to King as well. One of King's most famous sermons was addressed to Memphis sanitation workers and their supporters on April 3, 1967. His purpose was to support the strike and to encourage Memphis citizens to do likewise, but we now remember the speech as a premonition of his death. Sadly, this sermon would be his last, and the closing is familiar: "I just want to do God's will. And he's allowed me to go up to the mountain. And I've looked over, and I've seen the Promised Land. I may not get there with you. But I want you to know tonight, that we, as a people, will get to the Promised Land. . . . Mine eyes have seen the glory of the coming of the Lord."[57] Giardina has this sermon in mind when she creates Albion's final words to the striking miners:

> "But the Lord preserved [the children of Israel], and led them home to the Promised Land. Only he had hard words for Moses. Now Moses led the children of Israel through hardship and suffering. But the Lord wouldnt let Moses enter that Promised Land. God required his life before Moses could enter. . . .
>
> "But God let Moses see! . . . God took Moses up on the mountaintop and Moses seen the Promised Land." (216)

In portraying Albion's devout and politically engaged biblical theology, Giardina makes him her mouthpiece. And he voices her beliefs regarding a second important theological concept—possibly the most radical of all.

Albion's Christian Universalism

Albion first explains his theology of Christian Universalism to Carrie in the passage below:

> "I reckon I aint told you. I'm a No Heller."
> "A what?"
> "A No Heller. Hit's a kind of Hardshell Baptist. The Hardshells, you know, they believe God has it all set out who will be saved and who wont. Some go to Heaven, some to Hell, and they aint nothing a body can do about it. Me, I'm a No Heller. That's why I left Knott County, because they didnt want to hear the No Hell preached." (134)

Though a Methodist in her upbringing and an adult convert to the Episcopal Church, Giardina clarifies her personal theology with reference to Albion. Here is her description from a 2006 panel discussion, "Religion, the Sacred, and the Appalachian Writer": "I'm basically a Calvinist—I'm going to have to say this—but I'm a different kind of Calvinist. I'm a universalist. I'm Hardshell. I read about the No-Hellers in composing *Storming Heaven*. I'm a No-Heller, the Hardshell Baptists who think that God's got everything planned out for everybody but that everybody's going to Heaven."[58] Simply placing these two passages side by side offers substantial justification for considering Albion's theology as a window to Giardina's own. Her choice to portray Albion as a No-Heller, Hardshell Baptist is surprising but deft. Even among Appalachian writers, few have the background to place that option credibly on the table, and fewer yet have the facility to develop it in a way that is both theologically and historically convincing.[59] She could have more generically described Albion as "Baptist" or "Holiness" and let the details go in passing. But she does not, and the specificity of such a unique choice is a detail sure to draw attention to itself. Many readers may have heard the term "Hardshell," though they likely do not quite understand its implications and see it roughly, if not quite accurately, as synonymous with "strict fundamentalist." The term "No-Heller," however, is little known even among readers familiar with various Christian sects. Were Giardina a local color writer, we might assume that she chose it for the sake of its strangeness: that she wanted something quirky and quaint. But because she is a writer of literary fiction who takes theology seriously, we must assume that she made the choice with particular care.

Making Albion a No-Heller, a universalist, offers certain rhetorical advantages.[60] Most obviously, it makes him more sympathetic. Religion in the Appalachians and in many other rural areas is often associated with the fire and brimstone of Christian fundamentalism. As a Hardshell, Albion can *partially* fit this stereotypical expectation. But as a No-Heller, he avoids one of the most deeply off-putting aspects of fundamentalist Christianity: the apparent ease with which it condemns most people who have ever lived to an eternity of torment. Making Albion an outsider in his own sect and giving him the broadest view of divine love and acceptance makes him immediately more sympathetic.

An additional advantage of this choice is that it gives Albion's characterization an extremely sharp ethical focus. A persistent emphasis in Christian revivalism is inevitably to save souls from an eternity in hell. But a second emphasis is that the one doing the outreach is doing so for the sake of his or her own soul, trying to please God. But what if hell, as usually considered, is bracketed out of the moral equation? If the *otherworldly* aspect is removed, the intention of Albion's calling is focused on the here and now.

Theologically, *No-Heller* is a misnomer, a fact Albion's own statements make clear. As Howard Dorgan delineates the beliefs of Appalachian No-Hellers in his foundational study, *In the Hands of a Happy God: The "No-Hellers" of Central Appalachia*, the phenomenon called *hell* is experienced on earth. Because all humans sin, they "suffer the hell on earth that a separation from God's blessing institutes."[61] As Albion tells Carrie, "I shouldnt say I dont believe in Hell. . . . Hit's real. We all of us live in it sometimes" (134). It is the here-and-now separation from God's presence that drives Albion to take his gospel to his congregations, whether in Knott County (where his message was an offense to his church), at Kingdom Come, or in his final congregation beneath the tipple at Felco. His focus is not saving his fellow sinners from an otherworldly hell but leading his people into a way of life that brings fullness now. Some of these blessings are more vaguely spiritual. But he also knows that the miners are working under a sinful system that creates suffering and that the union can not only bring people together toward a single purpose but change the system that causes so much suffering—that creates such a hell. This intention also demonstrates the selflessness of Albion's ministry. He is not preaching to confirm his position as one of the elect but to share his experience of God's blessing. It is easy to see how this parallels the in-the-world emphasis of liberation theology. The power of the Christian faith is integrated into the immediate and has consequences in the present. And Albion himself is not working to earn some future reward—the reward of heaven is already guaranteed.

Another key ethical aspect of Albion's No-Heller theology is to change the way vengeance functions in the novel. A common perception of the Christian notion of God is that while a few are elected for eternal salvation, the rest are condemned to an eternity of suffering. Thus God becomes at least as closely associated with vengeance on the wicked as with love for the righteous. And it seems that humans tend to emulate the character of their God; or, to phrase it in a nontheistic way, humans create God in their own image. There is a certain gut feeling of righteous satisfaction gained from seeing evil people given what they justly deserve; doling out punishment thus takes on a kind of darkly ironic piety, and we therefore feel justified in taking vengeance on those who do what we consider wrong. But God in the No-Heller conception does not, ultimately, take vengeance. As Albion puts it figuratively, "One day Jesus Christ will wade right into Hell and haul out the sinners. Haul them out kicking and screaming" (134). And again, "Jesus will save ever last one. That there is Jesus's job" (135).

With all this in mind, Albion's theology certainly has a place for justice (the restoration of God's blessing) but no place for vengeance—not by God, not by the miners, not by Albion himself. This becomes most clear in his discussions with Carrie about the injustices perpetrated by the coal operators. She rightfully feels anger at the operators, and she is angry at Albion for not wanting vengeance. For example, when the explosion at Davidson Number Six kills hundreds of miners—an explosion that could have been avoided, since the operators knew there was gas in the mine—Carrie tells Albion, "Somebody ought to burn in Hell for this" (168). "His gentleness," she narrates bitterly, "was an affront to me. 'Go on then. And dont forgit to tote that Bible of yourn'" (168). Her view of the world does not yet have a place for Albion's theological strangeness.

This understanding of vengeance finds further expression in Albion's attitude before his trial. Carrie dreams of their being able to return to the Homeplace, which develops throughout the novel not only as an Edenic safe place but a type of heaven. She wants Albion to promise to return there with her:

> "I cant see that far ahead," he murmured. His lips moved against my finger. "After the trial." He turned his head toward me. "Hit's like the refiner's fire, this here trial. Hit will leave everything clear, if I do like God says. They'll be gun thugs at that trial, Carrie, and the brother of them two that was shot. And they'll be hating me and Isom. They'll look at me and I'll see that hate in their eyes. I got to look back at them without hate. I got to be able to smile and speak gentle, and when the lawyers ask me questions, I got to answer with respect. And ifn I can do that, maybe I can live at the Homeplace."
>
> I [Carrie] shook my head. "I dont understand. What does living as perfect as Jesus Christ have to do with the Homeplace?" (227)

Albion's spiritual goal is to see his oppressors, who would in fact become his murderers, as he believes God sees them, without vengeance in mind. Indeed, as explained earlier, his theology does not have a place for any easy either-or thinking that would separate the proverbial sheep from goats. He believes in the orthodox doctrine of the Fall, "the first sin, that it taints all of us" (134), but he goes beyond conventional Christian understanding in his belief that God ultimately forgives all and that Christians should therefore do likewise. And in the meantime, believers must faithfully work to bring about a human condition on earth as it is in heaven. It was toward this work that Albion was called when he claimed the Felco tipple as his church steeple.

Speaking Truth to Power

The Battle of Blair Mountain did not result in the organization of the southern West Virginia coalfields. On the contrary, the decade following the battle saw union membership fall dramatically, and the fields would not be organized until the 1930s. To say the work of people like Carrie, Rondal, C. J., and Albion was a failure, however, is simply not true. In Giardina's theological code, doing the right thing has a value of its own, regardless of the result. "Christianity," she told interviewer Thomas Douglass, "seems to be based on losing, a religion that grows out of a loser who lost everything. He preached that 'the first shall be last and the last shall be first.' I think I've always kind of resonated with that attitude."[62] The victory of Blair, then, was in speaking truth to power and, for once, making power listen. As Lon Savage has written, "For a few days, at least, they had gotten the nation's attention, had made the people of America a little more aware of the conditions of life of the Appalachian miner."[63]

At the suggestion of her editor, Giardina concluded *Storming Heaven* with an afterword in the voice of Rondal and Carrie's son, Dillon Freeman.[64] Set decades in the future, it ties up a few loose ends about what happened next to the characters left alive at the book's conclusion, and it offers fictional sources for the events that make up the novel. Like his father, Dillon is a union leader, and his local has been locked out for over a year: "I have used the time, when not on the picket line, to put together this story from the yellowed newspaper clippings of articles written by C. J. Marcum and the journal where my mother recorded the events of her life and the stories of my father" (292). This explanation is not especially necessary in terms of the structure of the narrative. But importantly, it suggests that the greater story does not end with the novel. Dillon figures prominently in *The Unquiet Earth*, and so does the continuing struggle for justice in the coalfields.

CHAPTER 4

The Unquiet Earth: Confronting the Coalfield Apocalypse

Dillon Freeman's afterword that concludes *Storming Heaven* (1987) does not read like the trailer for a sequel. It offers a moderately plausible explanation for how the elements of the story happened to be available for the book, and it notes briefly some events after Rondal's death. The effect is one of additional closure, not preparation for continuing the saga. Yet Giardina did decide to continue, to develop in three hundred pages what Dillon summarized in two. For readers of *Storming Heaven*, then, *The Unquiet Earth* (1992) offers many of the gratifications of a sequel, and it is hard to imagine how anyone who enjoyed the first novel could not begin the latter. In fiction as in life, we welcome a reunion with old friends, anxious to do some catching up, even to see how their children turned out. True to form, the book fulfills those expectations. But to be a successful work, a sequel must stand on its own merits.

The reception given *The Unquiet Earth* suggests that it stands very well. The book earned Giardina her second Weatherford Award, and it was honored further with the Lillian Smith Award for the year's best southern fiction and a prestigious American Book Award. Writing in the *New York Times Book Review*, Cary Kimble proclaimed it a "powerful sequel," judging it a "disturbing" book, then adding, "Ms. Giardina suggests that it is our obligation to be disturbed."[1] The *Chicago Tribune's* Madison Smartt Bell judged the book "as bitter as it is brilliant" and noted that it is so "skillful at matching damaged lives to the ruined earth that finally the two images merge and become the same."[2] Carolyn See in the *Los Angeles Times* praised the book's "cool sentences and engrossing narration" and termed it "uncompromising."[3] *Publishers Weekly* described it as a "compelling saga" that "starkly portrays the mining families' symbiotic, spiritual relationship with nature and their helplessness in dealing with the ruthless men who control their lives."[4] And summing up her long review for the *Nation*, Lillian S. Robinson offered high praise: "The narrative's power succeeded in making the world of Number Thirteen a permanent part of my literary, as well as my historical, memory."[5]

From History to Fiction

The historical period covered by *The Unquiet Earth* is twice as long as that of *Storming Heaven*. Giardina begins with events in Dillon and his cousin Rachel Honaker's childhood and adolescence, the 1920s and 1930s, then follows the lives of these characters and their circle all the way up to 1990. The expanse allows Giardina, within the two books, to give a fairly comprehensive panorama of the coal-mining era in West Virginia, from the earliest fraudulent acquisitions of land and mineral rights to the first stages of the devastation of mountaintop removal, and to do so in the context of the major world events of the twentieth century. World War II, the Cold War, the War on Poverty, and the fall of the Iron Curtain all play significant roles in the contextual fabric of *The Unquiet Earth*.

It has never been Giardina's practice simply to fictionalize history. She does not so much take a few liberties as use history to outline and generate a true story of her own creation. That said, *Storming Heaven*'s dramatization of the Battle of Blair Mountain is about as true to history as her genre and the available facts would allow; those who read the intentionally historical accounts will find few grounds for substantive complaint with Giardina's version. *The Unquiet Earth* plays more freely with historical events yet remains faithful to the social and moral significance of the period. For example, the novel's climactic event, the flood at Trace Mountain, is based on the tragic Buffalo Creek flood, but it is transposed from 1972 to 1990. Doing so places the disaster at the culmination of the strike in which the characters are engaged near the story's end, based on the Pittston Coal strike of 1989–90, an action in which the author took part.[6] Modifications like this one allow Giardina to capture an informative outline of economic and environmental devastation while still responding to the formal demands of the narrative.

Storming Heaven chronicles the early stages of the economic colonization of the coal regions, and *The Unquiet Earth* continues the story. It vividly depicts the economic degeneration, bringing to life what happens as the colonizers' methods of extraction become more mechanized, changes increasingly lucrative for the capitalists and economically devastating for the workers. By the time of this novel, the region is thoroughly captured by a single-industry economy, and the extraction of resources is accomplished with increasingly fewer benefits to the colonized. The characters are more deeply dependent on a system outside their control that cares nothing for their quality of life. Rachel, as one of the book's narrators, offers a telling reflection:

> I knew the machines and strip mines had taken the jobs of the miners, who were getting only one or two days' work a week. Every day I drove past the empty houses they left behind when they moved to Ohio or Michigan. I saw the weed-choked fields where entire camps were torn down to the foundations, saw the boarded-up stores and movie theaters in the smaller towns, the loaded coal trucks from the new strip mines rumbling through Justice like great iron elephants and shaking the buildings, as though the town was being ground to dust. I was sad that Jackie would miss the Italian bakery, the fish market, the tailor shops and little groceries, the dark maroon passenger trains with elegant white window shades. There had been wonderful things in the world, and they were no longer.[7]

Even as the causes of poverty are increasingly revealed as systemic, the inhabitants are made aware, especially through television, of their status in relation to broader society. And they discover, too, that the outside world has become more or at least differently aware of them. The mountaineers learn that they live in "a place called Appalachia," and Rachel notes that it is "a strange feeling to think my home had been named without asking anyone who lived here" (117). Appalachians had already suffered a history of belittling caricature, but here it accelerates with the speed of television signals. The local color writing of the past has been surpassed by a more sophisticated language of *othering*, replete with images reinforced by weekly episodes of *The Beverly Hillbillies* and the occasional documentary parading Appalachian poverty before the world at large. The demeaning "missionary boxes" of the past are replaced by "poverty programs" that include visits from well-intentioned if poorly informed soldiers in the War on Poverty, VISTA workers. Thus the ideological oppression that must be resisted in *The Unquiet Earth* is, if anything, more deeply embedded than that in *Storming Heaven*.

Aspects of Literary Form

"I write for people around here," Giardina told Tim Boudreau in a 1998 interview, "not for academics."[8] But even though Giardina's storytelling is straightforward, even plain by postmodern standards, it consistently offers the kinds of dense richness associated with the best literary fiction. As in *Storming Heaven*, she uses a repeating series of first-person narrators, but the list is even more extensive, with seven narrators giving voice to the story. Again too, as in the earlier novel, her choice to have each one speak in vernacular dialect enhances the novel's verisimilitude. The dialects are less prominent than those in *Storming Heaven,* but even that nuance is true to historical realism. As Stephen Mooney has observed,

> What makes the [two novels'] achievement still more impressive is her capturing the spoken language as it evolved over a hundred-year period. Whether one is reading a section of *Storming Heaven* set in 1895 or a portion of *The Unquiet Earth* set in 1985, the vernacular is delivered with equal ease and an uncanny sense of the unique rhythms that make the speech of people in the central Appalachian hills.[9]

A second particularly noteworthy aspect of Giardina's style is her rich range of literary reference. Her expansive knowledge of Shakespeare and the Bible, of theology and politics, and of a wide range of creative literature is never overplayed but always apparent. Representative of her careful but persistent use of literary reference and allusion, and of the way it deepens the book's effect, is her continual interplay with T. S. Eliot's *The Waste Land*. She alerts us immediately to this literary touchpoint with her epigraph from Ezekiel 37. It both provides a tonal context for understanding the world of the novel—a valley "full of bones"—and intimates the importance that Eliot's poem, which alludes to the same Bible passage, will bear on the text. Given Giardina's bleak portrayal of life in the colonized coal region, Eliot's collage of post–World War I devastation, alienation, and decay is a surprising yet fitting harmonic accompaniment to the world surrounding the failing company town called Number Thirteen. Both works detail the devastation of war on a place: Eliot's of World War I on London and Giardina's of the economic war on Justice County.

One particularly resonant set of echoes refers to these lines of Eliot: "I think we are in rats' alley / Where the dead men lost their bones."[10] In the poem, "rats' alley" suggests, among other things, the horrors of trench warfare and urban decay. Both images inform the novel. In Giardina's chapter entitled "Rats' Alley," for example, Dillon recounts for his mother the experience—and the dark absurdity—of his being shot in North Africa not by an enemy on the battlefield but by a delusional fellow soldier when he had stepped outside camp to "take a crap" (38). At the end of his account, he tells her he has applied for a job in the mines. In the very next paragraph, he is trapped in a roof fall, which he compares to being pinned down by the enemy (41). The juxtaposition suggests that the war zone and the coal mines are two places where dead men may indeed lose "their bones," and the term *bone* takes on a multifaceted density. In mining idiom it refers to slate that must be sorted from the coal, but during the conversation underground it carries additional meanings. The miners take turns banging a "chunk of bone" against a boulder, signaling their location to potential rescuers. Brigham Lloyd, one of the trapped miners, also refers to the coal they mine as "the Devil's Bones," but Sim Gore responds significantly, "Could be God's bones. God's bones a-holding up the world, and we got a powerful nerve to be messing with them" (44). Their exchange while awaiting death or rescue suggests that something in the whole coal-mining phenomenon—not only this roof fall—is deeply wrong, as eerily foreboding as any portrayal of war.

The roof fall is followed by a chapter called "God's Bones" (the first of two with that title) that recounts Rachel's wartime experience as a nurse in the American force occupying the Philippines, yet another scene of poverty and oppression resulting from war. She returns home with a human Japanese skull—a love token from her racist soldier boyfriend. Dillon is enraged at such disrespect for life. He takes it from her, and on his angry drive away hits and kills a red fox. He buries the bone and the fox together with the words "O Buddha O Christ O ancestors O God. The red fox died for our sins" (60). In the second "God's Bones" chapter, much later in the book, Dillon's family graves are being moved from the Homeplace so it may be strip-mined. It is during this scene that Jackie, Dillon and Rachel's daughter, rescues from remains dropped from a backhoe the hand of Dillon's father—most importantly, the thumb bone Dillon was holding when he died.

Like the multivalent *bone* symbol, water imagery is also developed in conversation with *The Waste Land*. In the first section of the poem, one of the warnings of "Madame Sosostris, famous clairvoyante," is "Fear death by water,"[11] and that fear threads throughout the novel. As a child, Rachel nearly drowns crossing a flooding creek as Dillon looks on, unable to help her (11–12). He recalls this incident as an omen when his mother tells him Rachel is on a ship heading toward the South Pacific: "It's bad luck for her, water" (37). A few years later, Jackie falls into an abandoned well at the Homeplace, and Dillon and Rachel struggle to save her (101). And most catastrophically, the flood at the novel's end occurs when the dam—made of dumped slate, the *bones* of Trace Mountain—gives way. By the end, not only Rachel, who drowns slowly in bed with congestive heart failure, but Arthur Lee Sizemore, Sim, Tom Kolwiecki, Dillon, and 125 others have died by water.

Such repeated and interwoven allusions and symbols, often with profound psychological and mythic resonance, intensify the depth of the novel. We are reminded of Mooney's judgment that "the more one reads [Giardina's] books, the more one realizes that nothing in them, not a single detail or image or line of dialogue, is without purpose. Giardina composes in recurring 'circles' or 'cycles' of images or symbols, which achieve a powerful resonance in the reader's consciousness."[12] A complex, multilayered aesthetic informs this apparently straightforward account. It is a testament to her artistry that the interwoven symbols and images noted here, along with many others, succeed whether or not readers recognize them as references to other literary works. But for those readers who do, their effects are enhanced and the work's significance is deepened and broadened.

Giardina's literary conversation with *The Waste Land*, the most well-known twentieth-century reflection of postwar devastation, suggests that while we necessarily read the novel as a story of the coalfields, its significance reaches beyond the borders of any region. Just as Eliot (who would *never* be called a London *regionalist*) offered his grave commentary on a war-torn culture through his visions of London, Giardina achieves a similar effect: the economic and environmental destruction of the coal region is a synecdoche for destruction that the broader world faces in an era of capitalism gone awry. In a 1992 op-ed article in the *New York Times*, Giardina called Appalachia the canary in the coal mine. Borrowing John Gaventa's term "the Appalachianization of America," she warned, "When the American people seek images of poverty and powerlessness on the nightly news, they now see their own faces looking back."[13]

Responses to Colonization

Giardina's continuing literary chronicle of Appalachian colonialism is compelling, but *The Unquiet Earth* achieves its greatest success in its characterization. A host of deftly drawn and memorable secondary characters—Louelly Day, Sim Gore, and Tommie Justice, among others—warrant novels of their own. But our discussion here will be limited to primary characters, especially the narrators who each embody a facet of the historical drama. In the process of considering what each voice offers, we will note the key ideas and themes that give the novel its particular richness and weight.

DILLON FREEMAN: THE RADICAL VOICE OF APPALACHIAN RESISTANCE

At the close of *Storming Heaven*, Dillon is the baby asleep on Rondal's chest, gripping his father's thumb even after he has taken his last breath. In the book's brief afterword, dated 1987, it is Dillon's adult voice that summarizes the decades of activity following the Battle of Blair Mountain. Most of the events portrayed in *The Unquiet Earth* occur between those two points, the death of Rondal and the labor struggles of the late 1980s. As a structural device, then, Dillon is well positioned as a believable narrator. But he is more than a link joining the narrative present with the era of the mine wars. Unlike Rondal's uncle Dillon for whom he was named—who, with the coming of coal, moved far enough back in the mountains to avoid the new way of life—the younger Dillon shows no sign of retreat. Through him Giardina puts a face on the seven-decade struggle the people of the coal region go through after the defeat at Blair, particularly as the struggle relates to economic justice. Both as a leader of the miners and a man who is bound to the mountains, he serves as the novel's most radical voice of Appalachian resistance.

Dillon comes to his role naturally, reflecting the traits of both Carrie Freeman and Rondal Lloyd, his passionate mountaineer mother and his radical, union-organizing father. From Carrie's family memories, as well as from his own childhood on the Homeplace, he inherits a devotion to the mountains and his community. The fused passion for place and kin, past and present, is a persistent theme in the tradition of Appalachian literature, but never more integrally than in Dillon: for him, the people and the place are of a piece. Throughout the novel, his care for the family graves and his attempts to interest his (presumed) daughter Jackie in the community and the mountains affirm that the two are indivisible. In a broader American culture that focuses on individual economic success, such devotion may be perceived as a regressive value, one that no longer makes sense; outside the region, the characteristic Appalachian tie to place has been perceived in a less than favorable light.[14] Popular opinion suggests that a more logical response to the devastation of coal country, then and now, is simply to leave. But for reasons more spiritual than pragmatic, Dillon does not consider leaving to be an option.

He knows the old ways cannot come back in the aftermath of colonization, but he refuses to concede the struggle for a decent life. From his mythologized version of Rondal, imbibed through family stories and community legends, Dillon inherits his father's focus on economic justice. Striving to emulate a man he never knew, he wraps himself in his father's mantle of organized resistance to the coal company's abuses and lack of concern for its workers. The economy depends utterly on coal, and what that industry chooses to do is determined by decision-makers who are distant, geographically and ideologically, from the region. Dillon knows that such a war is never finally won or lost, but waged in perpetuity.

The war fought with the economic weapon of hunger often becomes a war fought with more traditional weapons, not only by coal companies themselves but by governmental authorities under their influence. The corruption of local officials, as typified by Arthur Lee, should not surprise readers; forces of colonization are typically aided by some natives who turn the situation to their personal advantage. But the coal companies' deep collusion with the federal government, as demonstrated in the FBI's turning a blind eye first to miners being forced to work at gunpoint (142–3), then to the bombing of Dillon's home (154), may be harder to grasp for readers unfamiliar with the history of the region. The late-twentieth-century situation confronted by Dillon is as desperate as the one faced by his unionizing father in *Storming Heaven*.

It has commonly been suggested that, due to the difficulty of life in such a tenuous situation, coal camp culture creates a fatalistic dependency. But this is a suggestion Giardina subverts. Dillon represents the strain of Appalachian character in which the bond to family and place leads not to fatalism but to a persistent resistance, whether futile or effective, against those who value the region only for what can be extracted. His resistance, alongside that of his many friends and fellow workers, counters the stereotype. As Carolyn Neale Hickman has rightly noted, "Giardina's narratives may record a history of defeat, but they do not reinforce the fatalism and passivity to which the subordination of oppressed groups is often attributed."[15]

Concerns of family, place, and justice create the contextual fabric for the plot and sufficient motivation for Dillon's character. But equally engaging is the romantic plot that dominates the first part of the novel: Dillon's lifelong relationship with his first cousin Rachel. One of the more offensive and malicious Appalachian stereotypes is that of prevalent incest, and Giardina throws it in the readers' faces in ways that are inevitably unsettling, simultaneously quickening our distaste and, by using the name Rachel, recalling that a patriarch of Israel, too, had sex with his cousin. Giardina's choice is unquestionably a risk. Regardless, it successfully depicts a key weakness in Dillon's character: his apparent inability to look beyond his own immediate desire. He is either blind to the ramifications of the relationship or unconcerned by its potential consequences. Such a rash insistence is consistent with some of his other actions, such as blowing up the railroad bridge at Winco. While such violence may be necessary in a labor war, it is clear that Dillon's failure to think through the consequences often results in actions sure to cause problems.

That said, there is a Brontë-esqe appeal in the ferocity of Dillon's passions, and the taboo romantic plot is successful at least in part. Rachel returns his affections emotionally and, eventually, physically; but a key difference is that she wants to avoid the social condemnation associated with incest, whereas Dillon seems not to care. Throughout the novel, he is headstrong, stubborn, and too little concerned that others, even others whom he loves, might have concerns of their own, or even a better way of handling particular situations. When Rachel protests that she would pay far more heavily for their unconventional relationship than would he, she is clearly correct, and her later summation of Dillon's character is just: "There's some that would save the world and think nothing to hurt those around them, and you're that way" (190). That he ultimately finds it impossible to force Rachel into his version of a perfect organizer's helpmate—essentially, a version of his mother—testifies, as we will see, more to Rachel's own strength of character than to Dillon's growth. And his ultimate acceptance of his failure may have as much to do with the cooling passions of middle age as it does with better insight. What keeps Giardina from presenting him as utterly narcissistic is that, as egocentric as his drives tend to be, he simultaneously maintains an awareness that his life is not his own: for all his grasping and controlling, the risks he takes are grounded in his conviction that justice is pursued in relation to and on behalf of others.

Dillon comes to this awareness when, early in the story, he undergoes an epiphany presented as a conversion narrative.[16] This change of heart and mind is recounted when he returns from the war in North Africa. Wounded in body and spirit, he lies in bed for a week. When he is finally able to rise, he drinks a few beers and, sitting beside his mother on her porch, tells her the story of his wounding. As noted, one of Dillon's fellow soldiers became delusional and, thinking Dillon a German, shot at him. Dillon took a bullet in the leg and returned fire, first to wound but eventually to kill. While convalescing, he passed the time in the military hospital by reading the Bible. He tells Carrie that he laughed off its prohibitions, but other parts spoke to him:

> I believe in God, and I believe they's a fire running through everything that lives. When that Bible starts throwing rules at me, I laugh, but when it tells how sin burns and says turn the other cheek and when God gets hung on that cross, buddy I'm right there. I chose me and that's sin. I aint no better than a goddamn Nazi. That's what they do, choose themselves. And the rich people that keep what they got, they do the same. It's sin and the only way you burn it out is to die. Only it don't work if you just die for yourself, it's got to be for somebody else. (39)

This epiphany places Dillon, though as impulsive and headstrong as ever, on the road to self-sacrifice. His consecration is confirmed again when, after doing prison time for blowing up the bridge, he returns to Number

Thirteen. Though he had considered escaping the mountains for good, this was impossible:

> In prison I thought about going someplace where not a soul would know me. There are places where a man can go and be bitter, where it has been done before. . . .
>
> I came back here instead. I knew it was right when I stood in what once was my yard, beside the ruined wire fence where I buried the skull and the red fox. I have come back to watch over them and to keep company with the ghosts of my people who lived on this land, my Papaw, my great-uncle Dillon the hermit, and especially my daddy. (191)

As insufferable as he remains, Dillon lives according to his own principles, a code that retains deep elements of Christianity but is equally grounded in a transcendent love for his family (living and dead) and his home. Indeed, Dillon's spirituality becomes the primary medium through which Giardina directs attention to the significance of the land itself.

Trace Mountain: The Landscape as Character

The land is represented most clearly by an unconventional character: Trace Mountain. Given Giardina's deep allegiance to West Virginia and her outspoken concerns for the violence done against not only the people but the mountains—a complex she shares with and through Dillon—it is fitting that the features of place play an important role in the novel's progression. In a panel presentation at the Society of Environmental Journalists conference in 2008, Giardina stated,

> One of the things I've tried to do in this novel was to . . . have a mountain be a character. Trace Mountain is a fictional mountain . . . I treated in the novel like a person to me. It's like a character you follow through the novel and see the changes and so forth just as you do with the people in the novel. It's partly based on a mountain in McDowell County, West Virginia, where I grew up.[17]

Such a statement suggests that readers ought to pay more than typical attention to the landscape in the novel. As we do so, it becomes apparent that before ecocritical literary criticism had become current, Giardina had written what

Lawrence Buell would later term, in his landmark study *The Environmental Imagination*, an "environmentally oriented work." Though Buell's focus is on Henry David Thoreau, his criteria could have been generated with *The Unquiet Earth* in mind:

> 1. The nonhuman environment is present not merely as a framing device but as a presence that begins to suggest that human history is implicated in natural history. . . .
> 2. The human interest is not understood to be the only legitimate interest. . . .
> 3. Human accountability to the environment is part of the text's ethical orientation. . . .
> 4. Some sense of the environment as a process rather than as a constant or a given is at least implicit in the text.[18]

Particularly through Dillon but to a degree through the other narrators, Trace Mountain is portrayed as just such an entity, an agent and object of ethically resonant action: the mountain is bound in a doomed struggle with humans, and finally, it lashes out.

When Trace Mountain is introduced early in the novel, its imperiled condition is already evident. Carrie states that in climbing the mountain from her home in Jenkinjones, one sees that "the mountain below is covered with black slate from the mine. Smoke rises from it. . . . The fire will burn for years and cannot be put out. . . . It smells acrid, like singed raw sewage" (32). The image is realistic, yet it also suggests something mythic, a Hades-like vision, a foreboding netherworld near the bottom of the mountain. As she continues her description, she notes that the only way to escape the stench is "by rising above it toward the clean fog" on the top of the mountain. So Trace is simultaneously presented, at its summit, as a place of purity and refuge. Like the human characters, it is conflicted. Both physically and metaphorically, the degradation the mountain endures is rising.

Yet for a while, Trace retains remnants of the positive mythos associated with mountains, as suggested by the many important events that take place on its shoulders. It is there that Dillon and Rachel first consummate their lifelong passion, and they do so near the cabin where Dillon's namesake had fled to escape the tyranny of early colonization. Immediately following, Rachel refers to Trace as "a different world" and notes that it has long been a place of refuge for people who could not abide life in the coal camps (68). She later states, "You see the world differently on top of a mountain. Up there *you might think that you are safe*" (76, italics mine). Again, complexity and purposeful ambiguity: the mountain holds the promise of safety, but that safety may be an illusion. The changes suggested in Carrie's earlier description persist in Rachel's reflections.

Trace is mentioned again when Dillon drives eight-year-old Jackie up to see the ruins of his great-uncle Dillon's cabin. When she offers her fantasy that "bad things live" up the mountain (as suggested by the stench), she is not corrected by Dillon as she had anticipated (85). Instead, he agrees with her: "There are bad things living here." A few years later, Jackie laments her own loss of innocence, the time when "mountains were magic" (198). "When I was a kid," she continues, "I thought Trace Mountain was too powerful to be stripped, that anybody who tried would be cursed for all time. I wish I still believed it." Trace promises a power of its own, but it is confronting a perverse and more forceful antagonist, an enemy with no sense of the sacred.

Though Trace has no narrative voice, it finds a surrogate in Dillon. It would be typical to consider his relationship with the mountain as a more conventional romantic projection or even as a kind of pop spirituality discourse, but to the degree that we take Giardina seriously, we question those options. *Good King Harry* and *Storming Heaven* have demonstrated that places matter and mystery matters, and that unconventional spirituality is portrayed intentionally and must be interpreted with care. So when Dillon connects Trace with the mountains in Wales (a place often associated with Appalachia by the region's writers), calling them "ancient spirits," we assume he means it (209). And we assume it is more than metaphorical suggestion when he says, "I could hear the mountain above me groan and cry out, mourning its losses, screaming with pain when we cut away its bones. I knew when the roof fell and took a man it was no accident but the mountain lashing out like a wounded animal" (209). We are challenged still further when he tells us straightforwardly, "I can hear the mountains talk at night. It is a gift I have from my great-uncle Dillon the hermit. I lie on my bed with the window open and hear the cries coming off Trace" (209). The mountain is a character under attack, and the character is not invariably passive. It is difficult to be more precise regarding Dillon's spiritual understanding, but he is making his preternatural claims as seriously as his natural ones, regardless of whether readers' worldviews have a ready place for them.

As the story continues and Trace is illegally strip-mined, we see a foreshadowing of the abomination of mountaintop removal. On another trip up the mountain, this time with a teenage Jackie and the VISTA worker Tom, Dillon states, "But when I round the curve of the hill there is no laurel, no mountaintop to climb, no hermit's cabin, only a highwall, sharp like a knife, and a slice of empty sky" (213). Later, when he drives up alone to commemorate his first lovemaking with Rachel, Trace has been raped, flattened, "the core of the mountain barely concealed by sawgrass and the sprayed on green fertilizer that Arthur Lee will call reclamation" (273). The effect of this assault is intensified because of the spirituality Dillon has been associating with Trace and with mountains more generally. The place is for Dillon a "spirit land, sacred and dangerous" (230), and the vividness of Trace's characterization grows through the novel's conclusion. Near the end, when Jackie drives up the mountain to take pictures of the picket shack where Ethel Ray has been shot, she notes, "Night creatures keened high up on Trace, as though the mountain itself was alive and lamenting" (317). And when Dillon, warned by a dream, climbs the mountain for the final time to check on the dam, a "low moan swells from the water—it is the tormented spirit of Trace Mountain torn apart. I hear voices in the moan" (328).

Quite literally, Trace Mountain is moaning—part of the bone dam *is* Trace, the waste from mining operations. And finally as Dillon is about to meet his fate in the floodwaters,

> The water shrieks like all the lost souls, but it carries with it the top of Trace Mountain where I lived my life now dumped and scattered to the wind, the heart of it
>
> is there
>
> water reaches my thighs, pulls at my legs, I turn to face the wall and stretch my arms wide (335)

There is nothing natural about this deadly flood, so closely modeled on the events of the Buffalo Creek disaster, an event that was a turning point in Giardina's political thinking.[19] And though International Oil, Giardina's fictional name for the Pittston Coal Company, labeled the tragedy an "Act of God," few people familiar with Buffalo Creek or this novel can possibly accept such a claim. Few symbols have stood for the eternal more consistently than mountains, whether experienced in life or as mediated through myth and literature. Yet here the eternal is suddenly no more. Trace Mountain, like the people of Blackberry Creek, has proven no match for the power and deep perversity of economic and environmental injustice.

In terms of literary genre, Giardina's presentation of Trace is closer to magical realism than to romantic projection, but neither quite corresponds to what she is attempting. Nor does the depiction seem like a more typical religious pantheism, though Giardina edges closer to that in *Fallam's Secret*.

Still, however we regard the mountain ontologically, its presence as a character is integral to the novel. Recalling Buell's criteria, we may affirm that Trace Mountain is more than a framing device, that human interest is not the only interest in question, that humans are accountable for how the environment is treated, and that the mountain is clearly a process, not a constant.

That final scene even extends to the mountain something akin to volition. Carried by the flood, Trace Mountain comes for Dillon, to carry him away or to collect him into itself. His final thought—"I turn to face the wall and stretch my arms wide"—clearly alludes to Christ on the cross, dying for the sins of humans or giving his life to save his community (335) and to Dillon's own epiphany, that sin is only burned out by dying, "but it's got to be for somebody else" (39). Such self-sacrifice reminds readers of the words of Jesus, "Greater love hath no man than this, that a man lay down his life for his friends."[20] But the image may just as vividly suggest Dillon welcoming the mountain, opening himself to their shared fate. Readers need not choose between those two interpretations but may hold them in tension as a kind of indeterminate consummation unique to the relationship between Dillon and Trace.

Rachel Honaker: The Conflicted Heart

Rachel grew up alongside Dillon on the Homeplace, and like her cousin, she ultimately chooses to spend her life in coal country. She too is bound to the mountains, but she lacks the single-minded passion that drives his relentless resistance. Significantly, Giardina creates Rachel with heart trouble, using that traditional literary symbol to suggest the divided affections that define her. She knows firsthand the loss of Eden and she feels it deeply, but her adaption takes a less violent form. She states,

> I did lose the Homeplace when I went to school, and it had nothing to do with banks or coal companies. It was the inevitable loss known by those who are not tied to the same patch of earth for all their days. I mourned but I could not say I had done wrong. Land is so fragile—it can be taken by flood or fire or a piece of banker's paper—that it is best to build a life inside oneself that can be planted anywhere and held onto until the last breath. (15)

So as Dillon represents Appalachians whose passion binds them to the place and drives them to fight for justice, Rachel represents those who stay but create alternative ways to cope with the challenges of living in an oppressed place. She sees as clearly as he the injustice around her: as a county nurse, she treats ailments created by unfair labor practices, bad working conditions, and pervasive poverty. But she determines to find her own economic and psychological path as best she can and, most importantly, to do so in a way that does not disadvantage her daughter. For Rachel, building this "life inside oneself" even includes benefitting from the largesse of local powers that collude with the coal companies. She justifies her choice with the argument that her medical care serves those who would otherwise have done without, and that is true. Nevertheless, she inhabits the ambiguous territory between the oppressors and the resistant oppressed.

As symbolized by her heart condition, Rachel is developed throughout as the character most deeply divided, even in childhood. Looking at her family upbringing, we see her father Ben Honaker portrayed as simple, hardworking, and kind, openhanded almost to the point of being improvident. But his simple goodness is not the dominant force in the family. It may be more useful to say that Rachel is torn between the conflicting attitudes of two mothers: her controlling biological mother Flora and her psychologically forceful Aunt Carrie. Rachel is deeply drawn by both of them, even as they pull her in different directions.

Though a daughter of east Kentucky, Flora's values are developed as much by outside forces as by those native to the mountains. She pores over magazines and newspapers from Lexington and Louisville, and she formulates her understanding of normative culture based on what she finds there. She envisions a future for her daughter "better" than life at the Homeplace. From her, Rachel first imbibes an unarticulated but pervasive sense of Appalachian inferiority, and that sense is reinforced when she leaves home. To her nursing instructor in Justice, for example, Rachel and the other mountain students are the objects of her condescending philanthropy: the girls are her "mission work" (16). She informs them that "you must overcome your backgrounds," since Appalachians are, according to her reference, Arnold J. Toynbee's *Study of History*, "not better than barbarians" (16). Serving as an army nurse, Rachel feels her Otherness yet again, betrayed by an accent that prompts teasing about life in the mountains. The prejudice she experiences makes her angry but not in the way of Dillon. She resents the criticism but also accepts it, and she tries to adopt outsiders' attitudes, attitudes her mother has vaguely instilled.

Carrie functions as an alternate, equally powerful maternal influence. Their closeness is indicated by the fact that when Rachel suffers childhood scratches and scrapes, she does not run to Flora, who would have told her not to play so rambunctiously, but to Aunt Carrie, who offers intimate and nonjudgmental comfort (8). Carrie inspires in her niece the desire and strength to act in ways that are less conventional and more deeply grounded in mountain culture. And it is through Carrie's influence that she is inspired to become a nurse despite Flora's disapproval of nursing as a "common, nasty occupation"—meaning, in effect, that it deals intimately with the human body (14). If Flora inspired in Rachel a desire to move into a world outside the mountains, Carrie inspired the longing for adventure and the toughness that serving in a war zone demands. But as close as they are, Rachel never develops her aunt and Dillon's fierce love for the mountains, nor their radical sense of justice.

Rachel's divided heart is evident in her several romantic relationships. When she dates soldiers in the Philippines, she avoids physical intimacy—even after becoming engaged to her soldier boyfriend, Fred. Hers is not a choice based on personal moral convictions but on her mother's insistence that premarital sex is not something good girls do. Returning home, she succumbs similarly to the conventional idea that a young woman *should* get married, and her dividedness comes to the fore again. Tony Angelelli, who has been courting her, is an Italian, and Flora at first objects on the grounds that "they are not clean people" (34).[21] Carrie also discourages the relationship, though she does not share Flora's bigotry. Carrie, who has spent much of her life around traumatized men, perceives that Tony is a deeply wounded individual, "one of those damaged people" who will not be capable of the love Rachel needs (34). Torn between her two mothers' warnings and her own urge for independence, Rachel moves forward with this troubling dissonance into a doomed marriage.

Her divided heart continues to plague her in her affair with Dillon, whom she both loves and fears. It is difficult at first to see anything redeeming about the attraction to her cousin; nevertheless, the period of their physical relationship, though unconventional and brief, may be the only time Rachel successfully silences—at least in part—the internalized voice of Flora. Unlikely as it may seem, Rachel's affair with her cousin is not finally her most objectionable romance. Once Dillon takes himself out of the picture by refusing to communicate with his cousin-lover and presumed daughter during his years in prison, Rachel makes another troubling choice: she marries Dillon's nemesis, Arthur Lee. Just as Dillon is the focal point of Appalachian resistance to the coal companies' abuses, Arthur Lee, like Miles in *Storming Heaven*, is a type of the native who makes his fortune by serving the colonizers. In marrying him, Rachel literally places herself in bed with the enemy. Put so baldly, one might interpret Rachel as an opportunist who secludes herself from the sufferings of her community. But Giardina does not allow that easy categorization. Rachel has, on the contrary, shared in those hardships—and alleviated some of them, at least temporarily—through her work as a devoted nurse. Like Carrie, she has delivered babies, tended the sick, comforted the dying, and taken care of the old folks up in the hollers. And she does so with a deep sense of dedication to those she serves.

Dillon's insistence that Rachel forsake her career as a county nurse—he never lets her forget that she gained it through the influence of Arthur Lee—reveals that he does not begin to understand, let alone accept, her way of moving through the world. To her credit, Rachel understands Dillon far better than he does her. Furthermore, in the value system she has constructed, her greatest loyalty is to their child. She marries Arthur Lee not because of any particular feeling on her part; he offers her neither emotional nor physical satisfaction. But they strike a bargain: Rachel agrees to be his wife, and he agrees to take care of Jackie's needs, even sending her to the college of her choice, something neither she nor Dillon has the means to do. Finally, though in most people's—and certainly Dillon's—view, Arthur Lee is a traitor to his community, Rachel sees that while he has chosen a corrupt and corrupting position, no human is totally good or bad. Her passion to see her daughter cared for is as great as Dillon's passion for place, and her ethical gradations offer considerably more gray area than Dillon's. While readers may struggle with Rachel's choices, she is acting according to her own hard-won values in what she considers the most responsible way open to her. Both symbolically and literally, she pays the price of her divided self: after a few sad years with Arthur Lee, her troubled heart gives out completely.

The first half of the book centers primarily on Rachel and Dillon's romance, but it soon becomes clear that Giardina is portraying a broader social pale than any single love story. While their relationship continues to bear significance—even after Rachel's death—the novel is most accurately about the town itself, the community of Number Thirteen. Telling the town's story most closely are two very different narrators, the self-proclaimed mayor of Number Thirteen, Hassel Day, and Rachel and Dillon's daughter, Jackie.

JACKIE HONAKER: PORTRAIT OF THE ARTIST AS A YOUNG GIRL

Once Jackie enters the rotation of narrators (80), she handles forty percent of the remaining story, placing her experience at the novel's center. One advantage of this choice is that by using Jackie's point of view, Giardina, who also spent her first thirteen years in a coal camp, can draw vividly on direct experience. Giardina made use of family history in *Storming Heaven*, but Jackie's narration raises the merger of fact and fiction to another level. The similarities between Giardina and Jackie's childhoods are many: mountaineer mothers, Italian fathers, a level of affluence relative to their company-town neighbors, even a parallel fascination with books and writing. For example, Giardina told Thomas Douglass that as a child she simply took it as true that "other places were where things happened. I had no idea I could be a writer,"[22] a statement that parallels Jackie's ironic lament: "I'm not a real writer. Real writers live in New York apartments or sit at sidewalk cafés in Paris" (108). Then after two hundred words of winsome description of Number Thirteen—a full merger of author and narrator—Jackie laments the fact that "there is not a thing to write about, only hillbillies, and nobody cares to hear about hillbillies. I go inside to watch TV" (108). The young adulthoods of author and narrator follow parallel tracks as well: life-changing travel in England, working for West Virginia congressmen, living in intentional Christian communities in Washington, DC, writing for newspapers, and so on. Though our study does not place a virtual *equals sign* between the two, making Jackie "an autobiographical representation of Giardina,"[23] their similarities inevitably inform and enrich the text.

Just as importantly, this use of Jackie offers Giardina a new formal opportunity: her first extensive use of a child's point of view. *Good King Harry* presents a child narrator, but the perspective is that of a worldly wise and disillusioned adult recalling childhood on his deathbed; thus the story is related only bifocally through the child's eyes. Similarly, in the early sections of *Storming Heaven* narrated by a young Rondal Lloyd, Giardina sensitively uses the point of view of a boy; but again, his perspective is mixed with the interpretive insight of Rondal as an adult. In Jackie's early chapters, Giardina accepts the different advantage offered by keeping the narrative present within the child's naive but maturing vision.

A naive narrator offers a differently filtered perspective on events not otherwise attainable, a transparency that creates a particular flavor of irony. Jackie's perceptions of Rachel and Tony's marriage is telling in this regard, as readers are offered a relatively clear perspective on why and how that marriage does not work. We see, for example, how Rachel's understandable but unfortunate contempt for Tony influences Jackie's opinions of the man she assumes to be her father: "My mom hates my dad too. She tells me everything awful about him" (88). And we see how Jackie learns to use their discord to her own advantage. Even while she is attending a carnival with Tony and his girlfriend Jean, Jackie states, "I am already figuring how I can get back at my dad" (92). It is ironic, both sadly and comically, to witness the confusion with which Jackie interprets her mother's fire-and-ice relationship with Dillon, long before she knows that he is her biological father and unaware that her mother is meeting him for sex every Friday night: "One time I asked Dillon how he was kin to me, and Mommy said, Cousin, real fast. She said, Dillon is your second cousin. Dillon said, Hellfire, and looked real mad and went home in his truck so I thought he didn't like me to be his kin" (83).

The naive perspective also offers an unfiltered view of day-to-day life in a coal camp. Jackie's narration is not shaped by an articulated understanding of culture and history, allowing her a less prejudiced set of observations. As readers, we know that Number Thirteen is what is left of a village in decay, a company town built during the wartime coal boom, then left to suffer a slow asphyxiation at the mercy of an industry that no longer needs to keep it alive. The company is selling off or tearing down its houses, the miners are working limited days, families are scrounging a hand-to-mouth existence, and nearly everyone depends on some kind of tenuous public assistance. Jackie relates these conditions without an adult's apparatus for making meaning, and that allows her descriptions to be particularly believable regarding the hardships that come with injustice.

Number Thirteen is not only impoverished but isolated, as symbolized by the lack of a car bridge, but hegemonic influences nevertheless find their way in. Just as Flora read city newspapers and became convinced of Appalachian inferiority, Jackie becomes obsessed with what life should be like by watching television and, most poignantly, reading *Seventeen* magazine (182–5). It is not surprising that she judges her teen experience to be sadly lacking—any girl reading *Seventeen* likely feels the same way. But the realities of Jackie's world are more dire. These are the early years of the War on Poverty. The region has a name, Appalachia, and it can now be further objectified and caricatured by popular media. Particularly effective is the chapter in which a network television program invades the town to film a documentary about Appalachian poverty (123–6).[24] Jackie's perspective demonstrates just how such reports can be distorted. She portrays the desperate off-screen excitement, then the eventual anger of children who do not understand quite why they are being filmed and displayed, but know intuitively—and truthfully—that they are being called out for national contempt and pity (125–6). Such media images demonstrate not only the othering of Appalachia but, through Jackie's naive narration, the grave and immediate effects of this othering on children.

But as dismal as the situation is, what Jackie's narration shows us as well, with the unsettling clarity of naivete, is the goodness of the life she experiences in Number Thirteen. The community functions like an extended family, though a poor and often dysfunctional one. It offers, in fact, a faded image of the communitarian mountaineer culture portrayed in *Storming Heaven*'s delineation of life around the Homeplace. Life is challenging, but it is lived with the irreplaceable advantages of mutual concern and a distinct sense of belonging. When Arthur Lee marries Rachel and moves her and Jackie to Annadel, Jackie feels the loss: "I missed everything else about Number Thirteen. In Number Thirteen you could go right in someone's house without knocking, just sit on the couch and watch what was going on. No one would think a thing of it. *Out in the world you will be by yourself, but not at Number Thirteen*" (200, italics mine). As a teen and young adult, Jackie recalls the years at Number Thirteen as her happiest time (203, 244).

Later in the novel, when Jackie moves into a wider world, she becomes the representative of another type: the displaced Appalachian. The chapter following Rachel's death, appropriately entitled "Exile," details one of Jackie's attempts to leave the world of Number Thirteen. Like many Appalachians, she dreams of escaping to a world of broader opportunity; then, being away, she dreams of returning home. She has imbibed the idea that to be successful means to leave; to stay put is to accept as inevitable the poverty created by colonization. Yet even after years in Washington, DC, Jackie feels the pull to go home: "I crave the mountains. They invade my dreams, and so do my kin, living and dead" (250). Eventually she returns, taking a job editing the local newspaper, a position that allows her to take an active role in the community resistance and to exercise, to a limited degree, her profession as a writer. After the cataclysmic flood at the book's end, she leaves again and becomes a copy editor in Pittsburgh. But her dull life briefly suggested in the novel's denouement is hardly that of a talented young woman exercising her profession, but more indicative of a deeply hurting soul trying to manage her trauma. Had Giardina written a third Appalachian book, it is hard to imagine Jackie not playing a role and equally hard to imagine that part of her role would not have involved a return to Number Thirteen.

Hassel Day: Mayor, Caretaker, Pastor, Survivor

Exactly what is good about life in Number Thirteen, and maybe why it is good, is suggested by the fourth principal narrator of the novel, the appropriately named Hassel Day. Hassel begins his narration with the simple statement, "I am the mayor of Number Thirteen. . . . It's what I tell anybody that asks" (111). His little fiction does not reflect some pathetically cast will to power but the opposite: Hassel finds meaning in his service to others. And in the decaying coal culture, he finds no shortage of people in need: "American Coal owns the land and they used to own the houses until just here a bit ago. When they let things go, somebody had to look after folks, and I like to do that" (112). He is, by hook, crook, or a creative combination of both, trying to make the best of a world gone wrong. In doing so he represents another kind of response to postcolonial Appalachia.

Dillon is determined to resist the coal companies, and he organizes his fellow miners to work for justice; Arthur Lee all but ignores the plight of his neighbors and rationalizes making his own fortune at their expense. Hassel is as gifted and committed as either man, and he has an impressive nuts-and-bolts understanding of how systems work. But he trains his focus on the day-to-day struggles of people trying to survive. Poverty and injustice are the givens in his world, and his energy is directed toward helping his family and friends maintain a decent life in an indecent world. He is a force for building community among the ruins: as confidant, counselor, confessor, and all-around problem solver.

With a marked selflessness, Hassel deals with the complications—the hassles—that arise in Number Thirteen. Though his economic resources are as limited as the rest of those who make the dying town their home, he still manages to help friends and family as they struggle to make ends meet. But his economic contributions are secondary to the support he offers souls: "I set and drink coffee with everybody and they tell me their problems" (112). His trailer is located suggestively on the community's "free space," an area so designated because no one, including the county records office, knows exactly who owns it, thus removing it from the direct control of the coal company.[25] Hassel's home is the place where neighbors come to visit and speak their minds; it is a place where local kids find themselves hanging out, a home away from their own, often dysfunctional homes where the effects of poverty, alcohol abuse, and violence overwhelm. For example, when Jackie needs to talk with someone about Arthur Lee, she goes to Hassel's. When Ethel Ray needs to tell someone about her pregnancy, she turns to Hassel for consolation. When Tom moves to Number Thirteen, he rents a room in Hassel's trailer; and it is only through his friendship with Hassel that his community-building plans can have a brief and limited success. Hassel even manages to win a government grant to open a bar in town, yet another context where people may socialize, speak freely, and feel safe.

One symbolically suggestive goal that edges Hassel beyond the confines of home is his persistent campaign to have the road bridge rebuilt across the hollow that separates Number Thirteen from the wider world. He has determined in his heart that it will happen, and he pursues his hope in every context.

He begins by meeting with the county commissioners, but is there thwarted by Arthur Lee. He visits the governor's office but cannot gain a meeting. He brings up the topic with Tom's Catholic bishop, but the bishop's response is a painful irony: "I don't believe the Church is in the bridge building business" (286). But Hassel is. Most importantly in our conceptualization of the plight of the region, he finally determines to approach the United Nations. This is a significant detail because it underscores the fact that Appalachian coal country parallels other decimated colonized areas around the third world. While the book ends with the bridge no closer to being built than it was at the beginning, one can hardly experience Hassel's character without catching something of his persistent—if not very rational—optimism for Number Thirteen.

Hassel is, then, a beneficent survivor, a survivor who not only manages to keep himself alive but to make life possible for others. Such persistence and empathy owe something to another subtly delineated aspect of his identity: Hassel is a homosexual. This fact is gradually suggested but may remain overlooked by readers until one telling interaction with Tom in which the VISTA, along with the readers, realizes why we "don't see [Hassel] dating any women" (219). The subtlety is appropriately realistic. As in the case of Aunt Becka in *Storming Heaven*, the silent way Hassel's orientation is apparently accepted by his neighbors in Number Thirteen falls under the category David E. Wilson has termed "benevolent repression." Wilson notes that Giardina "masterfully engages the unspoken to script a subtext wherein lie the truths of her multiply marginal characters."[26] Though such a hesitancy may disappoint twenty-first-century readers, it is hard to imagine a portrayal that could be both realistic and overt. The quiet care with which Giardina suggests his orientation depicts the way the issue would have been handled in many rural communities of the era. It testifies to Hassel's quiet heroism that he sacrificially places the good of the community ahead of his own desire. And to Number Thirteen's credit, the people accept Hassel and his partner Junior without the overt homophobia often wrongly associated with rural communities.

Though Hassel fancies himself mayor, he performs something closer to a pastoral role—though without any particular religious affiliation or even angle. "I will go hear Homer [his brother] preach," he tells us, "but I aint religious in some ways myself. Still I will never question them that are. You never can tell what somebody else has seen or heard " (114). His pastoral role is most overt in his relationship with Tom, who first comes to Number Thirteen as a VISTA worker but later returns as a Catholic priest charged with a mission. In the same exchange that reveals to Tom and the reader Hassel's homosexuality, Hassel also acts as Tom's confessor, the one person with whom the Jesuit novice can frankly share his deepest struggles. It is fitting that when Hassel makes the neighbors practice performing a mass he engineers to fool Tom's bishop, Hassel plays "the preacher's part" (283). He is indeed the pastor of Number Thirteen, and Tom, though himself a priest, is one of Hassel's parishioners.

Theology in Number Thirteen

Hassel's counterfeit mass, along with the sequence of events immediately surrounding it, offers a useful window for viewing his role at Number Thirteen. But even more so, it brings together the several theological threads—from Pentecostalism to liberation theology—that are woven through the novel. As usual, Giardina's depiction of religious faith is both realistic and nuanced.

Hassel's faith—and his mass—might be characterized as inclusive communitarianism. He is not concerned with the theological implications of the Catholic ritual; his only concern is helping his friend Tom, and he unites the citizens of Number Thirteen to create the illusion of a successful congregation. When Tom looks shamefacedly around the packed house, Hassel simply says, "See here . . . all the folks that love you. And we want you to stay and we don't want them to send you to that Honduras" (287). That those present all love Tom is not fully true. What is true is that in Hassel's parish, maintaining relationships—even troubled ones—takes precedence; and Hassel has schemed together a congregation to convince Tom's bishop to let him stay in Number Thirteen. Significantly, he has even drawn in the patrons of his Dew Drop Inn with the promise of free beer for their participation, a reminder that Jesus himself was condemned for sharing a meal—a type of the eucharist—with publicans and sinners.[27]

In starkest contrast to Hassel's inclusive communitarianism is Doyle Ray's exclusivist Christian fundamentalism. In as harsh a statement as the pastoral Hassel ever offers, he has earlier referred to Doyle Ray as "a mean kind of Christian" (261). This is Hassel's term for the type of Christianity Giardina associates not only with fire-and-brimstone preaching but with the nationalism of the popular religious right. Not surprisingly, Doyle Ray is influenced by Pat Robertson and *The 700 Club* (278). Nevertheless, even Doyle Ray's church performs, though unwittingly, a part in the mass charade. When Tom is driving his visiting bishop to Number Thirteen across the railroad bridge, Doyle Ray's congregation is gathered along the tracks at the site of the mysterious kudzu Jesus. Doyle Ray wants to save Tom from the influence of "the whore of Babylon, the beast of Revelation, the Roman Catholic Church" (286), so he decides to test Tom's faith by asking whether he can see Jesus's face in the kudzu.

Significantly, Hassel testifies to Doyle Ray that Tom "even seen Jesus from his front porch the other day" (287), a true claim (281) that Tom falsely denies.

Giardina does not, however, let us see even Doyle Ray without a compassion-inducing complexity. He is the son of an alcoholic father, Brigham, who often beat him, his sister, and his mother. It was while trying to protect his family from Brigham's rage that Doyle Ray permanently crippled his sister, Brenda; for this he was sent to reform school, then directly to Vietnam. A chronic anger results, and his bitterness drives him to claim, "My only kin is Jesus" (313). This confession recalls Vernie Lloyd's escape into fundamentalism in *Storming Heaven*, when she, like Doyle Ray, is pushed beyond the limits of what she can psychologically bear. Though Giardina's aversion to this kind of Christianity is consistent in all six novels, she never lets readers divorce it from the wounds that sometimes push people toward it.

It is equally fitting that Dillon, too, has a role in Hassel's mass. Early on Dillon has stated, "I fancy a God that would as soon level a church building as look at it" (127). His personal belief, as noted earlier, maintains Christian ideas of self-sacrifice, but it has more to do with a mystical understanding of his people and place than with any institutional religion. Yet his attendance at the mass suggests that on a deep level he understands the value in what Hassel is doing. He and Tom have never liked each other, and Dillon has baited the younger man ruthlessly. But he knows Jackie cares for Tom, and he wants her to be happy. Despite their differences, Tom is now a part of the Number Thirteen community, and community takes precedence over personal antipathy.

To his credit, too, Dillon has never been blind to various shapes Christianity takes. Though there is no place in his thinking for company churches or the exclusivism of Doyle Ray (and particularly for the anti-union thinking that comes with nationalistic fundamentalism), he has recognized, like his father before him, the courageous and useful independence of the Holiness. During his years of union organizing, Dillon reflects that "there is one building where you are free of the coal company and that is a church" (127), referring particularly to Homer and Louelly Day's Holiness church. At Hassel's mass, the Holiness are represented by Louelly, and it is through Louelly that we are reminded of the high value Giardina places on religious mystery. The gathering reaches a fervor when Louelly speaks in tongues, but not in the apparent gibberish of glossolalia. Inexplicably, Louelly speaks in Church Latin, repeating an ancient prayer of thanksgiving and humility, "*Non nobis domine domine sed nomine*" (290). And it is after her message that Tom, appropriating Louelly's prayer, comes clean with his bishop not only about the mass but about his own falseness: "I lied. I lied to my provincial and I lied [to] you. I lied to my friends here." After a glance at Jackie, he turns once again to the bishop: "I want to go back to Honduras. It's more home than here. But I'm scared. I don't have the strength for it" (290). Tom does not, in fact, have the strength to return: only with the support of his weirdly syncretistic community does he admit his weakness and begin to regain the courage to follow his call. Mysteriously, God uses a Pentecostal Holiness woman speaking in supernatural tongues during a contrived Catholic mass to reinforce the divine call of a young Jesuit whose devotion is wavering.

Tom has every right to be fearful. To understand why, it is helpful to note two further strains of dangerous theology Giardina introduces through his character. Recalling Albion in *Storming Heaven*, we see in Tom both the radical discipleship of Dietrich Bonhoeffer and the politically engaged activism of liberation theology. Bonhoeffer's theology of complete surrender to Christ, even to the point of giving up one's life, is one that has long appealed to the heroic imagination of devout young Christians. As we will see in the next chapter, Giardina will play its dramatic implications to the full in *Saints and Villains*, her novel based on Bonhoeffer's life. But briefly here, according to Bonhoeffer, Christians must be completely willing to make the ultimate sacrifice, constantly ready to pay what he called the "cost of discipleship."[28]

One may imagine that such a concept is more appealing in heroic daydreams than in actual practice. And in fact, Tom's religious language throughout the novel has been tinged with arrogance. His grandiose approach to Christian devotion is suggested the night he reads Bonhoeffer's famous call to discipleship aloud to Hassel: "When Christ calls a man, He bids him come and die" (218). Hassel's response shows his prescient insight: "[Tom] will laugh at such things, like he wants to show he aint scared of nothing." Neither the bravado nor the fear is lost on Hassel. That is true not only during Tom's first stay at Number Thirteen as a VISTA worker but also during this second stay, when he has feigned feeling a call to Number Thirteen as a religious mission after his stint in, significantly, Honduras. This particular reference to Central America brings into play a second theological strain that appeared in *Storming Heaven*: liberation theology.

The final two decades in *The Unquiet Earth* take place during the era when liberation theology was at the peak of its influence in Central America. At this time many Catholic priests, real-life versions of Tom, found their ministry woven into the fabric of political unrest. Capitalist forces, often backed covertly by the United States, were trying to undermine Marxist-influenced activists there. And the liberation element of the Catholic Church was working on behalf of the common people against covert American interests. Giardina carefully directs us to this wider world association through the three posters Tom hangs on his wall when he returns to Number Thirteen: "Martin Luther King, Dietrich Bonhoeffer, and Sandino" (267).

The influence of the first two is already clear enough, but the third is equally important, though more obscure for most readers. Augusto Calderon Sandino (1895–1934) was a Nicaraguan revolutionary whose example helped inspire much of the revolutionary activity of the 1970s and 1980s, and whose name became the name of the *Sandinista* National Liberation Front, to which liberation theology lent its support. Eventually we learn that during Tom's first assignment in Honduras he, like so many other Catholic priests active during that time, had been kidnapped and tortured by American-backed terrorists; and again true to real-life detail, he knew that martyrdom might well be waiting for him should he return.

So it is in fact fear that brought Tom to his supposed mission at Number Thirteen. Hassel does not know the details of Tom's experience, but he has a pastor's insight into the condition of a soul and a closeted homosexual's understanding of the complexity of human nature, things that are felt but never spoken, that painful disjuncture between the surface and the depths. To Hassel, so accustomed to keeping his own inner life a secret, Tom's fear is apparent. Thus to save his friend from the thing he most fears, Hassel conjures the illusion that Tom has succeeded with his Catholic mission in the coalfields. The results of Hassel's stratagem are not what either man would have anticipated. But Hassel's motives, and the unexpected nature of his success, attest to what one person of good intentions may, however inadvertently or mysteriously, accomplish.

Readers may recognize the reference to the story of Jonah that serves as the text of the day during the counterfeit mass. He was, of course, the prophet who was swallowed by "a great fish"; but more importantly, he had "fled from the presence of the Lord" in order to escape God's call.[29] Significantly, in an earlier conversation with Jackie and Hassel, Tom, looking at the kudzu Jesus, had said, "Maybe Jesus is following me" (281). Clearly Giardina is directing us to see that like Jonah, Tom has been trying to escape his call to Honduras, and *call* is a concept Giardina takes seriously in her books and her life. As she told Martha Greene Eads, a call is what "compels you along. I believe more genuine calls make you say, 'No way am I doing that!' But it's the thing that just bugs you and bugs you."[30]

Previous chapters have noted this phenomenon in King Harry and Albion Freeman, and we see it once again here. The conviction Tom feels in the presence of the kudzu Jesus comes to a head in the mass and especially Louelly's message in tongues. Tom, like Jonah, cannot escape God's call on his life. So in an unconventional mass in a tiny West Virginia coal camp, Giardina convincingly brings together several important strains of twentieth-century theology. And she simultaneously connects world politics with the struggles of the postcolonial situation of Number Thirteen, successfully demonstrating, according to Mooney, "the parallels between colonialist, imperialist Reagan-era Central American policies and the federal government's longstanding policy of capitalist-industrial intervention in Appalachia."[31] When she performs such sweeps, she is giving her readers broader cultural referents, to be sure. But just as importantly, she is demonstrating that the world of her fiction cannot be dismissed as a kind of limited regionalism. Appalachia cannot be read as Other: Number Thirteen is the world writ small.

An Appalachian Apocalypse

The penultimate chapter of *The Unquiet Earth* is entitled "Till Human Voices Wake Us, 1990." The story thus moves toward its conclusion with another reference to T. S. Eliot, this time to the final line of "The Love Song of J. Alfred Prufrock": "Till human voices wake us, and we drown."[32] Giardina's omission of the final three words foreshadows what is to come.

Given Giardina's attention to mythic themes and biblical concepts throughout the book, it is fitting to understand the cataclysmic flood as a kind of apocalypse. Figuratively at least, the world of the novel has been destroyed by the deluge; its end has been brought about by a human sinfulness so great that the divine would no longer bear it. We are reminded, for example, of the Noah flood story, in which "it repented the Lord that he had made man on the earth, and it grieved him at his heart," and the Lord said, "I will destroy man whom I have created from the face of the earth."[33] Here a judgment has fallen on Blackberry Creek: the wages of sin—economic and environmental—is death.

Understood in biblical terms, the deluge should have eradicated sin and sinner, inaugurating a new age with the renewed possibility for a better life. But that was not the case in Number Thirteen. The denouement, narrated by Jackie, begins with the *New York Times* headline in which International Oil calls the flood an "Act of God"—and it may well have been (338). But what International Oil means by that phrase is anything but an admission that judgment has fallen on their sin; on the contrary, the company's phrase is legal discourse summoned to avoid responsibility.[34] In this coalfield apocalypse, the innocent have been sacrificed and the oppressors not only persist but thrive. Jackie notes that "the company has built a new road up Blackberry Creek, straight and broad because now there are no houses to take up space in the bottoms" (339)—a change that enhances profitability. The new age following this apocalypse seems no less depraved than the one that preceded.

Life in Number Thirteen, nevertheless, goes on. Hassel telephones Jackie in Pittsburgh, still trying to welcome her home, and he reports that those remaining—Louelly, Toejam, Junior, and himself—are scavenging the wreckage. He and Junior are cutting up metal from tipples and abandoned machinery to sell as scrap. And Louelly and Toejam gather the coal that falls from trucks now "running in fleets from the strip mines" to sell for house coal. So Hassel and his parish have once again endured and are working to survive in a postapocalyptic landscape. As he tells Jackie, "They's lots of people to look after. It keeps me hopping" (339).

Dark as the situation seems, Hassel's final words, "We'll still yet be here," reflect endurance under the thumb of oppression and may even offer hope (339). There is a deep and noble persistence that keeps Hassel and his people still loving their place in the world, however unconventional or even irrational their love. And maybe the suggestion here is that such love is stronger than anything International Oil can do. Lying in her dark room in Pittsburgh, Jackie tries "to see pictures on the ceiling"—pictures we may assume are visions of life in Number Thirteen.

CHAPTER 5

Saints and Villains: Conscience, Doubt, and the Call to Action

The Unquiet Earth (1992) confirmed Denise Giardina's reputation as an Appalachian novelist of the first rank, and nearly all the scholarly attention her work has received has addressed her two coalfield novels. Certainly some benefits accrue from acclaim as an Appalachian regionalist, but that particular classification may also have worked against a fuller and more accurate critical valuation of Giardina's work. Too often, praising a writer as a prominent regionalist is like proclaiming him a talented *minor league* baseball player: the compliment opens the door to a good many negative interpretations. And the descriptor *Appalachian* may, unfortunately, be a problem as well. The eminent novelist Lee Smith noted in a 2006 panel discussion that "regionalism is still a pejorative concept," and she added, "The way the rest of the country thinks about the South, even the South thinks about Appalachia."[1]

In Giardina's case, the situation is still more complex. Critics who gave her their attention in part *because* of her intimate engagement with Appalachian culture may have been less interested in works not grounded in Appalachia. Or they may have been discouraged by another trajectory her work takes. Just as some critics are slow to take an Appalachian novel seriously, others are hesitant to take a religious novel seriously, particularly a Christian novel. As Giardina told interviewer W. Dale Brown, "I think in some ways you can wrestle with the other faiths, but when you have a character who says, 'I am a Christian,' you have a problem. It is almost because Christianity is the dominant faith in this country and those words have been devalued by Pat Robertson types."[2] Brown may be correct in naming Giardina among those writers who "often fall abruptly between two worlds, too religious for a secular audience and too secular for a religious one."[3]

Such critical reticence is understandable. If by *Christian novels* we mean those sold primarily to a popular Christian market, carefully honed to avoid any language or situation that would make them awkward additions to a church library, it is likely that many do not return the investment of critical attention. But it may be helpful here to stipulate a necessary distinction. As noted in chapter 1, Giardina does not refer to herself as a *Christian* novelist but as a *theological* novelist; the two are not the same. The work of a Christian novelist adheres closely to the surface aspects of a Christian way of life, and the faith elements are straightforward and transparently portrayed. The work of a theological novelist attempts something more complex, both rhetorically and thematically. She necessarily engages in an argument that will demand that her readers question some aspect of belief, and maybe even revise their way of thinking. If the purpose of the Christian novelist is to confirm readers' faith, one purpose of the theological novelist is to motivate readers to understand their faith—or lack of faith—in new ways. The assumption that a novel's being Christian, as defined above, will narrow its thematic focus may indeed be correct. But a novel that struggles with great theological questions may be as broad as the eternal longing of humans to make sense of their place in the world—to consider and reconsider their responsibilities in it.

Saints and Villains (1998) is the fictional biography of the distinguished German theologian and martyr Dietrich Bonhoeffer. It is hard to imagine a slice of history better suited for the exploration of complex and challenging theological issues—or one more demanding on the skills and imagination of the novelist. Giardina has stated that she writes about "things that obsess me since they are with me for so long in the writing process," and it is clear that she obsessed over these theological questions and particularly Bonhoeffer for a long time.[4] The book took her six years to write, but the obsession paid off. Critic Sylvia Bailey Shurbutt has called it "Giardina's finest example of fiction writing,"[5] and few students of Giardina's work would dismiss that possibility.

Saints and Villains was awarded the 1999 Fisk Fiction Prize by the *Boston Book Review*, and it was longlisted for the International Dublin Literary Award in 2000. Bonnie Johnston's evaluation in *Booklist* is representative of many positive reviews. She called the book a "compelling, frightening, yet beautiful novel, written with passion, understanding, and eloquence."[6] Many reviewers noted particularly Giardina's achievement in taking on the challenge of making the story of a bookish intellectual an exciting read. Clea Simon in the *Boston Globe* commented that "to find a historical figure like Dietrich Bonhoeffer packaged in what is essentially a moral thriller is a surprising joy,"[7] and *Kirkus Reviews* agreed that "Giardina has the gift of making intellectual argument excitingly dramatic."[8] *Publishers Weekly* praised Giardina for managing "the extremely difficult task of giving a known story genuine tension and spiritual resonance."[9] Craig J. Slane in *Christian Century* called the book a "compellingly plausible psychological portrait," praising Giardina's "rich imagination" and "impressive historical knowledge."[10]

Other reviewers were less impressed. Susan Osborn panned the novel in the *Washington Post* as consisting of "static doctrinal and moral conversations,"[11] and the *Library Journal's* Caroline M. Hallsworth wrote that Giardina "fails to create a heroic or even compelling central character."[12] Whether or not one is ultimately taken by the novel, however, may at least in part depend on whether one finds nuanced theological and philosophical issues engaging, or even on how one values Bonhoeffer. He is more than an important theologian. Along with his writing, his brief, dramatic life—culminating in execution by the Nazis he faithfully resisted—earned him a place in the contemporary pantheon of cultural heroes. Today he is something of an industry among both theologians and popularizers: in addition to hundreds of academic articles and monographs at various levels of sophistication, hundreds of more popular titles, books, and even films about the man and his work repay the most casual internet search of his name. An advantage of writing about such a figure is that a ready-made audience exists. And that is also the disadvantage. Thousands of people, including reviewers, have some professional or deeply personal interest in how the author makes each move. It is a dangerous task to write the life of a saint, especially a recent one.

From History to Fiction

Even more so than with Giardina's earlier books, then, critics have weighed how tightly or loosely she handles historical facts and situations. Betty Smartt Carter, in a laudatory review for *Books and Culture*, claimed that Giardina "cut herself free from all but the basic structure of Bonhoeffer's life" and instead "chose the broader path of imagination and instinct."[13] On the opposite pole, Paul Baumann in the *New York Times* called the book a "painstakingly reconstructed historical narrative" that fails in part because it is more "a predictable dramatization of the facts than an original reimagining of life."[14] One suspects that those most familiar with the biographical accounts tend to note the broadness of the speculation, and those less familiar with Bonhoeffer's life focus on the historical constraints. The truth may be somewhere in the middle, but as reviewer Elinor Langer noted, "Much more important than the exact balance of history and fiction is that the two flow into each other so naturally."[15]

In any case, most would agree with *Publishers Weekly* that Giardina has "an admirable grip on her panoramic story,"[16] and to the panorama she remains true. She has kept close to the most widely known events, at least in part because changing them would create an off-putting distance in too many readers.

(It is one thing to relocate the breaking of a dam as in *The Unquiet Earth*; quite another to relocate a war.) But Giardina has taken a storyteller's liberty with the lesser-known events, and she has given herself the freedom to create and manipulate the details she needs to realize her formal and thematic intention. Multiple reviewers point out the cinematic nature of her method,[17] and it seems only fitting that greater license be exercised as the camera zooms closer and closer in and the historical record becomes more sparse. Indeed, much of what makes *Saints and Villains* an effective psychological novel is its portrayal of Dietrich's inner life and his most intimate interactions.

Our purpose, then, is not to examine the book as an artifact in the Bonhoeffer debates (though it is) or to measure it against any version of the historical record, but to understand how it works—and how *well* it works—as a novel that strives for truth in relation to a historical context. As Giardina writes in the afterword, "This novel is a work of the imagination, first and foremost, and yet I hope it is also true. Some 'facts' have been altered because of the demands of the story."[18] In a particularly insightful comment, Lee Congdon writes that in *Saints and Villains*, Giardina "is after something other than scholarly accuracy. She wants to understand and present the 'truth' of her subject's being."[19] Whether she succeeds should be the primary measure of the novel's success.

Biographies of Bonhoeffer continue to proliferate, and certain periods of the protagonist's history are well documented. Giardina's portrayal of his years in prison, for example, has considerable substantiation in the biographical record; his *Letters and Papers from Prison* remains widely read, and Giardina herself has testified to its influence on her life.[20] A different kind of creative act was necessary for the depiction of his time in the United States, however, because much less is known about it. This gap in the record gave Giardina liberty to create events that work formally to complement and enhance what is known historically. Her incorporation of the Hawks Nest Tunnel disaster in West Virginia may serve as an example, if not a paradigm, of the freedom she takes with history in the service of literary art and the truth art can offer.

In 1930 Union Carbide began the tunnel through Gauley Mountain to redirect the New River to a hydroelectric plant. In the process, the drills encountered silica, and its dust filled the confined air. Though the company was aware of the deadly health concern, they continued sending unprotected workers, most of them African American men desperate for a Depression-era paycheck, into the tunnel. Hundreds died of silicosis, an untreatable condition, and their bodies were dumped in makeshift graves.

Dietrich's experience at the Hawks Nest Tunnel is one of those occasions in which Giardina works creatively with history to serve the overall progression of the novel, wedding a lesser-known period of his life with a too-little-known event, and doing so in a way that does not violate the historical frame. Students of Bonhoeffer agree that his understanding of the Christian faith changed during his time in the United States at Union Seminary. It is known that during this period he was deeply troubled by American racism, even to the point of comparing it—unfavorably—with the then-current German treatment of Jews. And it is known that near the end of his stay in the United States he took an extended trip through the South, though details of his itinerary are lost. Further, we know that Bonhoeffer had a friend named Frank Fisher—Giardina's inspiration for Fred Bishop—who was from the South and returned there after studying at Union.[21] Another of his seminary friends, the labor activist Myles Horton, was working with miners in the Appalachian coalfields. And his professor and friend Reinhold Niebuhr was traveling to the region during that time.[22] So while Dietrich's fictional journey to Gauley Mountain is something short of a likelihood, it is not an unreasonable possibility.

Nevertheless, it is a segment of the narrative some reviewers have criticized. In her generally laudatory review mentioned above, Simon referred to it as "a false note in an otherwise stirring adventure,"[23] and Patty McCarty in the *National Catholic Reporter* dismissed the section as something to "please Giardina's hometown crowd."[24] What such readings fail to perceive is the importance of this incident in foreshadowing Dietrich's opposition to Nazism. Hawks Nest is his first experience with large-scale homicide wrought against people for the sake of profit, a crime perversely allowable because of the victims' race. Neither should it be overlooked that to cover Dietrich's accent and scholarly look, his friends pass him off as a mute, intellectually impaired person, dressing him as a hobo and making him keep his expensive eyeglasses in his pocket. Thus for a brief period he is trapped in a position of being able to see only with difficulty, to experience human depravity at its worst, and to have no voice in the situation. He is symbolically silenced and humbled, even as he observes a horror that will be magnified exponentially in his home country—where again he will see only in part, suffer humiliation, and be silenced.

Martha Greene Eads has rightly noted that Dietrich's "encounter with dying Hawk's Nest tunnel-diggers [is] vital to the discovery of his own dangerous vocation in Nazi Germany."[25] To direct readers' attention to its significance, Giardina gives two related chapters the same name, "White Tunnel." The first recounts this adventure at Hawks Nest, and the second depicts Dietrich's journey toward his own execution. Fred plays prominently in both. As noted,

Dietrich experiences Hawks Nest alongside Fred, and as he reaches his deadly climax, it is that adventure with Fred—not the weighty words of Niebuhr, Jean Lasserre, or any other theologian—that comes to mind: "He lies still and tries to recall Fred's voice. He can't hear it. But somewhere between black night and gray dawn he is riding in the back of a truck upon a bed of corpses and Fred is tracing a cross on Dietrich's forehead with a dusty fingertip."[26] Whether or not she executes it perfectly, we can hardly dismiss the Hawks Nest Tunnel scene as "a false note."

Just as Giardina must choose which liberties to take with history, she must, as we have already suggested, make choices about her cast of characters. Major historical figures cannot be radically altered, but she has the options of leaving people out, of portraying less-known historical characters loosely or closely to the record, of manipulating or blending historical persons to better serve the story, or of creating wholly new characters. Each option carries its own risks and advantages. When Giardina varies most broadly from the historical record with her cast of characters, she does so with clear and effective artistic intention, some of which is explained in the novel's brief afterword. Most noticeable for those familiar with Bonhoeffer's life is the absence of Eberhard Bethge in the novel, given his close relationship with the protagonist. Concerning that choice, Giardina states, "I can only hope that the friendships of the fictional Bonhoeffer with Fred Bishop, Elisabeth, and George Bell have captured some of the special nature of this relationship" (486). What makes her explanation helpful is that it invites us into her reasoning. The book is about Dietrich, and she chooses to use or conflate or create other characters based on how they allow her to develop the roles those relationships played in Dietrich's interior life—and, of course, on how they move the story along.

Aspects of Literary Form

Much could be written about Giardina's execution of her craft. Our discussion here will be limited to three elements that may be important for readers who are trying to gain a fuller understanding of her accomplishment: her use of the doppelgänger, the mass, and the play within a play.

The Doppelgänger

One thing that moves any story along is an engaging antagonist, and Giardina fills this need through the creation of Alois Bauer, a character inspired by several of Bonhoeffer's historical interrogators. If making a saint into a human has a certain risk, turning a powerful Nazi into an object of at least limited sympathy and moral complexity is riskier still. Giardina confronts the challenge in the most direct manner imaginable: she creates a doppelgänger, she *tells* the reader (through chapter titles) that he is a doppelgänger, and she then proceeds to make him, at least early in the novel, more sympathetic than her iconic protagonist.

Any reader who attends to the implications of class feels an immediate sympathy for Bauer. He is reared in poverty by a drunken father, who, in the first chapter, beats the boy and kicks his dog to death, even as the child prays, "Please God make him stop please God make him stop" (14). If ever a child needed to find a way out, it is Bauer. As in our own day, for a poor young person with ability and drive, a military career may be the most readily available—and sometimes the only—opportunity to make his or her way in the world. That Bauer chooses this route during the rise of the most perverse military and political machine in modern memory is a historical misfortune—almost secondary to the fact that, at least early on, he is doing what he can in his situation.

Family and fatherland have given Bauer nothing. In contrast, they have given Dietrich everything. He reeks with privilege of which he is barely aware. The aristocratic Bonhoeffer family has wealth, class, and education; Dietrich is offered every opportunity imaginable to excel and succeed. He has been raised for success by a supportive family with virtually limitless resources; he need only choose his field and pursue it. Yet the two characters are in some ways similar, as they must be for the doppelgänger device to work. Both are talented, even brilliant young men striving toward accomplishment and success in the avenues available to them. The difference is that Dietrich has choices. Together but by different roads each seeks the best way of moving through a complicated and dangerous world. Curiously both live lives centered on their relationship to their nation, a nation both men serve and then, in opposite ways, betray. Materially, Bauer rises as Dietrich falls. Spiritually, Dietrich rises while Bauer lives out the murderous trajectory of his horrific childhood.

Mozart's Mass in C Minor

The most overt formal device that brings Dietrich and Bauer together is Giardina's use of Mozart's Mass in C Minor, a work that plays significantly in both men's lives. Giardina uses the parts of the Mass as section divisions throughout the novel, a choice that offers mixed success. Some of the headings do have apparent ties to the content or tone of the sections. For example, the section *Kyrie eleison* is made up of scenes from Dietrich and Bauer's youth, the childhoods that would lead to the struggles both men would face. As such, "Lord have mercy" seems an appropriate designation. Functioning similarly is *Et incarnatus est* ("and was made flesh"), the section that begins Dietrich's time in prison, when a life of privilege is replaced by a life of suffering lived among the suffering: here Dietrich, at least loosely, takes on the Christ role that culminates in his passion. That Dietrich, like Christ, is "made flesh" supports the thematic progression.

Making these headings the focus of section divisions, however, claims more attention than their significance will bear. This may explain why one otherwise positive reviewer referred to the section headings as "a rather fussy construction" that "strikes a pretentious note."[27] In fact, the placement suggests that the narrative is structured as a mass, and that does not seem apparent. The titles are closer akin to a leitmotif in a piece of music than to an actual structuring framework. As motifs, they work well enough. One cannot always articulate what the precise relationship is between the section of the novel and the section of the Mass; still, the reading experience is richer for their complementary presence, and that may be sufficient. Readers are left to experience their own associations.

As a plot device and as thematic reinforcement, the Mass is more successfully incorporated. It is richly suggestive that the two men's lives intersect in the context of a grand but incomplete piece of religious music. For Bauer the Mass is the object of his heart's desire, a veiled longing for spiritual wholeness. The power and influence he gains as he rises in the Nazi ranks he invests in pursuing his grail—the original manuscript. He claims that he does not believe in God, yet he seeks to fill the void he feels within by making a fetish of a great religious document. His longing, the text suggests, is a spiritual longing; unconsciously, he knows something is missing or broken in him, and he knows it is something present in the Mass (taken in all its rich connotations). Similarly, Dietrich's perfect but lifeless execution of the "Kyrie" for Leonid Kreuzer is what ended his youthful aspirations to become a concert pianist (8). The passionate spirituality Dietrich develops through the novel finds an appropriate culmination when he is playing this great but incomplete Mass at Schönberg; his performance on a battered piano, improvised from a precious but confusing orchestral score, is suggestive of the imperfection synonymous with any striving to know the divine. Progress is made, but imperfection remains. At the end, Bauer "weeps openly" and Dietrich's own eyes fill, for reasons that may not be too different. Mozart never completed the Mass, but what he completed is enough; that his great work may only be partially realized, for Dietrich at least, must be enough. Bauer's quest continues.

A Play within a Play

One of Giardina's most purposeful alterations of a famous historical figure is her use of T. S. Eliot (whose work was so significant in *The Unquiet Earth*) to illuminate Dietrich's inward struggle. She brings the two men together at the bishop's palace of George Bell, a mutual friend, and she shifts the timeline so that their visit may correspond to Eliot's composition of *Murder in the Cathedral*, the story of Thomas Becket. Thus she is bringing a writer (Eliot) who fictionalized a famous martyr (Becket) together with a man who would a decade later become a martyr himself (Bonhoeffer)—and who is himself being fictionalized in this very text. Though one reviewer called their meeting "another distraction,"[28] closer attention to the function of the relationship reveals its important formal and thematic role. Once we suspend our disbelief about—or are delighted by—the imaginary pairing, we see that again Giardina has confabulated a historical sequence that works effectively to forward Dietrich's self-knowledge and ultimately his transformation.

Would the real-life Eliot have asked his hosts and their German friend to dress in tails and do a dramatic reading of his rough draft, almost as a kind of writerly thought experiment? It does not seem impossible. Certainly Giardina's Eliot is abrasive, self-absorbed, completely willing to let others suffer for his art. And he is also a literary genius of extraordinary psychological insight, a characterization that rings true to students of the historical Eliot's work.

Those familiar with Eliot's play will recall that after Becket's return to England from exile, he is confronted by four tempters and what they have to offer: the temptation of physical pleasures like those he enjoyed as a young man; the temptation to strive for personal power; the temptation to overthrow the government for the good of the country; and, most importantly, the temptation to seek eternal glory after death, the glory that comes from being a martyr. Dietrich senses how closely these temptations, most especially the last, parallel his own. When he, Eliot, and the Bells are doing a dramatic reading of the draft, Dietrich—confronted by Eliot acting as the fourth tempter—experiences a deeply discordant epiphany. He throws down the manuscript and shouts at Eliot, "What the hell are you doing?" (185).

After a few more accusatory lines, Eliot stops the reading and speaks directly to what he has intuited about Dietrich's condition. He offers him a bit of cold comfort, assuring him that Becket was a true martyr "because he stops trying to be right and simply is. Suffering is action, and action suffering" (186). To Dietrich's protestation that "I have no desire to be a martyr, nor do I expect to be one," Eliot responds, "No . . . it's not likely. But you're no stranger to spiritual pride, are you?" Not only, then, does Giardina present us with a fascinating imagined meeting, but she prefigures through Eliot's twelfth-century hero the temptations Bonhoeffer encounters as he works to discover and follow his call.

Heeding the Call

The theme of following one's call has been significant in all Giardina's previous books, and here that theme is moved appropriately to the center of the story.[29] *Saints and Villains* is, after all, the fictional biography of an important theologian who made following the call of God the focus of his most famous theological treatise and, at least in Giardina's telling, the focus of his life. Though it contains intense action, this is ultimately a psychological novel in that the movement centers on the inner struggles of a single brilliant mind to discover his best way forward. Such a narrative situation allows Giardina to deal directly and in depth with one of her own concerns and to do so without violating the realism of the narrative. The rest of this chapter will focus on that theme and in the process explore several complications that impact Dietrich's pursuit as he struggles to discover and live into his call.

Two Conceptions of Call

In the most foundational Christian sense, *call* refers to a responsibility that bears on the life of *every* believer, a topic the historical Bonhoeffer explored extensively in his writings. The theological concept most famously associated with Bonhoeffer is that of "costly grace" in contrast to "cheap grace"—phrases that have taken their place not only in scholarly but popular religious parlance. The terms are the subject of his book *The Cost of Discipleship*, written during the rise of Nazism and still in print 80 years later. It is, in fact, the book alluded to when Dietrich is pastoring in England (171). He writes the famous first lines when he is visiting Bishop Bell: "*Cheap grace is the deadly enemy of our Church. We are fighting today for costly grace*" (183), and the entire first chapter of what is now a Christian classic is spent discussing these two types of grace. "Cheap grace," the historical Bonhoeffer writes, "is the preaching of forgiveness without requiring repentance, baptism without church discipline, Communion without confession, absolution without personal confession. Cheap grace is grace without discipleship, grace without the cross, grace without Jesus Christ, living and incarnate."[30] In other words, cheap grace means appropriating the apparent advantages of being a Christian without paying the cost; that is, without actually living according to the principles, demands, and way of life laid out by Jesus. The opposite of this *cheap grace* is *costly grace*—the intentional, radical pursuit of doing what one perceives as God's will no matter what the cost, suffering the consequences of a countercultural stance and then, when the struggle reaches its inevitably imperfect consummation, depending upon God's grace.

Such a radical discipleship is suggested in the portrayals of many of Giardina's religious characters, possibly King Harry but most certainly Albion Freeman and eventually Tom Kolwiecki. So it is no accident that when Tom is struggling with his own vocation, he is reading from Bonhoeffer's *The Cost of Discipleship*. The final sentence in the following passage will be familiar to readers of *The Unquiet Earth*, since Tom shares it with Hassel Day: "As we embark upon discipleship we surrender ourselves to Christ in union with his death—we give over our lives to death. Thus it begins; the cross is not the terrible end to an otherwise god-fearing and happy life, but it meets us at the beginning of our communion with Christ. When Christ calls a man, he bids him come and die."[31] Such an ultimate commitment, Bonhoeffer states, is the foundational call on every committed Christian.

A second understanding of call moves beyond the foundational call to the conviction that God has called a particular believer to a particular path of action. When King Harry feels his call to unite Christendom, when Albion feels his call to organize the miners at Felco, and when Tom feels (and flees) his call to return to Honduras, they are sensing a call in this second sense. They have responded to a foundational call to faithfulness, and then they are discovering and following (or not) the specific task God would have them do in their lives. This particularity might be understood as the call to discipleship instantiated into a specific life situation. It takes into account the responsibilities, the advantages, the possibilities, the inclinations, and the gifts that a particular human owns, and practically speaking, those things themselves may create one's particular call. But we must not exclude, in Giardina's worldview, a mysterious, preternatural dimension—as if one's way forward had somehow been determined in advance. The challenge of discovering and following such a call is the struggle that animates Dietrich's story.

Discovering or understanding one's call is no simple task, and as Giardina presents her protagonist, the process begins even before any awareness of the phenomenon. From the beginning of *Saints and Villains*, this particular, mysterious idea of call is already at work in Dietrich's life. His childhood and adolescence are spent pursuing excellence as a pianist. But when his parents have him evaluated by Leonid Kreuzer, the master concludes that while Dietrich's technical prowess is beyond question, that prowess is not enough. Kreuzer judges that Dietrich does not play with the passion characteristic of a great concert pianist. "What is missing," Kreuzer states, "training cannot provide" (8). At home that evening, Dietrich's father gathers the family into the study for the final verdict and asks his son, "Would you still wish to study music?" and Dietrich dutifully responds, "No, Father." With those words, his past and his future as a pianist fall immediately away.

This strangely fatalistic sequence is partially explained by the fact that Dietrich's family is one in which eminence in some field—at least for the men—is the highest value. His father is not simply a good psychiatrist but "Germany's leading psychiatrist" (4). Dietrich's brother Karl-Friedrich is not simply a good scientist but one "who had already been noticed for his research on splitting atoms" (16). And Dietrich's twin Sabine's husband is not simply a good lawyer but "one of the most brilliant young legal minds in Germany" (16). When it is determined that Dietrich will not be a pianist of the first rank, that vocation is no longer a worthwhile pursuit. But that night, a distraught Dietrich taps three times on the wall between his room and Sabine's, their private signal that means, "Think of God" (8). A page has been turned, and it turns mysteriously toward the divine.

When to the astonishment of all Dietrich chooses to pursue theology, he does not do so based on any apparent religious devotion or even a conscious passion for the subject itself. He makes his choice for the challenge, explaining to his family that theology is "an intellectual pursuit, like philosophy, only more specific and therefore more rigorous" (9). In response to his brother's sharp dismissal—"I can't imagine anything more fuzzy-minded, or irrelevant"—Dietrich responds that "if theology seems irrelevant . . . then it is because it has been improperly presented. I shall change that." Rationally, he has deemed it an area in which he may be a leading contributor, and readers must wonder if his theology will lack the same element his piano playing lacks: passion. But later in the conversation he explains his choice more mysteriously: he confesses to his family that when he made his pronouncement in response to a teacher's question, "It just came out suddenly, but I realized I'd been considering it quite a while." The decision seems at least as intuitive as reasoned. A call is already working its way into Dietrich's future.

The Call Foreshadowed

As noted above, Dietrich's Union Seminary friend Fred Bishop—in life and death—plays a key role in Dietrich's progression. Most significantly, Dietrich is influenced by Fred's understanding of call. He is frustrated with the lack of intellectual rigor he finds at Union, and intellectual achievement is at that point still his highest value. During one classroom outburst, he upbraids his classmates and even his professor: "It is not just jokes. It is your theology. Or lack of it. There is no critical thinking here" (29). As the conversation continues, Fred tells of a poor but faithful woman in his church who has lost two sons, one to the prison system and one to disease:

> From what she knows, there's no sense to any of it, and tell you what, that's as much as you know too. So don't go to Ruth Jones with that intellect stuff. Know what she'll say? Woman will ask you if you love Jesus. Intellect! Take your intellect and argue her any kind of theology you want to. She won't pay you any mind. Mourns her sons. Loves Jesus. Won't let go of any of it. (30)

As Fred speaks, Dietrich "relaxed as though the anger were visibly draining from him" (30). A change is taking place. In Fred he begins to see how a living faith goes beyond theology. He does not lose interest in his discipline's rigor or even in his need to make a great contribution, but he begins to understand that there are facets of faith he knows nothing about but toward which he is drawn. Through his work at Abyssinian Baptist, an African American church in Harlem, he realizes that people there have something vital in their lives that he lacks, and he begins, in a way that is beyond his volition, to pursue it. The coldly rigorous theologian even finds himself weeping when the choir sings (35). He later confesses to his friend Lasserre, "I have theology. But very little of the sort of faith I witness among my Harlem churchgoers. They seem to feel the presence of God, and I feel nothing. I only think" (39).

But that is changing. Though his fellow theologians, particularly Niebuhr, remain important and influential for Dietrich, it is not through a revised understanding of academic theology that he begins to intuit his new direction. It is instead through Fred's friendship and his mysterious approach to the faith that Dietrich's transformation edges toward fruition, and Fred is persistently described in relation to his call, a call with which he himself remains utterly ill at ease. He is talented enough and well connected enough to have been offered an important pastoral charge right out of seminary: he has a *call* in the occupational sense. But it is not his call. As Fred struggles to be faithful, Dietrich is gaining awareness of how a call is experienced.

In a way that goes beyond the rational, Fred knows his own way forward is somehow linked with the injustice occurring at Gauley Mountain. And after he, Dietrich, the idiot savant Earl, and Doc Booker (readers of *Storming Heaven* may remember that Doc moved to Charleston) visit the workers at the Hawks Nest Tunnel construction site, Fred's call becomes increasingly clear and unsettling. In a sequence that parallels Albion Freeman's call to the coal camps, where the tipple becomes his church steeple, the tunnel at Hawks Nest becomes Fred's parish, and service to the suffering people there is his dreaded call. As they return to Charleston, he warns Dietrich about the weight of his experience, and he shares the burden of receiving a call, a leading he cannot evade:

> "When we arrived yesterday I told Earl there wasn't any church here," [Fred] said. "What if there is? What if it's my church?"
> Dietrich felt his mouth go dry. "You have a church," he said.
> "A church that never has felt right. Never felt the hand of the Lord on my shoulder when I walked in that church. I felt it back there. Heard the voice in my inner ear. That's what a call is, and it's a terrible thing. I don't want it, not at all." (75)

And he adds, "I hope you never get a call. . . . I wouldn't wish it on you." Fred's statement, though it reflects his longing to spare Dietrich anguish, in fact quickens the faith silently growing in the theologian's heart.

Following the Call in Germany

Dietrich is changed by his American experience with Fred. In fact, he writes to his sister Sabine that he has experienced a kind of conversion (51). But once he returns to Germany and moves, however tentatively, in the direction of following a call, the way forward is not clearly marked. This likely explains his increased melancholy and Dietrich's father's comment that "America . . . seems to have turned Dietrich's brain to porridge" (80). As noted in our previous chapter, for Giardina a call "just compels you along."[32]

The foundational call to discipleship, according to the historical Bonhoeffer's theology, is clearly an absolute. But the specific call to a particular work, as experienced with Fred at Gauley Mountain, may mean a lifetime of seeking that includes as much confusion as faith, a lifetime of following whatever "just compels you along," struggling to do the right thing, to make the best choice in any situation. Even setting aside the intrinsic mystery of discerning a preternatural leading, for a call to be perfectly clear would demand that Christian theology speak with a consistent message. And that has never been the case. Even among Christians, conflicts arise in clarifying just what it means to do the right thing in any particular instance. What happens if doing the right thing in relation to one aspect of a situation means doing the wrong thing in relation to another? A particular call is utterly personal, but it inevitably demands action in the world: one is called *to an action*, and performing or not performing an action inevitably affects others. As Brian Cole has written of Giardina's use of the concept, "The call always flings a person into a community, however welcoming or unwelcoming that might be, and clarifies that person's involvement in a very troubling and uncertain event."[33] Necessarily, the call is shaped by the life situation of the individual called: the material advantages, the social advantages, and psychological makeup of the individual. Dietrich is already a theologian with an international reputation, a would-be pastor, the son of a wealthy and influential family. And he is discovering his call during the ascendancy of the most depraved political force in modern history. Having been called by Christ "to come and die," he must still discern what particular actions to take, given his resources and his context. Whatever Dietrich determines is his call will be carried out in tension with other competing obligations, some of which themselves are weightily binding. To follow his call, then, is to be at odds with other important claims on his life, including those of his family, his friends, his lovers, his fellow conspirators, his fellow churchmen, and even his country.

The Nation, the Church, and the Call

Dietrich is a patriot who refers frequently to his love of his country. He shares something akin to that deep Appalachian tie to place we associate with Giardina's most sympathetic heroes. Cole has even argued that "Bonhoeffer's decision to return to Germany is closely connected to a belief that one cannot divorce call from place."[34] But Dietrich's ultimate allegiance is to Christ, and he holds deep-felt convictions about Jesus's teachings on nonviolence. Thus he suffers through several complex questions: How, particularly during a time of war, can love of country and love of Christ be harmonized? And what if that war is being aggressively executed toward evil ends by a perverse regime? And what if the individual Christian finds himself at odds not only with the government but with his Church? Most confusingly, what is the simultaneous relationship of a Christian to the Church, to his nation, and to his personal call? This ethical triangulation reaches beyond *Saints and Villains*, beyond all

Giardina's fiction, and deep into the author's life. She is here engaging head-on an issue of her own lived concern, and it may help our fuller understanding of the text to hold in mind Giardina's own, very American historical context.

Historically Americans, though formally insisting on the Constitutional separation of church and state, have often—at least tacitly—been ready to identify what is good for America with the will of God. Whether dressed in language of Divine Providence, Manifest Destiny, or any other form of religiously toned American exceptionalism, the transformation of *America* into something like a divine entity has been persistent. And the broad landscape of American Christianity has inevitably led to various religious and political factions coupling to support agendas they believe to be mutually beneficial. Such thinking was dramatically evident in the late twentieth century, the two decades when Giardina was most engaged in political action and writing her strongest fiction.

During these years, what is termed the religious right had not only made common cause with the most conservative wing of the Republican Party but gained a dominant popular religious status in the process. Suddenly conservative fundamentalism, an often overlooked faction of American Christianity, found itself with new political power. Regardless of how one might judge the intentions of either agent in this coalition, any critically thinking Christian—and Giardina is one—must inevitably have perceived the looming tensions and dooming contradictions of identifying a political faction's agenda with a faction of Christianity. The reasons for the tension are straightforward; they are not, however, simple. At its foundation, the problem is one that concerns a distinction between nationalism and patriotism.

Dietrich's Union Seminary friend Lasserre offers a useful perspective on the distinction, one that Dietrich eventually comes to share: "One thing you must understand about me, Bonhoeffer, and if you grasp it, perhaps we may get along. I am no nationalist. I love France. And sometimes despise it. As I love and despise Germany, and love and despise America. I am a citizen of the Kingdom of God, Bonhoeffer. And one cannot be such a citizen and also a nationalist. *C'est impossible!*" (39). Serious Christian theologians may debate how or whether it is possible to be a Christian and a *patriot*, but it would be hard to find a thinker of any sophistication who sees the possibility of being a Christian and a *nationalist*. Typical usage is likely to see the latter as a more intense, extreme version of the former. But as Giardina uses the concepts, the distinction is a difference not only of degree but of kind. Patriotism is the love of or allegiance to the political ideals, the way of life, the cultural characteristics of a particular nation; as such, patriotism may be one legitimate and useful set of beliefs held among others. Nationalism, in contrast, deifies those characteristics and makes allegiance to one's nation the ultimate value to which other loyalties must finally give way. That distinction reveals an irreconcilable dilemma. It is the nature of Christianity to demand ultimate allegiance; it is also the nature of nationalism to demand ultimate allegiance. But two *ultimate* allegiances are inevitably contradictory, and each will follow its own agenda until one distorts or subsumes the other. When the mandates of a nation and the mandates of Christianity differ, as eventually they must, the question of ultimate allegiance is not only pertinent but inescapable. The words of Jesus will resound for many readers: "No man can serve two masters: for either he will hate the one, and love the other; or else he will hold to the one and despise the other."[35]

The rising agenda of the religious right during Giardina's most productive period veered perilously toward the path of nationalism. This is the tendency Giardina associates with historical phenomena such as Pat Robertson's *700 Club* and Jerry Falwell's Moral Majority.[36] She prefigures these religious leaders in *Saints and Villains* with a parallel historical figure, Frank Buchman. Buchman is the popular American evangelical who sings Hitler's praises as an anti-communist—the man whom Dietrich confronts at a London lecture (164–5). The dominance of such popular nationalists and their movements left many Christians, including Bonhoeffer in his time and Giardina in hers, suddenly outside mainstream Christian expression. As Giardina stated in a 2014 interview, before the rise of the religious right, "being a Christian meant walking with Martin Luther King and speaking out against the Vietnam War like the Berrigans and William Sloane Coffin. Then liberal Christians grew quiet and the media looked elsewhere. Unfortunately now, both the media and liberal secularists seem to equate Christians and fundamentalists."[37] Pushed to the margins, non-nationalistic Christians had to choose whether to accept insignificance or speak an unpopular prophetic message from the margins. Like Bonhoeffer, Giardina has persistently opted to speak.

Resistance is challenging work in part because clear distinctions demand nuanced thinking. In popular discourse, the essential nuances of responsible theology are inevitably sacrificed to the generalities of utilitarian expediency demanded by political factions and institutions. This was true of American Christianity in the last decades of the twentieth century, and it was true during the rise of Hitler's National Socialism (with still more dire consequences). In both periods, the ascending religious faction initially perceived the political alliance as an avenue for self-propagation, even for evangelism; but the political faction understood the religious faction as a tool to be manipulated and altered as necessary.

THE CALL TO RESIST NATIONALISM

Such was the case in Nazi Germany, where the nationalistic "German Christians" soon came to believe, as Dietrich explains the situation to his lover Elisabeth, that "the church exists to serve the Fatherland. That the Fatherland is a gift to us from God, and that God has blessed the Fatherland by raising up Adolf Hitler to lead us to our divinely ordained place at the head of the nations" (84). Though Dietrich strives to take a public oppositional stance in speaking to the Church and the nation, he is variously ignored, ostracized, or silenced, even by many who had been his closest allies. As represented in the text, most tragically by the failure of Martin Niemöller, the Confessing Church decides it must adhere to a public patriotism in order to compete in the popular mind with the nationalistic "German Christians"; as a result, much of the Confessing Church slips into what Dietrich and eventually other believers come to understand as an ideology of nationalism. The Church could not serve two masters.

In theological terms, nationalism is a kind of *idolatry*: placing one's allegiance to nation before one's allegiance to God. During his first conversation with Elisabeth, Dietrich offers his evolving understanding: "God does not play favorites with nations, and anyone who claims a divine blessing for his country is guilty of blasphemy and idolatry" (85). Later in a radio address, he warns that when "*a people, a nation, make an idol of authority, then the leader shall become a misleader*"; the radio broadcast is cut off before he put it most succinctly: "*The leader who makes an idol of himself and his office mocks God*" (102). Most telling may be the confession he places before his confidant, Bishop Bell, later in the novel when his thinking has become more radically articulated:

> "All my life I have listened to the teaching of Luther. . . . The state is ordained by God and therefore is sacred and must be obeyed. Loyalty to one's own country comes before anything else. But I no longer believe this. Germans, Americans, English, Italians, Russians, all believe it and all are wrong. The nations have become idols, and I will not worship them. I have brothers and sisters everywhere on earth. I have another country."
>
> "The Kingdom of God," Bell said. (327)

The transformation of patriotism into nationalism, and therefore from a viable Christian perspective into the sin of idolatry, is something that Dietrich perceives long before his fellow theologians and pastors. In retrospect, today's readers may wonder how the religious people of a nation could have been so slow in understanding the danger of Nazism. Dietrich's witness, like Giardina's fiction, should encourage reflection on how easily patriotism may be perverted.

In summary, then, as Dietrich pursues his call—both the foundational call of complete dedication to God ("costly grace") and his particular call to resist the Nazis—he finds himself in the most difficult dilemma: he is a deeply patriotic Christian whose true Christianity and true patriotism both demand that he speak out against German nationalism and, eventually, even work to overthrow it. Following his important Reformation Day sermon in which he warns the congregation about the peril the Church is facing, Elisabeth stops him and delivers the book's clearest expression of his call: "'What you did today,' she said, 'was what you were put on earth to do'" (93). Her phrase is a direct echo of Earl's question to Fred Bishop, when Fred is trying to discern—or to avoid—his own call to Hawks Nest: "Preacher, you know what you come on this earth to do?" (74). Whether Dietrich gives Elisabeth's words the weight they deserve is uncertain. He hugs her but has nothing to say. Nevertheless, he eventually finds himself drawn more deeply into a confusing conspiracy in which he must sort out and act upon his most deeply held convictions.

QUESTIONING THE CALL

Only once is he tempted to verge toward the popular nationalism. On the night Hitler is named chancellor, Dietrich walks through downtown Berlin in a scene that recalls the manic wildness of Goethe's *Faust*. The streets are alive with a celebration lit by the glow of burning books. In this mad context, Dietrich enters "a sorcerer's fantasy": "He would never admit to anyone, not then or later, that he loved the drums, that they stirred him and roused him and made him long to join the marchers" (100). Aside from that night, his temptations to question or to stray from his call are more subtle, and because of their subtlety, more treacherous. They often come, if not from within, from the people he loves most and whose sympathies are closest to his own.

Through fictional versions of several real historical figures, Giardina suggests the complexities that haunt Dietrich as he works to realize his call to oppose the idolatry of nationalism. Niemöller, though a patriot, a World War I hero, and a faithful pastor who has acted as Dietrich's spiritual mentor, encourages him to check his prophetic message and remain within the institutional Church. Early on, Niemöller understands something of the danger in Hitler's interference in the Church, yet he tells Dietrich, "I look for some good in [Hitler]" (123). Later he discourages him from officiating at the funeral of Sabine's Jewish father-in-law. He argues that if Dietrich does so, the nationalists within the church will "use that against us to sway opinion during the church election" (142). Dietrich complies. By taking Niemöller's advice he betrays his call, his closest sibling, and his extended family. Just as significantly, he loses the respect and confidence of Elisabeth, a character Giardina has created to represent his conscience. "Go away," she tells Dietrich after his failure. "I hope someday you find some courage. That's what you need, you know" (147). Her dismissal is brutal but true. And when he loses Elisabeth, he loses not only his best friend but his lover and, aside from George Bell in faraway England, his only confidant (146–7). He soon apologizes to Sabine for his failure: "How could I have been such a coward? Sabine, I no longer understand myself. Worst of all is the knowledge that *one never makes up for something like that*" (161, italics mine). Significantly, that final phrase is quoted verbatim from the night he and Sabine, as teenagers, accepted the hospitality of a country cottage but failed to confront their hosts' anti-Semitism (13). Eventually Niemöller recognizes the truth in Dietrich's warnings, and the two work together against Hitler's influence on Christians. But by the time Niemöller comes to comprehend the danger, it is too late for effective resistance from within the Church, and he himself is imprisoned.

Dietrich is also strongly drawn to—or, ironically, tempted by—the radical Christian peace testimony of his friend Lasserre, with whom he shares so many strong convictions about nonviolence. During their last meeting, he even tells Lasserre, "You'll be proud of me. I've become a pacifist" (197). That radical alternative is so appealing that at one point Dietrich plans to leave Germany for India, learn from Gandhi, and use what he learns to resist the Nazis. The temptation is strong because it makes sense. How better to learn the ways of nonviolent resistance than from one who has used them so effectively? On the surface it seems like a faithful way forward. Yet Dietrich cannot feel clear to make the trip; it is, he senses, yet another kind of evasion. In a visit with Bishop Bell, Dietrich discerns that only returning to Germany would be, in Bell's phrase, "faithful to the call of God" (205). So he returns—prompted by a call from Niemöller and his own love of country—to help train pastors for the Confessing Church, the group that still hopes it will be able to muster a dissenting alternative to nationalism.

Through these struggles, Giardina highlights how difficult it is to choose among possible pathways in discerning one's call. Each time Dietrich leaves Germany or is tempted to leave, motivations seem mixed. And if the reader at times questions whether Dietrich is leaving his homeland to follow his call or to avoid it, we may assume the protagonist himself is going through a similarly challenging process of discernment. This is at no time more true than when Dietrich's family, with Niebuhr's help, enables his return to Union Seminary, a move that allows him to avoid conscription. As a guest lecturer at Union, he can escape the moral complicity of serving the Nazis, continue to write theology, and likely have a long, productive life of serving the Church as a prominent theologian. His only responsibilities at the seminary are to prepare lectures, teach, and write—the tasks to which he is most suited. Yet he has no peace of mind. Instead of doing his work he spends his days "PRAYING PACING DRINKING SMOKING SWALLOWING SLEEPING PILLS PASSING OUT then again and again" (254, sic).

Weighing heavily on his mind at Union are memories and dreams of Fred Bishop and their trip to Gauley Mountain. Significantly, he is housed in the seminary's "Prophet's Chamber," and the ironic symbolism is apparent. As with Tom in *The Unquiet Earth*, the allusion is to the biblical prophet Jonah, who flees his call to preach the word of God to Nineveh. After one night of especially drunken escapism, Dietrich hears Fred's voice calling him to his fate through "a tunnel of white fog," an image that recalls the deadly silica at Hawks Nest (256). At last, to the frustration and disgust of Niebuhr, who has worked with the Bonhoeffer family to help Dietrich escape conscription, he decides to return and to accept a position in the German military. Not surprisingly, Niebuhr cannot understand Dietrich's choice, and he even doubts Dietrich's moral fiber. Because of its covert nature, Dietrich cannot tell his American mentor that he returns as part of the resistance, though ironically his choice to participate in the resistance is closer to Niebuhr's own theology than to the pacifism of Lasserre. But it is closer still to Albion Freeman's perplexing charge to his fellow miners: "You carry those guns in God's freedom. You cant escape your sin, so sin boldly and know God loves you. Only try to do good for the glory of God."[38]

Other circumstances, too, would dissuade Dietrich from his call. Even after he discerns that his call includes participating in the plot to assassinate Hitler, he is still somewhat at sea. He daydreams about his participation as a gallant work of great Christian heroism (272), but in practice his role is anything but that. He does not have the skills or position that would place him in the inner circle of more effective conspirators, and his limitations frustrate his coconspirators as well as himself. Though his brother-in-law and fellow conspirator Hans von Dohnanyi assures him, "You do us great good by being our pastor, by giving us counsel and encouragement" (270), Dietrich does not see his assigned role as enough—possibly another way in which his ego struggles to accept his particular call. As the plot progresses, he is given important, trusted tasks. Yet his skills as a secret agent, while they improve, are at times comically inept. There is a good deal of irony in Giardina's calling him a *V-Mann* (322).

But more importantly, his coconspirators, like his family, never understand his motivation. His actions are driven by theological convictions they do not share or particularly care about; his work is a sometimes floundering response to a call they cannot understand. Indeed, as he tells Willem Visser 't Hooft, the general secretary of the World Council of Churches, "Most of my fellow conspirators dislike my views" (288). So even among this dedicated band with whom he is destined to share the gallows, he is emotionally and spiritually alone. His family, his friends, his fellow theologians, his fellow patriots, none of them—with the exception of Bishop Bell—ever understand what directs his course. The isolation that results from following his call is summed up well by Visser 't Hooft: "Indeed, you are the loneliest man I know" (288).

FOLLOWING THE CALL IN PRISON

The more faithful Dietrich remains to his convictions, the more he is estranged from those around him. Oddly enough—or maybe not so oddly—Dietrich finds a less conflicted way forward in pursuit of his call during the last two years of his life, his time in prison. His incarceration marks significant growth in his understanding of what it means to experience costly grace.

The sequence begins with an unsettling calm. When a strange voice answers his telephone call to Hans's home, Dietrich knows immediately that their plot has been compromised, and he understands at once the fatal implications:

> Dietrich froze, then set the phone slowly back on its cradle. He stared straight ahead for a time, seeing nothing. A dull thud at the back of the house brought him back to himself. He went outside and found a robin lying on the veranda. It had crashed into the glass windows of the sun-room. Dietrich picked it up and its head fell limply across his finger. A broken neck. He laid it off on the grass and, on an impulse, covered it with dry leaves. Then he went inside and climbed the stairs. (385)

The scene is richly symbolic. Dietrich's apparent calm, even though it is a kind of shock, suggests his embrace of the inevitable, and the bird's broken neck foreshadows the death he will suffer. Yet it also suggests that during his final years, he will accept his suffering with care and a concern that reaches beyond his own welfare. Just as importantly, it alludes to the passage in Saint

Matthew's gospel in which Jesus comforts his followers—"Fear not them which kill the body"—with the assurance, "Are not two sparrows sold for a farthing? and one of them shall not fall on the ground without your Father."[39] His last act before the Gestapo arrives is to eat a second large breakfast, telling the cook, "It may be the last for a while" (385). This symbolic "last supper" suggests Dietrich's awareness of the sacrifice to come and at least a preliminary sense of acceptance.

Early in the novel, Dietrich reacts to Fred's understanding of call with puzzlement, and at one point confesses to his friend, "I've never felt such a call" (55). As the book continues, he has an increasingly strong intimation of the task before him, but he has never been free from at least some level of confusion, frustration, and psychological distress. In the prison sequence, many of these distractions disappear. Certainly the temptation to rationalize flight—even justifiable flight—is gone. He would never again return to New York, never again to London; he would never be tempted to go to India; he would never again be tempted, on a mission for the Abwehr, simply to remain in Switzerland. It is not only the confinement, however, that sharpens Dietrich's call to a finer point.

What Giardina presents in the prison narrative is a fairly traditional progression toward spiritual wholeness, a version of the *via negativa* that is closer to Job than Aquinas: the things in which he has taken comfort or even found his human identity are stripped away. Most importantly, before he can fully live into his call, he must lose his pride.

The pride the Bonhoeffers take in their heritage and the advantages such status brings is clear from the first pages of the novel and continues throughout. Even as Germany takes a desperate turn for the worst, they see their clan as powerful and sacrosanct. "The thing is," Karl-Friedrich says, "to look after the family. If the times are as unsettled as Hans believes, and certainly he is in a position to know these things, we must circle the wagons, as they say in America" (130). In prison such illusions of inviolability are shattered. Dietrich's place in the aristocracy is exchanged for the degradation of a prisoner. His keepers are aware of his family status and wealth, and that fact buys him a handful of advantages; but even some of these he refuses, since they would be gained at the expense of his fellow prisoners. Only when imprisoned at Tegel Wehrmacht Interrogation Prison does he become, not in theological theory but in fact, one of the poor Jesus preached to and about. In Tegel, he is just one of many unwashed, half-starved prisoners, eating rotten food, sleeping fitfully on a filthy bed, and relieving himself in a bucket, half-expecting at any time to suffer interrogation, torture, and execution.

Formerly too, he has taken great pride, or found his identity, in his distinction as a theologian and writer. Even in prison the longing for intellectual achievement never leaves him. Yet there it is a struggle even to find pencil and paper, let alone the books or peace of mind he needs to do scholarly work. In frustration he bargains with God, finding delusional comfort in his desperate reasoning: since he cannot not complete his *Ethics* in prison and since that book is destined to be "the crowning achievement of his life's work," he must, ergo, inevitably be released (395). He needs to believe that "his stint in captivity is not time lost" (420) from his academic career. Dietrich eventually comes to understand, however, that his most important life's work is not a theological tome but weighty letters to his parents and former students. Most importantly, the process of his writing has changed, as Giardina portrays in this interior view:

> There is some essence of God he longs to get at, which can only be approached at a slow pace with shoes in hand and eyes cast down. In the past, he thinks, this has not been his way. He has always possessed too much pride in his own intellect. This will no longer work, perhaps has never worked. The more one makes such a search for God the more everything dissolves. . . .
> He scribbles, runs out of paper, lies on his cot and burns. (420)

Through this spiritual refining—demonstrated in humility and frustration—Giardina indicates that Dietrich is coming to a new understanding of what matters most. If as a teen he chose theology as simply a demanding discipline in which he could achieve prominence, here it has become a sacred passion, the very stuff of life.

As a final blow, Dietrich is even stripped of any potential satisfaction he could take in having been part of the resistance. If at one time he has imagined himself in a heroic world-saving role, he loses the fragments of that fantasy. Near the beginning of his incarceration, the prison commander Maetz assures Dietrich, "It's not as though you're considered a great danger to the Reich" (394). Any vestige of self-respect is further stripped away through interrogations with his own "grand inquisitor" and doppelgänger, Alois Bauer. Bauer is as brilliant as he is perverse, and he knows exactly how to make Dietrich suffer: through a humiliating coming-to-terms with his own smallness. On their first interview, the "most unholy confessor" forces Dietrich to admit, "Yes, I am a coward" (405). Next he forces Dietrich to claim that he will take an oath of loyalty to Hitler if requested, and Dietrich says truthfully that he will—another sin that would "risk the destruction of his soul" (406). And during their final interview at Tegel, when Dietrich has been emboldened by the assured hopelessness of his situation, Bauer pushes the point still further. "Pastor Bonhoeffer," he chides, "'your involvement in these matters was quite enough to earn you a likely death sentence, but not nearly enough, perhaps, to assuage your pride. You may be Hitler's enemy, but not a very important one.' Though Bauer was lighting another cigarette, he did not miss Dietrich's wince" (453).

As imprisonment is burning away anything in which Dietrich can take pride, he has no direction left but to bear his situation and try to stay sane. To do so, he must accept the prison as "his pastoral charge" (399). Aside from a lackluster year in London, he has never held a pastorate, though he had tried and failed to get an occupational call. And during the last Christmas Eve meeting of the conspirators, when Dietrich swears, "I will kill Hitler with my bare hands if necessary," he laments that "I shall never be able to be a pastor again" (282). That was not, apparently, his choice to make. In prison the charge he had longed for has found him, and he becomes a faithful, if deeply flawed, pastor.

It is a testament to Giardina's realism and psychological acuity that Dietrich does not suddenly become the perfect suffering servant. Bereft though he is of those former attributes in which he found a proud identity, sainthood does not come easily. He is at his best when he is offering comfort, and he does so with such heartfelt concern that he becomes not only popular but necessary in the prison. He is a source of solace for his fellow prisoners, for the dying, for the guards, even for the prison officials. He has learned to step away from his own misery and do what he can on behalf of others, and the consolation that "Pastor Bonhoeffer" offers is appreciated by his parishioners and satisfying for him as well. Though an intellectual and a man of words, he learns that at times they mean little. When his guard Linke, who has become his friend, is lamenting the loss of his home to Allied bombing, "Dietrich says nothing. He has learned in prison that words of comfort are little more than gibberish. A hand on the shoulder is better" (432).

His pastoral ministry is least effective when he lapses into his former self, when he lets his own intellectual battles color his interaction with people who are simply not part of the intellectual conversation. He at times lashes out at their nationalism, at their anti-Semitism, and at their requests for self-serving prayer; and he insults them in ways that they cannot possibly understand. If he is a saint, he is a saint to whom we are more likely to offer sympathy than adoration. Still, though far from a perfect pastor, he is authentically engaging the task at hand. He is acting on his call. Most discomforting is his continuing relationship with Maria von Wedemeyer, which he pursues in a way that seems delusional and self-serving, though understandably so. He acts like a doomed man clutching for a romanticized lifeline—which is exactly what he is.

Fulfilling the Call

During his last days at Tegel, Dietrich tells his sister Suze about his coming death: "I can better face that possibility if I accept it, not if I try to avoid it. It's a new sensation, the acceptance of impending death" (443). He is accepting his death, to be sure, but on a more foundational level he is accepting his call. It is after this change that he drops all pretense in his conversations with Bauer. He begins to speak truthfully and frankly to his doppelgänger, confronting the Nazi's arrogance, upbraiding him for blaming his own immoral choices on a God whose existence he denies. A full study could be made of the prison sequence as a kind of theodicy. Dietrich becomes, maybe for the first time, a frank prophetic voice confronting a particular Nazi with his sin. When Bauer takes offense at Dietrich's directness—"Pastor Bonhoeffer, I will not be mocked"—Dietrich responds with a true piece of spiritual advice: "I am not mocking you, Alois. I am telling you, you cannot escape the love of God. That is a warning" (456). The exchange continues:

> Bauer stepped closer. "And this also is a warning. Whatever happens to you from now on for good or ill depends upon me. Your fate, your destiny—" he came so close Dietrich could feel Bauer's breath on his cheek—"in my hands."
>
> "Then you must fight God for possession of me," Dietrich said. (456)

In this sequence, Dietrich is unselfconsciously living fully into his call, speaking what he perceives as his deepest truth and embracing the consequences. He does not evade or equivocate. "The two men stared at each other," Giardina writes, "as though a gauntlet had been thrown down between them" (456). From this point through the progression toward his execution, Dietrich has little dread or—even when it is dangled before him—hope. He has accepted his call. And in his conversations with Bauer, he treats the Nazi more like a wildly wayward parishioner than an enemy. Indeed, when Bauer asks him to perform his treasured Mass in C Minor, he "starts to refuse, but something in Bauer's face, something of a lost soul, causes him to change his mind" (477). When the Mass is played, both men weep.

Years before, Dietrich had written, "When Christ calls a man, he bids him come and die." In the steps toward execution and the acceptance of his fate, that general, foundational call to all Christians becomes in fact Dietrich's particular call. He has been discerning it throughout his lifetime and has lived into it at last. His final bold message to Bishop Bell and to the world, "For me it is the beginning," speaks to the wholeness he has at last found in responding to Christ's call—a stark contrast to his doppelgänger, whom he leaves hiding in a closet.

In *Saints and Villains*, Giardina achieved her most complex and fully realized psychological portrait. She wrote the novel when her powers as a storyteller were at their peak. And the life of Bonhoeffer offered a context in which she could realistically incorporate and test her expertise in theology, politics, and history. Her next novel would not lay aside these concerns, but it would handle them in a mysterious way that would leave many critics and readers in the liminal space between puzzlement and delight.

CHAPTER 6

Fallam's Secret: One True Sermon

In the wake of the weighty and complex *Saints and Villains* (1998), it is not surprising that the time-travel fantasy *Fallam's Secret* (2003) would receive less critical approbation. The novel is very different from anything Giardina had previously published and, by the most apparent indicators, not only less serious but less ambitious. Given the dramatic change of direction, our critical challenge—and it is a difficult one—is to see the book for what it is and not for what one may have been expecting. Speaking broadly, *Fallam's Secret* is, like the previous books, historical fiction. But regarding the nature of the story, that is where the similarity seems to end. All previous books were essentially realistic and securely situated in history: they had defined, if malleable, parameters to press up against. By placing this work in the arena of fantastical romance, Giardina dismissed such limitations and gave her imagination free rein.

The story begins in a contemporary, somewhat reconfigured version of West Virginia's New River Gorge. But with passages through a wormhole, the setting shifts to seventeenth-century Norchester, a fictional village in England during the era of Cromwell's Commonwealth. Protagonist Lydde Falcone is a West Virginia native who has spent her career making a living on the British stage, but she travels back in time for the role of her life: the middle-aged actor finds herself enjoying a twenty-year-old's body, masquerading as a fourteen-year-old boy, and falling utterly in love with Noah Fallam's alter ego, the Robin Hoodesque Raven. Given the remove such a narrative situation presents, the departure from the earlier books goes without saying. Far more surprising is the degree to which the novel recasts many key themes that have been the mainstays of Giardina's career: the battle between haves and have-nots, the continual dialectic between the individual conscience and political authority, and a complicated portrayal of gender roles, all enacted within her theologically sophisticated understanding of the world.

When the book was published in 2003, most reviewers agreed that Giardina had spun a good tale. But beyond that, assessments varied broadly—even on the same aspects of craft. Robert L. Reid, writing in *Appalachian Journal*, praised the author's "impressive ear for speech-rhythms," an attribute long considered one of Giardina's strengths.[1] Michael Shannon Friedman, on the other hand, asserted in the Charleston *Sunday Gazette* that the Norchester characters "speak, for the most part, in a robotic, stilted fashion that simply rings false," even comparing Lydde's time travel with "a particularly bad episode of *Fantasy Island*."[2] Reviews were similarly mixed on the central romance. Jeff Zaleski for *Publishers Weekly* found it "hard to swallow ... [Lydde's] instant love for the Raven,"[3] while Friedman, despite his reservations, claimed the courtship of Lydde and Fallam to be "perhaps Giardina's finest achievement as a novelist."[4] Concerning the pacing of the story, *Library Journal's* Karen T. Bilton praised the "swift plot and imaginative descriptions" that "keep the reader involved in this generally engaging narrative."[5] But *Kirkus Reviews*, though conceding the book's "neat surprises," claimed that "things drag toward the end and dawdle to the finish line."[6] Responses to the book's thematic force were also conflicting. Carolyn Kubisz for *Booklist* criticized the author's failure to develop the "underlying themes, regarding faith, a woman's place in society, and environmental responsibility."[7] More charitably, Belinda Anderson noted that while the book reveals "threads of serious themes ... it's clear the author is mostly enjoying herself."[8]

That such assessments were so widely varied may indicate more about the novel than do any of the evaluations taken alone. At the risk of oversimplifying something as complex as a novel's initial reception, one might suggest that the book's early reviewers did not quite know what to make of it. A fast-paced time-travel romance coming from the desk of a novelist well known for historical realism of the weightiest kind? Giardina's name on the cover naturally led reviewers to anticipate a little more of what they were accustomed to receiving. They did not see in it the "literary weight"[9] they were expecting or the "epic scope"[10] that had characterized the author's first four efforts. It was natural simply to consider the book as one of her "weaker novels"[11] and let it go at that. An unfortunate outcome of this initial critical assessment is that the book has never received the kind of scholarly attention that might allow us to see beyond the witty, relatively light surface into its thematic density. In the most insightful review offered to date, Reid seems to anticipate this very problem, stating that *Fallam's Secret* is "full of secrets, more than any reader is likely to uncover."[12] Our aim here is to offer a way into the novel that brings some of those secrets into critical conversation.

If great literature pleases and instructs, *Fallam's Secret* is at least halfway successful. Time travel in fiction is great fun, and all the more so when the story is as competently told as this one. One may certainly enjoy the book without giving its philosophical foundations a second thought. The weight of the novel, however, is revealed in its theological fabric. Though it never slips into didacticism, it is, in its own way, a thesis-driven novel. With that in mind, this analysis will begin by examining the sermon that appears, almost as a summation, near the story's end.

Fallam's Sermon

Many fans of time-travel romance may understandably pass over Noah Fallam's final sermon without much reflection. It occurs, after all, when he is about to be dealt a death sentence, and we are anxious to see what happens. Here, however, his message will be considered in detail, with the hope that a nuanced reading may begin to reveal the method and message of the book.

Even late in the novel when Fallam and Lydde have become a couple, she continues to feel concerns about his attitude toward women. Because he is a Puritan pastor—and because concealing his Raven identity includes concealing his more enlightened beliefs about gender—Fallam has persisted in preaching the Puritan party line from the pulpit. He has even referred to women at one point as "neither elect nor unelect but unworthy of any consideration by God."[13] But he promises Lydde that he will not always speak that way, that someday she will hear him preach what he really believes. His promise prepares us for the final sermon and foreshadows its significance.

Fallam introduces the sermon by saying, "I promised someone I love very much . . . that I would one day preach a true sermon, from my heart. Today is that day" (317). This opening is key. It signals that, for once, neither the readers nor Lydde herself will need to question the various levels of reality and irony that have been in tension throughout the text. It seems, too, a fitting way for a theologically engaged novelist to voice the guiding moral principle of the book. Fallam begins,

> I take as my text the fourth chapter of Luke's gospel. Jesus is baptized and undergoes temptation in the wilderness, then reveals himself for the first time. He says, "The Spirit of the Lord is upon me, because he hath anointed me to preach the gospel to the poor; he hath sent me to heal the brokenhearted, to preach deliverance to the captives, and recovering of sight to the blind, to set at liberty them that are bruised, to preach the acceptable year of the Lord." Then Jesus told the people, "This day is this scripture fulfilled in your ears." (317–18)

Fallam's choice of this biblical text and its context is telling. In the wilderness Jesus had been tempted to take power in the typical ways of revolutionaries, by gaining broad popular, religious, and political power. But he refused these temptations, and at that point in his ministry, he revealed his true mission: to be a king of a very different kind of kingdom. Nevertheless, in the tradition of the Old Testament prophets, he put forth a strong message of social justice: deliverance for those who have been most gravely oppressed. Fallam continues to explain Jesus's words: "What is this 'acceptable year of the Lord'? It is the jubilee year, the time of freedom and justice, of the liberation of the poor and oppressed, indeed the liberation of all of us" (318).

The phrase "jubilee year" is not familiar to most readers today. But it would have been familiar to Fallam's listeners, and Giardina has chosen it with care. In Old Testament history, Jubilee was the most radical element of a complex religious economic system. According to a statute outlined in Leviticus 25, every fiftieth year (the Jubilee), land that had been lost or sold was restored to its original families. This law had several important purposes. It worked against great disparities of wealth because every Jubilee the economic playing field was leveled. Significantly too, it was a way of caring for the land, of letting it rest so that its fertility would not be depleted by over-farming. The Hebrews were commanded to let the land lie fallow every seven years for this purpose, but Jubilee was a grander instantiation of the Sabbath principle: the Sabbath of Sabbaths. In addition, Jubilee was intended to remind the faithful that ultimately, the earth does not belong to individuals. It belongs to God and humans are its caretakers. Finally, with the coming of the Jubilee, Israelite slaves were set free. So even that most desperate form of poverty was eradicated.

The term has since been used by Jews and Christians in less absolute and binding senses, but it always carries the significance of equality, freedom, and forgiveness, both physical and spiritual. Fallam's sermon next equates Jubilee with another key theological concept: "It is nothing more nor less than the proclamation of the Kingdom of God, a kingdom which is not *coming*, my friends. No, Jesus says it is already here. We live *at this very moment* in the Kingdom of God. Only we have not eyes to see it" (318). With this statement Giardina dives into still deeper theological waters. The Kingdom of God has been defined in many ways, but it always refers to the divine reign on earth. In particular, what Fallam is voicing here is an interpretation modern theologians call *inaugurated eschatology*: while the fullest revelation of God's rule on earth is yet to come, the *final* state of things (eschatology) has already *begun* (has been inaugurated). Though this is a complex idea, it means in essence that the final reign of God is already taking place in the lives and the work of Christian believers; they are already living by the principles of the Kingdom, hence already living *in* the Kingdom, invisible and partial though the Kingdom may be. The logical link Fallam is making is based on the idea that the Year of Jubilee is a kind of prefiguring of the Kingdom of God.

Fallam continues with a very natural question: "'Why can we not see the Kingdom of God? Because we avoid living in it. We do not heal broken hearts, we do not deliver captives, we abuse the poor, and we do not free *anyone*.' He was looking at Lydde again" (318). This passage speaks directly to a central message of the novel. As a young man, Fallam was disinherited—and jailed—for writing a pamphlet that argued for democracy, universal education, the redistribution of wealth, the equality of races, and universal salvation (228). And his interest was not only that of an academic theologian. When due to his parents' death and his older brother's expatriation he came into control of the family estate, Fallam inaugurated a policy of forgiving his tenants their rent and allowing them to remain freely on the lands—creating his own Jubilee. Still more dramatically, through his Robin Hood avatar, the Raven, he has been placing his life in peril by robbing from the rich and giving everything stolen to the poor in his district of Norchester. But by this point in the novel, there is yet another group whom he knows to be in bondage: women. Through his relationship with Lydde, Fallam has realized more fully that to be a seventeenth-century woman is effectively to be a slave. No wonder, then, that he "was looking at Lydde again" after he suggested that no one is free; as noted, he had promised Lydde this true sermon as a corrective confession for the way he had previously preached Puritan beliefs about gender.

The final sentences of the aborted sermon keep Giardina from falling into didacticism by merging the theological gravitas with the fantastical plot:

> Though the Kingdom of God is here, it lies just beyond the surface of what we see. It is like another dimension present with us always, though we are separated from it by the thinnest of membranes. But sometimes it trickles through into our wounded world in sublime moments of beauty, of truth, of peace, like water trickling through tiny fissures in a dam. We perceive it when we love. And someday it will burst through in its entirety and its goodness will wash over our world and transform and renew and restore everything we know. (318)

The language here obviously speaks to the metaphorical conceit of the book. Lydde's uncle John, a physicist, has taught her that multiple worlds coexist, that time is less like a straight line and more like a bowl of pasta. That concept is what allows the time-travel motif and the suggestion of multiple dimensions. John's metaphor for time and reality also presents an apt metaphor for the inaugurated eschatology Fallam preaches. (And as we will see later, it does so in the language of Celtic Christianity that subtly but significantly permeates the book.) But there is one more word in the sermon: "Someday—." The sentence—and the sermon—is suddenly cut off, but even that final word suggests and affirms something important about the concept of inaugurated eschatology: "Someday—," in time, the multiple worlds will come together in the culmination of the Kingdom of God, the instantiation of that Kingdom in its fullness. Why the Kingdom comes in such a graduated way is not, thankfully, a question Giardina attempts; she avoids a morass of theological confusion by allowing the question to persist as a mystery in the text, just as it does in Christian theology.

The reason the sentence is cut off in the story, however, is no mystery at all: unknown to the congregation, while preaching his sermon, Fallam has been watching Major-General Elisha Sitwell ready his troops to enter the church. Fallam has in fact been delivering his final message from a pulpit that may as well be his gallows. At the word "Someday—," Sitwell crashes into the church to apprehend the Raven. To avoid revealing Lydde's sex during a strip search of all *men* in the congregation for his betraying birthmark, Fallam confesses and Sitwell immediately condemns him to death. This sequence carries us toward the exciting conclusion of the novel, but it does more than that too. Recalling the context of the biblical passage Fallam has been explicating, it is worth noting that after Jesus's sermon in Luke 4, Jesus also upbraids his listeners for not hearing his message. In response, they drive him from town and try to throw him off a cliff.[14]

Fallam's final sermon takes only one page of a 331-page novel. One can enjoy the novel and understand it on some level without paying this scene more than passing attention; the sermon may be read as a simple message of hope. But it pointedly offers Giardina's powerful intention behind what is simultaneously a fairly light, often humorous piece of fantasy. Throughout the novel, we are persistently reminded that, on many levels, things are seldom what they seem.

Appearance and Reality

Having looked briefly at where the novel goes—the thematic climax—we can now take a step back and see in detail, more formally, how Giardina carries us there. My approach to form derives from a concept drawn from the work of

Kenneth Burke, who defines *form* this way: "*Form* in literature is an arousing and fulfillment of desires. A work has form in so far as one part of it leads a reader to anticipate another part, to be gratified by the sequence."[15] Analyzing *Fallam's Secret* with this principle in mind, we see that one of the ways Giardina builds her plot is through the repetition and variation of a single concept in a broad variety of instantiations, each one conditioning readers, sometimes sequentially, sometimes simultaneously, for another. Whether we intuit such a pattern unconsciously or attend to it consciously, it continually raises expectations and fulfills them. So while incidents and situations differ widely in their surface features, a pattern emerges revealing the deep structure of the book. The particular formal motif Giardina repeats and varies is a continual play between appearance and reality. Once we become aware that this is one way the text works, a closer reading demonstrates that the form, almost like a geometric pattern of fractals, works consistently throughout, sometimes in the smallest details, sometimes in longer plot sequences, and eventually in the whole book.

A flashback early in the novel presents Lydde's father Carlos as a Sicilian immigrant living in the coal-mining region of West Virginia. His parents had emigrated to the region when he was a child, motivated by the poverty that drove many southern Italians to the coalfields and, significantly, fleeing the vengeance of the Black Hand, the Sicilian mafia, which his father had antagonized. Carlos's dream in his adopted state is to create the illusion of the childhood farm he left behind, thus suggesting at once the appearance/reality motif: "When he bought his land on Fallam Mountain, he knew he wanted more than a house. He wanted to recreate Italy" (21). So he builds in the mountains of West Virginia a white stucco house with a red tile roof, a stone barn, a smokehouse for prosciutto and pancetta. Brutal reality breaks into his fantasy when the Black Hand, having apparently become aware of Carlos during his wartime service in Italy, burns the house down with his family inside. His wife and all his children but Lydde are killed in the fire.

Or maybe they only appear to have been killed. The children's bodies are never found, and Carlos spends the rest of his brief life in a vain search for them, leaving his remaining daughter in the care of her uncle John and aunt Lavinia. Lydde's hope throughout her childhood, too, is that her siblings may have somehow escaped. When fifty years later she learns of Uncle John's discovery of the wormhole, she has further reason to hope that in reality they may not be dead at all. It is worth noting that the church that covers the seventeenth-century end of the wormhole is named after Saint Pancras, a patron saint—the protector—of children. Though Giardina never tells us that fact, she does state that Lydde thought "Pancras was a silly name" (36). At least in retrospect, the author has signaled her readers to pay attention.

Clear indicators of the appearance/reality pattern are the wall hangings in Uncle John's home office. In retrospect Giardina has presented something little short of an outline: a print of Salvador Dali's *Christus Hypercubus*, in which the artist attempts to visualize the fourth dimension, time; a photograph of an opening blasted in rock that is Hawks Nest Tunnel, near the twenty-first-century end of the wormhole; a print of a church in Norchester, the seventeenth-century end of the wormhole; and a print of the historic Batts and Fallam expedition in the New River Gorge. Along with the prints that foreshadow events to come hang two quotes that direct our attention to the theme:

> *Magic is any sufficiently advanced technology.*
> —Arthur C. Clarke

And—

> *There are more things in heaven and earth, Horatio,
> than are dreamt of in our philosophy.*
> —William Shakespeare (36)

Uncle John's disguising of the wormhole with the Mystery Hole offers another instantiation of the play between appearance and reality. Few of us who pay to see a roadside attraction, such as Uncle John's Mystery Hole, do so because we think there is some actual violation of natural law tucked conveniently alongside the interstate. Instead, we pay for the performance of the ruse, for the kitschy but funny theatrics of the proprietors. In the novel's case, however, the illusion is doubly complicated. The Mystery Hole only seems to be a typical roadside attraction. Instead of being a theatrical illusion that draws travelers to look at a very natural divot in the rock, the Mystery Hole is an illusion of an illusion: Uncle John has built a false illusion to distract people who might otherwise stumble onto the real anomaly. The illusion, then, is that what appears to be a bit of kitsch theater actually disguises a preternatural phenomenon. The Mystery Hole is the stage and Uncle John the chief actor, one of many repetitions of theater to suggest the primary formal technique.

Giardina repeats her appearance/reality pattern yet again by creating Lydde as a professional actor: a person whose profession is to fuse what is with what seems to be. This choice works in several ways to move the plot along. Most obviously, her training prepares Lydde for the role she plays when she steps through the wormhole into seventeenth-century Norchester. But more subtly, in what seems at first only incidental to Lydde's backstory, we learn that she had her greatest twenty-first-century triumph playing Prince Hal in Shakespeare's *Henry V*. With a mix of desperation and chutzpah, she had convinced a director to cast her in the role of the fourteen-year-old prince. In doing so, she became a kind of reverse *ganymede*. In Elizabethan theater, a ganymede was a boy who played a woman's role. In the case of Lydde, she was a woman playing a boy's role, a reversal Shakespeare himself used in the character of Rosalind in *As You Like It*.

The form continues with further reversals when Giardina depicts the reception Lydde receives on her arrival in Norchester. When she falls through the wormhole, she is dressed in Reeboks, blue jeans, and a Duke Blue Devils sweatshirt. While not gender-specific attire in the twenty-first century, her clothes immediately brand her as a strangely dressed boy, the role she would play in public through most of her time in the seventeenth century. Due to the strangeness of her clothes, she is accused of being an actor—and because of her youth, a ganymede. The reversals keep piling up: Lydde is an adult female actor who is not dressed as an actor who is perceived as a boy actor who then must act the part of a boy who is not an actor to save himself from the religious authorities. The Puritan rulers of Norchester have no use for theater, no use for actors, and, because of Puritan gender beliefs, certainly no use for ganymedes.

The complexity of the appearance/reality form compounds still further as Giardina presents the weirdly indeterminate conflation of individual family members in Norchester. She maintains an intentional lack of definition about the precise relationship of the apparently parallel characters in her worlds, preferring various suggestions of mysterious connections between the worlds and their inhabitants. Through Lydde Giardina refers to connections as "the drawing up of odds and ends of colored thread to weave into a magical tapestry" (242), and this is the method Giardina manipulates through her suggestive parallels. Uncle John is not Dr. Soane (his seventeenth-century parallel) exactly, though the two are in many ways doubles: they are sagacious, they are men of science, and they look alike. Similarly Dr. Soane's servant Mary is not Lydde's sister exactly, but the two are in some ways one and the same: both girls come from families with five children, four of whom have the same names and all of whom died a kind of death by fire, Lydde's siblings in a house fire, Mary's from a fever. We even learn late in the story that Fallam's first wife was Margaret, Lydde's mother's name. She was Lydde's mother—but not exactly.

In contrast to a more specifically defined pattern of parallels, Giardina's method of suggestive connectedness offers several advantages in pushing the plot forward. First, it allows her to reflect the characters' own lack of clear knowledge about the other world into which they have entered through the wormhole. That is part of the mystery. Through most of the story, Uncle John does not know whether they have regressed temporally, moved sideways into a parallel universe, or shifted into some combination his mathematical formulae have not yet revealed. He is not sure that the phenomenon he, Lydde, and eventually Fallam experience has been primarily temporal until, at the book's conclusion, he finds the Celtic cross once again on the skeleton at the entrance to the wormhole—the very cross that Lydde had first noticed there, then recognized on a chain around Fallam's neck in seventeenth-century Norchester. But more important thematically, Giardina goes out of her way, in both the lighter and the weightier threads of the novel, to leave open the space of unknowing. She affirms connectedness, but she maintains the attribute she values in all her novels, especially when spiritual and physical worlds intersect: mystery.

This play between appearance and reality is one of the most gratifying aspects of the novel, both as a formal device and as a bond that ties together plot, theme, and even theology. And it creates a natural entryway for another important recurring theme: the dialectic of gender indeterminacy.

Gender Questions

As we move to this aspect of our analysis, it is important not to lose sight of the fact that on one level *Fallam's Secret* is just what it appears to be: a romantic, occasionally even erotic, romp through space and time. As such, it revivifies many of the clichés associated with a dime-store romance: an exotic location, a dashingly dark and mysterious hero bursting with masculine energy, a desirable young heroine who cannot resist being swept off her feet and into bed, and so on. That the heroine is masquerading as a fourteen-year-old boy and the hero as a Robin Hood knock-off adds to the fun. And that was, at least in part, Giardina's intention. After completing *Saints and Villains*, a long and weighty novel by any standard, she stated that she was ready to create something lighter: "I finally reached the point," she told Belinda Anderson, "where I thought, you know, I don't have to prove anything writing some big, heavy, serious thing anymore."[16] Were this *only* a popular romance, we might simply conclude that Giardina uses Lydde's protestations about gender equality as an attempt to bring the typical romance genre up to date or simply to make her character more sympathetic. It is gratifying, if not very believable, to read the way Lydde-as-Lewis speaks truth to power: the brave but vulnerable youth confronts the stern Puritan governor who may well respond by having him/her drawn and quartered. When examined closely, however, the novel offers a much more complex understanding of gender construction, cultural bias, and the psyche.

That gender is socially constructed and performed is a common idea in much current literary critical thought, and Giardina is working with that notion here. Most obviously, Uncle John warns Lydde that to survive in her life-and-death masquerade, it is not enough to look like a boy: "you have to be male just by the way you act" (87), and again, "It really will be safer, as long as you're here, if you pretend to be a boy. It's that much harder for women. Very little freedom, lots of hard work, and you're not supposed to know anything" (87). Uncle John does not intend his warning to be ironic in its narrative context, but clearly Giardina is referencing some of the darker aspects of acting the part of a woman in our own complex and confusing reality. Rereading the novel we see that whether intentionally or unintentionally, Lydde makes gender choices in a way that suggests a level of complexity and ambiguity in her character.

In a flashback to one unsuccessful London romantic relationship, for example, Lydde's lover tells her that he liked her "better as Hal than as Lydde" and adds that "she would have made a great lesbian," to which she responds a little too easily, "Too bad. . . . I've never had the remotest interest in women" (45). The potential gender indeterminacy continues in that context: "She ran from safe, sweet guys because they seemed boring or wimpy. But she let herself be swept off her feet by jerks who turned out to be sleeping with two other women at the same time. She fell hard for gay men, and fended off married men, who seemed to find her intriguing because she wasn't like their wives" (45). In Norchester the indeterminacy is repeated and varied: on arriving in the seventeenth century and being forced to explain her presence to the townspeople, Lydde identifies herself as—or becomes—her brother Louis (later Lewis), even assuming his name. Readers will recall that when she had transformed herself to play Prince Hal—her most successful twenty-first-century role—she made herself up to look like this same brother and occasionally passed as male not only in the theater but on the street, once even daring herself to use the men's restroom. Clearly Giardina has created her as a woman ambiguously fascinated with the complexities of her own gender: "She looked often into mirrors—a handsome boy. She was falling in love with her own face" (46); in other words, she loved herself as a man.

Though less overtly, there is at least an implication of orientation ambiguity in Fallam as well. After his Raven alter ego has tricked Lydde into coming to one of his hideouts—and determined her gender by running his hand under her clothing—he states, "And since I guessed you to be a woman, I must confess, I have lain awake at night with longing for you. At last my desire for you overcame my judgment" (159). His statement here may be understood as self-deceptive. He had, after all, lured her to his hideout to determine *whether* she was indeed a woman. The sexual longing to which he refers preceded his knowing her sex. Beginning then with two lovers who at least on some level and to some degree suggest a state of orientation ambiguity, it is all the more engaging to watch their romance develop. Their evolving relationship portrays in both characters a new way of acting in relation to gender, whether or not they fully understand their own changes.

At first Lydde serves as a simple mouthpiece for fairly standard twenty-first-century progressive thought. Over time, however, her feminist voice becomes more complex and nuanced, and she must examine more deeply her own prejudices in relation to Fallam. Giardina initially presents Lydde as evidencing a kind of cultural blindness, becoming a time-traveling version of the "ugly American." She considers the locals who do not share her twenty-first-century views of gender as simply stupid. And after the first quarrel of their secret marriage, she complains to Uncle John that even her new husband is a "Neanderthal" (268). But as she learns to grow beyond her own cultural constraints, she finds, despite Fallam's unsophisticated understanding of gender, many positive qualities often missing in her twenty-first-century contemporaries. As Uncle John reminds her, "He's a good man. He's a better man than a lot of the ones back home who talk a good game but treat women like dirt. He's human, though. You can't make him over into someone from our time" (268). Though progressive in his own day, Fallam has a long way to grow. Lydde never accepts his sexism, but she learns to value him for who he is, and she learns to stand a little less self-righteously on the moral high ground of her twenty-first-century conscience.

Like Lydde, Fallam too grows in his understanding. He is fascinated by Lydde at first because she demonstrates attributes he considers masculine: she is outspoken, opinionated, foolishly courageous in her gender performance. And because of her lack of inhibitions, she is a more fascinating sexual partner than the women of his own time. But Giardina pushes Fallam's understanding by forcing him into positions where he must see Lydde not as a lover but as a fully functioning part of his outlaw gang. In the mummers' robbery, for example, he chooses her over her male peers to participate in his plan because she is the most levelheaded, a trait he previously would not have associated with a woman. Finally in the climactic prison breakout, traditional gender roles are completely reversed. Though he has previously seen her as the lover and wife he must protect, it is she who risks being burned at the stake to protect him, breaking him out of jail, saving him from torture and a hideous execution, and making possible their escape to the New World. She gives him back his life, and, significantly, he is not resentful but proud of what he would once have perceived as a too-"masculine" performance—the performance of an equal.

Fallam is clearly created as a man ahead of his time. And he has been willing to pay a price for his progressive convictions, as evidenced in the political tract that resulted in his estrangement from his family and its fortune. But he is nevertheless a seventeenth-century man. His intentions are good—he tells Lydde that he considers himself one who holds egalitarian "Quaker" views regarding gender—but like Lydde he is limited by his cultural biases. He holds enlightened ideas, but he struggles to make his practice live up to his principles. Before their marriage, for example, he does not object to her gathering with her actor friends to perform Shakespeare on the sly. But after they are married, he tries to forbid her from doing so: "I said, you must stop. Indeed I had forgotten, you must forgive me for that. But it was one thing when you were simply a woman who intrigued me. It is quite another when you are my wife" (266). After their mutual anger dies down, Fallam is able to say, "I suppose I cannot ask you to stop acting any more than you can ask me to stop being the Raven. Keep on with Mossup [her fellow actor] if you must" (270). By the book's end, not only does he not try to forbid her but, as noted above, uses her theatrical expertise and cool-headedness to further the Raven's work.

What Giardina presents, then, is a couple transcending their own culturally bound ideas about how men and women relate. As Reid states, the story "portrays the dangerous but beneficial interaction between two social cultures widely separate in time."[17] Just as meaningfully if less overtly, Giardina may also be suggesting a deeper understanding of gender often associated with Jungian psychology: that all individuals are on one level both male and female, and that it is only through the male's recognition and acceptance of his *anima* (inner feminine) and the female's recognition of her *animus* (inner male) that individuals may further their journeys toward individuation (wholeness). What we see in the Lydde-Fallam relationship, then, is an example of two people who are not only passionately in love but who enable each other's full expression. A relationship that began in healthy mutual arousal progresses into healthier trust and matures into wholeness, not only of the relationship itself but of the two individuals.

Through her love for Fallam, Lydde learns to be less judgmental about a culture different from her own. She accepts the fact that in learning to know a man from a very different culture, she has to look deeply within, come to terms with who she is, then demonstrate her equality, not simply demand it. Through his love for Lydde, Fallam comes to a fuller understanding of the capacities, even the equality, of women. To really know a woman from another culture, or maybe to understand women at all, he needs to question his own socially constructed views of gender. In doing so he begins to accept his inner feminine: he learns to share domestic duties, to come to terms with his own weaknesses, and to accept Lydde not simply as a woman to protect and enjoy but even as a fellow outlaw, a complete equal. Finally in the jailbreak scene, he accepts her very literally as his savior.

Celtic Connections

For reasons that will become apparent, consideration of the gender theme leads us directly to another stratum of thought that informs the novel: Celtic spirituality. Our point is not that Giardina's understanding of gender is *derived* from Celtic Christianity; the progressive views put forward by Giardina through Lydde are standard fare on the progressive side of present-day thinking. They are, if you will, in the air. But as a writer who thinks like a theologian, Giardina would inevitably be engaged by the confluence of newer thought with the various strains that have waxed and waned in the history of theology. And in fact, if we attend closely to the novel, we see that she is nudging us into seeing her connections. But the key word here is *nudging*. Though I have called the novel "one true sermon," Giardina is careful to avoid preachiness. The reader unfamiliar with Celtic Christianity can read the novel with a gratifying understanding. But for the audience that follows the allusions to more nuanced theological possibilities, the novel offers additional weight and spiritual resonance.

Readers will recall that Lydde ventures to the wormhole following the directions John Soane has left with the mysterious keys on a rolled piece of parchment. When she reaches the opening,

> the movement of the flashlight caught a dull glint of metal near the breastbone. She leaned closer and saw the tangle of a necklace among the ribs. Carefully she tugged on the chain, pulled it up to the light and cradled it in the palm of her hand. It was a tarnished silver cross, a Celtic cross. She placed it back in its bony nest.
> So she had found the skeleton. (70)

The narrative here is clearly focused on the skeleton itself, not the cross. Nearly a hundred pages pass before we see it again when Fallam is interrogating the young "boy Lewis" and Lydde sees around his neck "a small Celtic cross identical to the one she had found with the skeleton in the cave. Lydde gasped" (146). This detail forwards the plot by suggesting to Lydde that this same Fallam may be the skeleton she had found over three hundred years in the future. And at the novel's conclusion, it is this cross on the twenty-first-century skeleton that convinces Uncle John that he has certainly been in the past. But for the theological theme, the importance of the cross is in Fallam's explanation of it. Significantly, he explains to Lydde, "I got this in Ireland, as a matter of fact. It seemed to me a symbol of an earlier, *purer form of Christianity*" (146, italics mine). As previous chapters have suggested, it is not an overstatement to say that all Giardina's novels are, on some level, an attempt to portray a "purer form of Christianity." With this Celtic cross, she directs us toward at least one potential confluence with or influence on the "purer form" portrayed in the novel.

Ancient Celtic Christianity held a different understanding of gender than the Roman, Augustinian Christianity that has been the most important source of Western theology and determined the direction of secular Western thought. The trajectory set by Augustine and his influential followers was one that placed women in a subservient role in every aspect of life, resulting in the deep gender biases that have for so long characterized the patriarchal understanding not only of the Church but of contemporary culture more broadly. This is a situation still evidenced in many religious and social groups today. Too often overlooked is the fact that there were other Christian traditions, both ancient and modern, that followed different trajectories. One of those mentioned in *Fallam's Secret* is the Quaker tradition, which argued from its inception for the equality of men and women. But Quakerism is comparatively recent, dating only from the mid-1600s (about the time of the novel's historical setting). A far older tradition with a pronounced egalitarian approach to gender is the theology of the ancient Celts.

Religious historian J. Philip Newell, a Church of Scotland minister and former warden of Iona Abbey, notes that "the Celtic world was one that gave much greater scope to the role of women and more fully incorporated both the feminine and the masculine into its religious life and imagery."[18] Focusing on the works of Pelagius (ca. 360–418), the first great Celtic Christian theologian, Newell points out that it was characteristic of that tradition to take a more egalitarian approach to gender than its Roman counterpart. In fact that vision of comparative equality, as evidenced in the education of women to read the Scriptures for themselves, was one of the beliefs that drew harsh criticism from the dominant Roman Church and certainly played a part in Pelagius being declared a heretic in 431. It is not surprising that elements of such a strain of thought would be appealing to Giardina and that her most admirable characters embody it. As we have noted in her other novels, many of Giardina's characters embrace ways of thinking that are Christian but often in versions that straddle the fringes of orthodoxy and are at odds with the institutional Church.

In addition to Fallam's cross, another clear indicator that Celtic Christianity informs the ideational fabric of the novel is Giardina's introduction of the Celtic concept of *thin places*. Whatever kinds of super-realities fantasy writers may create, they usually ground them in some connection to the familiar, to the real world of everyday thinking and experience. This merging of the fantastic with the ordinary offers all kinds of possibilities for interesting (and often comic) details. But just as importantly, it helps readers suspend disbelief in ways that allow them to engage more fully in an imaginative reading experience. For readers to enter fully into *Fallam's Secret*, they have to perceive the idea of a wormhole as at least *imaginatively* plausible. Giardina gains her plausibility through the concept of thin places. Her definition within the text is characteristically brief and cogent:

> Uncle John explained about thin places. A thin place, he said, is located at the boundary between heaven and earth. A place where you can ever so briefly glimpse what lies beyond, perhaps even talk to God. When Moses met Yahweh in the burning bush he was standing on a thin place. The Celtic monks who came from Ireland to pagan England identified thin places, like the island of Iona, for their monasteries. (128)

And for the less mystically minded, like Lydde and many readers, Giardina offers another definition in the words of Uncle John:

> Okay. You don't want thin places. How about a combination of relativity and quantum theory that posits ten or more dimensions including more than one dimension of time? Each dimension separated from the other by the thinnest of membranes pierced by wormholes too small to be detected. How about space-time so elastic that you can't even get an agreed upon sequence of events? Time not as a straight line but like—like a handful of shaving cream? How about universes that continually split off one from another into an infinite number of universes that proceed in infinite parallels? (129)

While her definitions within the narrative are sufficient, by the time Giardina was writing the book she could assume at least some previous familiarity with thin places. Especially over the last few decades, interest in Celtic spirituality has surged, and the concept of thin places has become increasingly common in many circles, both formally religious and more vaguely spiritual. Recent usage of the term was certainly influenced by George MacLeod, founder of the modern Iona Community mentioned above. But the concept has been around for a good deal longer, maybe for as long as humans have had any sense of the sacred. The religious historian Mircea Eliade writes in *The Sacred and the Profane* about the nature of sacred places: "For religious man, space is not homogenous; he experiences interruptions, breaks in it; some parts of space are qualitatively different from others."[19] A sacred place, Eliade offers, is most elementally a place where *"something sacred shows itself to us."*[20] Giardina's thin places are a part of the continuum of sacred space to which Eliade refers. Most contemporary usage follows, at least at a distance, the concept of the fathers of Celtic Christianity. As Eric Weiner writes in a 2012 *New York Times* article, "It's not clear who first uttered the term 'thin places,' but they almost certainly spoke with an Irish brogue."[21] This Celtic idea of thin places, of "the intertwining of the spiritual and the material, heaven and earth, time and eternity,"[22] serves as a metaphorical complement to the more conventional idea Fallam addresses in his "one true sermon": "the Kingdom of God is here, it lies just beyond the surface of what we see. It is like another dimension present with us always, though we are separated from it by the thinnest of membranes" (318).

Another Celtic Christian concept that pervades the novel has also received increasing attention in the last half century: the notion of *panentheism*, that God is somehow *in* all things. This concept is distinct from *pantheism*, the idea that God *is* all things. The ideas are not the same, yet without some careful theological nuancing, one who claims the former is likely to be accused of the latter. In fact another influential Celtic theologian, John Scotus Eriugena (ca. 815–77) had work condemned by the Church for this very reason. With panentheism in mind, some of the easy-to-overlook aspects of *Fallam's Secret* take on a greater weight. Early in the novel, for example, Uncle John is discussing with the child Lydde the death of her family members:

"Do we go to heaven when we die?" Lydde asked.

He shook his head. "No. Heaven is just what people settled on because they don't have enough imagination to think of anything else. We go to more than heaven. We go everywhere God is, and that means everywhere."

"Is that where my brothers and sisters are? Are they everywhere?" (61)

It would be easy to read this passage simply as Uncle John comforting his young niece or as a throwaway line from a speculative physicist. But understood in the light of Celtic Christianity, it seems more likely that the devout Uncle John is telling Lydde exactly what he believes to be the truth: God is everywhere.

This panentheism is particularly significant as it leads directly to another Celtic Christian concept that pervades the novel and for which, in our day of widespread environmental destruction, Celtic Christianity may be best known: the belief that all creation is sacred. In the Celtic tradition, creation—whether the stars in the sky or the rocks by the side of the road—is inseparably intertwined with God. Drawing on the work of Eriugena, Newell writes that "creation is essentially a theophany, a showing or revealing of God's Soul to our souls."[23] Creation and the Creator are not one and the same, but they are inseparable, and therefore creation, too, is holy.

One significant fantastical element of the novel is what happens on each end of the wormhole whenever one of our heroes passes through. In Norchester, each passage restores the obliterated paintings in an Anglican chapel. The whitewash with which the Puritan antagonists have covered the images miraculously disappears, and the celebratory story paintings on the walls reappear. And on the West Virginia end, each passage pushes the valley fill, the destructive result of mountaintop removal, back toward its proper place. These two effects seem at first widely different, almost accidental in their juxtaposition. Aside from the fact that both phenomena are apparently good, there seems to be little relationship. The Norchester phenomenon is more readily seen as an integral plot device. It furthers the Puritans' suspicions of witchcraft associated with the condemned Anglican church, it creates sufficient hubbub to raise the tension level of Lydde's arrival, and it characterizes Cromwell's Puritan government and his theology as one suspicious of beauty and perplexed to the point of anger by mystery. More thematically, it offers a mysterious promise that the current religious oppression will not last forever.

The West Virginia phenomenon is harder to place coherently in the overall narrative progress. But if we consider it in light of the Celtic theological concept outlined above, the pairing does not seem accidental at all. Creation and the Creator are not one and the same, but they are inseparable. All creation is infused with the divine, the mountains no less than that sacred space we call a chapel. Giardina's message, then, seems to be that the offense, even the repugnance, we feel when we read of the desecration of a temple or an ashram, a mosque or a synagogue, is similarly warranted by the desecration of a mountain. And neither manifestation of evil will ultimately prevail.

That the formally sacred church and the natural landscape are spiritual parallels is demonstrated most clearly in the labyrinth motif that recurs throughout the novel. After his discovery of the wormhole, Uncle John has been performing various mathematical calculations to determine its nature and also to learn whether other such phenomena may be discoverable. Part of his method is to overlay a labyrinth pattern onto a map of the New River Gorge. Asked by Lydde about his use of the labyrinth, he responds, "It's a geometrical figure ... but with spiritual implications. I've tried other things, squares, trapezoids, rectangles, but didn't see much of a pattern. With a labyrinth, with its entrance superimposed over the Mystery Hole, some interesting things show up" (132). Giardina explains little about the nature of the "interesting things," but what is presented is sufficient to affirm direct if mysterious connections between the physical and the spiritual realms. As we learn late in the novel, Uncle John's calculations have been faulty because he has been using the traditional Chartres (Western) labyrinth instead of the older pattern present in the Norchester church, a "carryover from the Celts, maybe" (51). This apparently incidental inclusion both affirms the way Celtic theology informs the text and emphasizes the idea of the physical and spiritual as connected realms. With this connection in mind, we begin to more fully understand Giardina's point that a single design governs both. To blast the natural landscape, then, is to attack simultaneously the spiritual dimension of reality, even to disrupt the parallel worlds.

Throughout the book mountains are characterized as ancient, even eternal phenomena, present "since the beginning of time" (53). Giardina's language becomes still more explicit in this regard. Describing the valley fill (the remains of blasted mountains) to Lydde, Aunt Lavinia states, "If the Devil built a fortress in the middle of your daddy's land, that's what it would look like" (67). Uncle John says mountains offer "the thinnest of all places, where the jagged crests of those old mountains touch the sky. Stand on such a place and you're close to true reality. Destroy it and you rip a hole in the fabric of creation" (9). The Raven's description of mountaintop removal after his trip forward in time puts it succinctly: "To flatten an entire range of mountains. . . . It is an affront to God" (197). More than simply figures of speech, what Giardina seems to be putting forth in such statements, particularly with the term *fortress*, implies a kind of war between good and evil that somehow involves the places where physical and spiritual realities are separated only by "the thinnest of membranes."

That phrase—"the thinnest of membranes"—carries us back to Fallam's preaching at the beginning of our discussion. In his sermon Fallam uses these words in relation to the Kingdom of God, which "lies just beyond the surface of what we see. It is like another dimension present with us always, though we are separated from it by the thinnest of membranes" (318). Because much popular Christian thinking often confuses the Kingdom of God with a locality called Heaven that is elsewhere, having little to do with the earth, it is easy for readers to miss the point the novel is making. The eminent theologian N. T. Wright's more precise understanding of the Kingdom better fits with the intention of the novel: "Earth—the renewed earth—is where the reign will take place, which is why the New Testament regularly speaks not of our going to be where Jesus is but of his coming to where we are."[24] Even more to our point, Wright offers, "Heaven and earth are not after all separated by a great distance; they are certainly not different locations within the same spatial continuum. It is more appropriate to think of them as overlapping and interlocking dimensions."[25]

In this light, the parallel phenomena of the restored paintings in the Norchester Church and the recession of the valley fill near the Mystery Hole make consistent sense. The promise in both cases is one of restoration: the restoration of a fuller religious expression from its Puritan repression and the restoration of the earth from its desecration by mountaintop removal. Giardina's implied claim is that they are not simply parallel phenomena but two instances of the same phenomenon. Each is an expression of the coming Kingdom of God; each is a motion in the inaugurated eschatology that affirms that the Kingdom of God both has come and is yet to come in its fullness. The restoration of the church paintings and the recession of the valley fill are, mysteriously, two sides of the same cloth. Each is a step toward renewal that is both physical and spiritual, temporal and eternal. In the language of the novel, then, we must understand mountaintop removal not simply as an unfortunate corollary of economic necessity but—to use the traditional Christian term—*sin*. And what stands behind that sin is spiritual blindness.

Giardina's Sermon

It is worth recalling here that Giardina is not only a novelist but also a political activist and an Episcopal preacher. In 2000 she ran for governor of West Virginia on the Mountain Party ticket. Winning that election as a third-party candidate was out of the question, but her purpose was to call attention to the devastating effects of mountaintop removal and to force the issue into public discussion. One might suggest that Giardina's candidacy was itself a kind of sermon: the use of her prophetic voice to call attention to an environmental catastrophe, a spiritual catastrophe. *Fallam's Secret*, in addition to being a fantastical romance, is a sermon of another kind preached to another audience—another attempt to speak prophetically on the most important environmental crisis of our day. And it may well stand as a kind of call to action.

After Fallam's journey through the wormhole to West Virginia, he tells Uncle John about his experience of the "affront to God" that is mountaintop removal. "Your leaders are as foolish as ours," he tells him. "Perhaps it will take more than one person *going forward* to undo such damage" (197, italics mine). In this passage, "going forward" refers to moving through the wormhole, since each passage causes the valley fill to recede. But it is impossible not to see the contemporary political suggestions of the phrase, implications grounded in Giardina's theology. In a 2007 article in the *Charleston Gazette*, she parallels Fallam's sentiment: "I will be as blunt as I can be. Mountaintop removal is evil, and those who support it are supporting evil. The mountains of West Virginia are God's greatest gift to West Virginia. To destroy the mountains is to spit in the face of God Almighty."[26]

It will indeed take many people *going forward*—through protest, through environmental restoration, and even through gubernatorial campaigns—to begin to restore the damage that has been done and is being done to Giardina's home state. And such a massive going forward will demand a new awareness. "We live *at this very moment* in the Kingdom of God," Fallam preached in his one true sermon, "only we have not eyes to see it" (318).

CHAPTER 7

Emily's Ghost:
The Making of a Giardina Hero

"I think *Wuthering Heights* was the first Appalachian novel," Denise Giardina stated in an interview with *Still: The Journal*. "Of course Emily Brontë never got near the mountains, but if she had, I think she would have fit right in."[1] In fact Emily has been fitting in, at least in Giardina's fiction, throughout the novelist's career. *Wuthering Heights* has been a suggestive reference point for several of Giardina's heroes, offering them a vision of romantic freedom and wildness, a way of reflecting on their own external and internal landscapes. In retrospect it seems fitting that Giardina's most recent novel, *Emily's Ghost* (2009), would direct attention to the world of the Brontës.

Though few would rank its achievement alongside the Appalachian novels or compare its scope with the more ambitious *Good King Harry* or *Saints and Villains*, most reviewers agreed that *Emily's Ghost* is a satisfying read. Mary Ellen Quinn in *Booklist* called the novel "a convincing imagining of the Brontë story, perfect for Brontë fans,"[2] and Kathy Piehl for *Library Journal* praised the book's "unconventionality and passion," deeming Giardina's version of Emily a heroine that fans of historical romance "definitely will want to meet."[3] In the same journal, Neal Wyatt, in a review essay of books based on classic texts, praised Giardina for "bringing the Brontë sisters to life with great sensitivity" and allowing readers "an intimate glimpse" into the imagined world of the Brontës, "while evoking the same passionate sensibility present in Emily's *Wuthering Heights*."[4] *Publishers Weekly* judged the book "a solid biographical novel," noting in particular that "the relationship between Emily and Weightman is nicely nuanced, and the insights and inferences about Emily and Charlotte's relationship are convincingly rendered."[5] And Jean Westmoore in *Buffalo News* praised the work as a "fascinating reimagining of the lives of the Brontës" that "weaves a stunning tapestry of fact and fiction around the lives of this famous literary family." It is, she concluded, "impossible to begin and not finish it, and just as impossible to lay it aside afterward and say nothing about it."[6]

Not all reviewers, however, have been so taken with Giardina's presentation of the "famous literary family."

From History to Fiction

One of the more extensive commentaries on *Emily's Ghost* is Jennifer L. Holberg's unflattering review essay in *Books and Culture*.[7] Holberg establishes her disapproving tone by leading with an allusion to *The Sixth Sense*, a popular Hollywood thriller about a young boy who converses with dead people. She then proceeds to pan the novel for its use of ghostly voices, for the liberties it takes with the known and unknown history of the Brontë family (particularly Emily's relationship with William Weightman), its negative portrayal of Charlotte Brontë, and its over-the-top gothic elements. Regarding the last point, many would agree: the scene, for example, in which Emily's father Patrick breaks open the sides of Weightman and Emily's coffins and pushes them together (thus allowing their romance to continue in the hereafter) is not likely to wear well. Holberg's judgment that it is "cringe-worthy in its Gothic over-indulgence" may not be too great an overstatement. Much of her critique, however, as we will see, is more disputable. But it did have the unintended consequence of eliciting a lengthy response from Giardina on the magazine's website.

Giardina began by admitting that it is "bad form for a novelist to respond to unfavorable reviews" but felt it necessary to do so: "The reading of my text and the reviewer's challenge of my research require me to defend the book against distortions of both book and historical sources."[8] Giardina's breach of literary decorum is not hard to understand. Parts of Holberg's review are misleading and even insulting, as when she states, "Alas, Giardina seems to have never met a conspiracy theory about Charlotte that she didn't like."[9] But one suspects Holberg's essay is not simply a review but an opportunity for her to weigh in, often very thoughtfully, on what she terms "the Brontë family literary sweepstakes"—the plethora of scholarly and less-than-scholarly speculations on the family. In her reply to Giardina, she notes that her review was based in part "on a desire to put this work into the larger context of Brontë studies,"[10] and she does so.

The most important aspect of this exchange is the way it frames a foundational difference in how two capable and committed students of fiction and history may disagree on the responsibility of the fiction writer to the historical record—a question pertinent to much of Giardina's work. Holberg asserts that "fiction should be allowed a measure of invention, but with real subjects the parameters must be carefully limited."[11] Giardina would no doubt agree. But she and Holberg disagree on where to draw the lines. Regarding Giardina's portrayal of an Emily-Weightman romance, for example, Holberg notes that "not a shred of evidence exists in contemporaneous sources that points to Emily Brontë ever having even a romantic interest of any kind."[12] And her implied conclusion is that such a romance therefore ought not to be fictionally drawn. Giardina's practice in this book and elsewhere follows a different principle: she determines it appropriate to imagine details that, given silence in the historical record, seem in harmony with her best historical judgment and creative insight. She manipulates fact in the service of the truth that fiction may offer. This is particularly apparent as she details the interior life of her characters.

What Giardina does in *Emily's Ghost*, then, is not so different in kind from what she has done in other novels. For example, having Emily experience a romantic attachment for Weightman, a man well known to her, is less a departure from the historical record than having Dietrich Bonhoeffer discover his deepest romantic love in Elisabeth Hildebrandt, who did not exist, or creating for him a life-altering exchange with T. S. Eliot, though there is no record of the two meeting. Regarding the latter, Giardina has stated, "I think it is very legitimate to ask the 'what if' question."[13] She makes such choices to serve her craft. To the degree these choices succeed, they serve the truth that her craft serves and possibly allow a depth of understanding that might have been missed without the "what if" question. Whether we are comfortable with such an approach determines our response to her novels. That is a choice readers must make, book by book. In regard to *Emily's Ghost*, the novel's essential value is not its successful or unsuccessful finish in or contribution to "the Brontë sweepstakes," but how it works in its own right. In that regard, far more troubling than the argument about the Brontë history is the misunderstanding of the ghostly voices and the significant role they play in the text.

Understanding the Voices

Possibly because of the book's title or maybe because the name *Brontë* brings with it vivid gothic associations, few readers are surprised by the appearance of ghostly presences in the novel. They keep readers turning the pages and push the plot along in engaging, often moving ways—even if these are what Holberg calls "*Sixth Sense-y*" ways. But students of Giardina's work are unlikely to let the preternatural pass by so lightly. In Giardina's response to Holberg, she affirms that the ghosts "are not meant to be some cheap special effect"; on the contrary, "The central point of *Emily's Ghost* is how we continue on with those who have died, our understanding that we are still connected through God's loving promise that death is not the last word. I have felt that with loved ones who have passed on; I suspect so have many people. This is not a subject to be treated trivially."[14]

Clearly Giardina has intended something more significant than Holberg believes is achieved. Her use of the ghosts is certainly not trivial—she wants to suggest a continuing connection. But serious intention does not guarantee success. Martha Greene Eads, an acute critic of Giardina's work, has observed of the Appalachian novels that "often their strength emerges from her commitment to speaking for the dead. . . . Giardina brings back to life her departed neighbors and the communities they populated—communities that are passing or are past."[15] Such a continuity with the past, Eads observes, is "similar to the one Holberg detected and found so dissatisfying."[16] Eads affirms, in fact, much of Holberg's criticism of the novel: her judgment is that the strategy in *Emily's Ghost* "flop[s]," that the "ghostly presences" are "unconvincing."[17] She thus judges Emily's ghosts as a failed attempt to do what the author successfully accomplished in the Appalachian novels.

While Eads's and Holberg's criticisms cannot be dismissed, neither can they be wholly accepted. It is insufficient to dismiss the ghostly phenomena as a failed evocation of ancestral influence or as an unfortunate extra-historical confabulation. What Giardina is attempting in *Emily's Ghost* is less akin to what she has done in the Appalachian novels and closer to what she has done in her fictional biographies: that is, to show the development of the interior life of her protagonist. As such, the experience of preternatural presences functions as one device for portraying the psychological experience of a complex historical figure, first as a traumatized child, then as a mature woman. As in Henry James's *The Turn of the Screw*, the ghosts might better be read, whether ontologically or psychologically, without final judgment. Recalling her previous novels, it is clear that Giardina often walks such a mysterious edge. But in the tradition of Nathaniel Hawthorne (obliquely referenced in the name of Maria Brontë's physician, Mr. Hawthorne[18]), who offers readers alternate ways to understand the scarlet *A* (or *lack* of a scarlet *A*) carved (or *not* carved) on Arthur Dimmesdale's bared chest, she usually, if not always, constructs her telling in a way that makes space for both natural and preternatural mystery. Allowing *Emily's Ghost* its own integrity, we may understand the voices best if we simply observe their significance for the protagonist who hears them.

In chapter 1, three "invisible friends" unknown to Emily tell her stories from "many hundreds of years ago" (18). Holberg interprets these as real presences, and because they *tell* Emily the story that would be the seed of *Wuthering Heights*, Holberg asserts that the sequence "reduce[s] Emily's imagination to mere channeling, not true creativity."[19] The text gives sufficient grounds, however, to interpret them in less paranormal ways. Most obviously, the visitors speak to Emily while she is in the state between wakefulness and sleep, when the mind is more susceptible to hallucinations. From the chapter's first line, Emily is portrayed as a little girl who relishes the privacy of her own imagination and the freedom that bedtime affords her: "At night, the door to other worlds opened wide. Emily waited as darkness fell, so ecstatic she shivered and wrapped her arms tight about her chest" (17). Once she is in bed, the scene turns particularly Hawthornesque:

> The rush candles on the tables cast their shadows upon the walls. The flames wavered, and the light danced across the rough stone with each icy draft that blew through the cracks in the old latticed windows. Emily watched and was lost in the movement of light and shadow across glass and stone. When all the girls were settled, the candles were blown out. But often there was enough of a moon to keep the shadows alive.
> Then the ghosts came and told the stories. (18)

The stories told by the ghosts are largely a manipulation of folk motifs that would have been familiar to a little girl whose childhood had been rich with her father's Irish folktales. That such details would reconstruct themselves in the hypnagogic state is not abnormal; neither is it atypical that they would be fully real to her.

Further, Emily's storymaking and storytelling fill many needs in her life at the Clergy Daughters' School, a dreary life at best. Making stories allows her an activity that she loves and that cannot be taken away. And telling them gives her a way to gain affirmation from the other girls, especially the older girls. As we see at one typical session, they "sighed at the final denouement, and several applauded. Everyone agreed that not only was the story fine but that Emily ... told it with a great deal of presence" (21). Emily's stories propel her from a place of insignificance to having a role to fill at the school.

Still more importantly, the stories allow Emily to cope with hardship. Consider her life thus far. She has little memory of her late mother. She was separated from her father, whom she loves, when he sent her and her sisters away to a boarding school. Once at school, she suffers not only cold and hunger, but psychological and physical abuse. Escape into stories and retreat into an interior world may be read as adaptive responses to past and current trauma. And the tactic is effective: within her paracosm, Emily can exercise the creativity she loves, maintain psychological stability, and withstand external events that are fundamentally out of her control. The unconscious is particularly creative in protecting people from traumatic experiences, and Emily's unconscious is a storyteller.

This does not mean that she is mentally ill, only that she is psychologically complex. Her imaginings do not keep her from having a "normal" life; on the contrary, they enable normalcy amid chaos. This is most apparent when she is punished by the school's headmaster, Reverend William Carus Wilson. He orders that Emily be shunned by the other girls and forced to stand in front of the class on a stool. While on display, she quickly falls into a reverie about what it is like to be so tall, and that leads her "to write a story about a giantess." The next line is telling: "The giantess said her name was Agatha, and the conversation began. So the time passed rather quickly" (30). Note that Emily begins by consciously creating a story, but the story immediately takes on a life of its own. This occurrence does not appear to be preternatural or psychotic, but rather resembles the way creative writers often experience their characters: as speaking to them. Emily bears her isolation more easily because the silence imposed "could not shut the mouths of her friends. The ghosts and the fairies and, yes, the devil were as noisy as ever" (30). Even as Emily is humiliated and shunned, Agatha, along with her other invisible friends, makes the situation bearable.

Significantly, in this sequence the six-year-old Emily is already developing both the adaptive behaviors and virtuous responses that she will carry into adulthood. Her courage is demonstrated when she bites Miss Andrews on the leg to stop her from abusing her sister (25). Her ethical sense is expressed in her resentment at Wilson's indulgences while the girls do without necessities—and in her willingness to take direct action (stealing bread) to address the unfairness (24). And when the headmaster accuses her of being "possessed by Satan," she responds in a way that indicates a strong and precise sense of self: "'I'm not,' she whispered. 'I tell stories'" (27). Indeed, storymaking is already the center of Emily's identity, her way of maintaining a full and freeing interior life in a world that constrains her: "Only to her invisible friends could she speak freely" (32).

The ghostly presence of Maria in chapter 2 and of Weightman in chapters 15–18 is a distinctly different kind of potentially preternatural phenomenon: the voices of departed loved ones that continue to influence her life. The single visitation from Maria is understandable given its traumatic context. The sisters have been called home from school due to Maria's death; then sister Elizabeth dies as well. In the distraught household, Emily is left to suffer her way through the grief alone: "No one could be bothered with Emily" (34). Furthermore, though she might have been able to deny the Reverend Wilson's existence while at school, she could not forget what he told her concerning her Maria's death: "It is your fault. It is a warning to you" (33). Going forward, Emily has two options: believe the story told by Wilson or tell a new story in which she is not to blame for her sister's death. It may be, then, that Emily's imagination once again provides respite in the form of her dead sister's voice: *"It wasn't your fault"* (35).

The experiences of Weightman's voice that occur in the final four chapters are similar in kind to those with Maria, though far more extensive and complex. But here there is a range of viable explanations for the phenomena at hand and Giardina, true to form, keeps things carefully ambiguous. Interestingly, Holberg dismisses the possibilities of the voices being "evidence of schizophrenia or a matter of purely imaginative inner dialogue" by noting that when Anne Brontë suggests those possible causes, "Giardina has her Emily affirm quite forcefully the reality of her auditory companions."[20] In fact, what Emily says is "If I am not talking to Willie, then I am mad" (322). True, this is a forceful statement, but it is most plainly read as the author offering her readers an either-or. We may believe in Weightman's preternatural presence, or we may believe that Emily is mad. We may even believe both. In the narrative context, Emily has been seeking his advice, and again, hearing the supportive counsel of a trusted, departed loved one during a traumatic period may not be typical, but it is not rare.

And it is certainly not rare in Giardina's fiction. Whether we consider these voices as real ghosts, psychological manifestations, uncontrolled figures of speech, or spiritual realities, they are a part of the intertextual worldview Giardina constructs in her novels. In *Good King Harry*, the voice of Merryn speaks to Harry the night before he plans to massacre the French chivalry: "Deep within me a still voice said, Stop now, Harry, else it shall be too late."[21] In *Storming Heaven*, Aunt Jane senses Alec May's ghost, and she is assured that he "walks for joy, not for disquiet."[22] (Interestingly, that happens in a passage preceded by a reference to *Wuthering Heights*.) Albion Freeman even ministers to the dead, comforting the ghost that haunts his farm. "I speak to it," he says, and "soothe it."[23] And in *Saints and Villains* when a distraught Dietrich is grappling with the question of whether to return to Germany and resist the Nazis, he sees a trusted (and departed) friend: "Fred is transparent, seems to waver and fade, returns for a second, then disappears. Without saying a word."[24] "Perhaps," the narrator adds, echoing Hawthorne, "Dietrich has dreamed all this." But even as Dietrich wonders, he hears Fred's voice encouraging him to be true to his call: *"Go on in go on in."*[25]

Weightman's voice stopping Emily from killing a threatening constable is similar: *"No. If you wish to hear more"* (312). The voice later tells her to go to Ponden Kirk, where she is reunited briefly with Nero (her merlin) and his mate—Giardina's symbols for Emily and Weightman. Walking back to town, it is evident that she has experienced a kind of ecstasy. John Brown tells his wife: "I saw Emily Brontë coming down off the moor just now. . . . It was—well, she looked as though she'd seen the God Almighty" (316). Giardina's audience may differ on whether Emily's experience should be understood as paranormal or hallucinatory, or even as authentically religious. Regardless of interpretation, readers may agree that these experiences offer insight into the interior life of a traumatized and brilliantly creative woman.

The use of preternatural phenomena, then, is not a handy contrivance to push the plot along with a splash of gothic flair. And while the presences do suggest, in Giardina's words, "how we continue on with those who have died,"[26] they are more than an attempt to repeat what was accomplished in the Appalachian novels. Finally, though the knowns and unknowns of their history provide an engaging context, the book should not be read primarily as an installment in the Brontë saga. We understand the book most fully if we read it as the development of one woman's interior life as she struggles against the constraints of her era to achieve something like wholeness. Understood in this way, Emily becomes Giardina's most complex and closely limned feminist hero.

The Giardina Hero

Giardina's fiction has consistently featured strong female characters but never a hero like Emily. Merryn in *Good King Harry* and Elisabeth in *Saints and Villains* act heroically, but they often do so in service of male protagonists; they add complexity and interest to the stories, but they function primarily as conscience figures for the development of Harry and Dietrich. Rachel and Jackie are among the protagonists in the multivoiced *Unquiet Earth*, and they portray strategies women of their respective generations have used to make their way through a postcolonial Appalachia. But again, they are presented in relation to—and at times as controlled by—the men they love. Carrie Bishop bears part, even the greater part, of the heroic weight in *Storming Heaven*, but the multiple first-person narrative structure necessarily divides the focus. She is a hero, but so are C. J., Rondal, and, though not a narrator, Albion. Many of Carrie's defining actions are performed in causes championed by her partners; her heroism is understood in relation to theirs. As the narrator who survives to tell the tale, she is left playing Ishmael to Rondal's Ahab, maybe even Saint Luke to Albion's Jesus.

Previous to Emily, Lydde Falcone of *Fallam's Secret* was the female character most clearly created as a hero. Hers is the point of view we follow most closely; her development is the transformation most expansively delineated; and in the final scenes she is, in fact, the most daring of the swashbucklers. The fantastical nature of that novel, however, does not provide the kind of realistic psychological landscape offered to Harry or Dietrich, to Rondal, Albion, or Dillon. As Giardina told Thomas Douglass while she was writing it, "I want [*Fallam's Secret*] to be kind of a mystical book, maybe a funny book in some ways. Maybe a book where the characters are still alive at the end, as opposed to a book where they are all dead at the end. I'm tired of those."[27] This does not mean that the book lacks weight. As noted in the previous chapter, it has a great deal to say about theology, gender, and humans' relationship with the natural world. But, experienced as fantasy, *Fallam's Secret* does not cultivate a fully realistic psychological engagement with Lydde. It took Giardina's return to realism in *Emily's Ghost* to provide the narrative context—and the hero—for that kind of exploration.

The discussion that follows below, then, has three interwoven intentions. The first is to delineate seven attributes of a Giardina hero that have crystalized through her career. With those in mind, we will observe how Emily, embodying many—if not quite all—of those attributes, becomes Giardina's most fully realized feminist hero. Finally, as a way of furthering our discussion of all six novels, our reconsideration of her heroes will reprise many of the important themes to which she consistently returned over nearly thirty years of fiction writing.

Deep Christianity

Giardina has been candid throughout her career about the importance of her Christian faith. Silas House and Jason Howard's description of her as having a "Christ-centered identity" seems accurate.[28] Yet she has been equally frank in acknowledging the narrowness that identifying as Christian can suggest. Her faith, she states, is in a God "far larger than the God of the religious right."[29] How, then, might we best understand the unique version of faith that informs her novels and particularly the actions of her heroes, some of whom make little or no pretense of religious faith? I am offering the concept of *deep Christianity*—a Christianity that is grounded in Christian principles but not necessarily put forth in Christian language.

One of the clearest statements of this *deep Christianity* preceded Giardina's birth by some two hundred years. The eighteenth-century Quaker John Woolman drew the concept with a humble precision that has not been surpassed. He observed,

> There is a principle which is pure placed in the human mind, which in different places and ages hath had different names; it is, however, pure, and proceeds from God. It is deep and inward, confined to no forms of religion, nor excluded from any, where the heart stands in perfect sincerity. In whomsoever this takes root and grows, of what nation soever, they become brethren, in the best sense of the expression.[30]

Woolman, like Giardina, was a believer who recognized a deep structure in Christianity more foundational and more extensive than any single historical articulation. Such a principle may function within Christian language, but it transcends that language, operating and motivating at a structural level that precedes any particular creed, liturgy, or institutional expression. Though Woolman's work was likely known to Giardina's Quaker ancestors, a more probable influence on the author herself was Dietrich Bonhoeffer. His *Letters and Papers from Prison*, one of Giardina's formative texts, introduces the related terms "unconscious Christianity" and "religionless Christianity."[31] These concepts intimate a kind of faith that does not limit itself to the confines of any institutional nomenclature but belongs wholly to the world, and it may be evidenced in those who have no religious affiliation at all.[32]

It is just such a deep Christianity that motivates and guides Giardina's heroes as they work for justice. Obviously some of her heroes are traditionally Christian. For example, Albion heeds the call of God to organize the miners, Dietrich follows God's inescapable leading to play his part in the Nazi resistance, and Noah Fallam risks his life for the poor of Norchester. Other heroes make no claim to Christian faith, yet they think and act according to principles consonant with deep Christian thought. Rondal, though apparently holding no articulated religious beliefs, embraces the spiritual dimension of people working together for the common good, and he dedicates his life to furthering the cause of justice. Hassel Day, possibly the most effective pastoral character of all, simply admits, "I aint religious in some ways myself. Still I will never question them that are."[33] And Dillon, though he states, "I fancy a God that would as soon level a church building as look at it,"[34] spends a lifetime laboring on behalf of his fellow workers and ultimately sacrifices his life to save his community.

Temperamentally and maybe religiously, too, Emily is similar to Dillon, and she even seems to echo his language when she states, "I would sooner burn a mill than profit from it" (325). As a curate's daughter, she participates in the forms of Christian orthodoxy. But in her heart she remains wild, even antinomian in the tradition of Hawthorne's Hester Prynne. She is never depicted speaking or practicing in the ways we associate with striving for sainthood, like Albion or Dietrich or her beloved Weightman. She is, however, portrayed in Christian action: feeding the hungry through her distribution of bread and helping the poor by acting as Weightman's conduit for communication with the Chartists (192). And significantly, her worldview includes the Christian idea that the world we see is not the only world that is; she believes in a reality that exists on the other side of earthly appearances, which one may enter fully only after death. Yet her way of understanding it, as closely tied to the moors as Dillon's spirituality is joined to the mountains, would be as scandalous to many Christians today as it is to the bewildered Reverend Mr. Dury, who cautions her, "Dear Miss Emily. . . . Do you wish to sound a Hindoo? You are a good English clergyman's daughter" (149). Such unconventionality, however, does not place her belief outside the pale of deep Christianity—a way of being religious in the world that is not so much professed as embodied.

GROUNDED IN PLACE

Considering Giardina's own passion for the West Virginia mountains, it is fitting that her heroes share just such a bond. The author ranks her mountains right after God in her own list of allegiances,[35] and her heroes do about the same, though at times reversing or merging the elements. This relationship with place is more than the love for a particular landscape. It includes a grounding with a real piece of earth, to be sure, but also with a history and culture, a tribe, even the spirit of the place. Through this essential identification, the place shapes the hero's way of valuing and moving through the world.

Emily Brontë's bond is with the moors; they are a part of her essential identity, just as the mountains are part of Dillon's: "She loved knowing every square inch of a place. She loved the way the wind roiled the grasses upon the heights, the company of birds and other wild creatures, the glimpses of fairies out of the corner of her eye. Emily could imagine herself nowhere else, no more than amputating a limb" (80). Indeed, the wildness Emily shares with the moors is one of her dominant and most successful characteristics. Like Huck Finn rafting down the Mississippi, it is only in wandering the moors that Emily transcends the social conventions that inhibit the realization of her deepest self. Emily on the moors is wild, expansive, mysterious, and utterly free. Her nighttime rambles are one of her two "times most precious . . . to escape into her fictional world of Gondal"—that is, into her paracosm and away from the world that continually chafes and limits her (70). The interior landscapes Emily traveled as a little girl at boarding school have become increasingly embodied.

In one telling sequence, both poignant and comic, the Brontë sisters are making their way over the moors back to Haworth after an awkward and exciting evening, first of suffering the banalities of the Durys' parlor, then of being inspired by Weightman's lecture on *Antigone*. Accompanied by Weightman and the Reverend Dury, the sisters are discussing the nature of heaven:

> "I don't want to go to Heaven at all!" [Emily] cried. I want to come back here. To the moors."
> "Come back?" Dury was shocked again.
> "Yes," she said. If not for her support of Anne, Emily would have turned in a circle waving her arms over her head, crying, Here! Here! Here! and then run off into the dark. She was forced to imagine doing it. (149)

In this rare instance, Emily, who in public usually "said not two words to anyone" (127), edges toward religious ecstasy. Later, when she is feeling guilty about her sisters going off to work as governesses while she stays at home on the moors, Anne assures her, "No, no. It would be terrible for you to leave. You have tried it before and it kills a part of you, you know it does" (155). Anne's words are more than a metaphor—the moors are part of Emily.

Like Dillon's love of the mountains, Emily's love for the moors is associated with more ancient, more elemental beliefs about nature and the divine. So inevitably she is drawn to people she associates with preindustrial life; hence her deep friendships with Tabby and Old Dean. They embody something ancient and true and grounded in the place, signified through the stories they tell of the fairies, stories that suggest a way of living and believing before the industrial world closed in:

> "I wish I could see fairies," Emily said. "When I go out at night and watch the stars, I wonder if they have fled somewhere there, to the Pleiades or beyond."
> "They have fled," Tabby agreed. "Sometime after I was grown. It were the factories as had driven them away."

"Indeed they did, Tabby," Weightman said. "Indeed they did. And a great much else besides." (185)

After Weightman's death and the sisters' return from Belgium, it is to the moors that Emily flees to find him. It was on the moors that their romance had blossomed, and it is there that their love continues, even after death: lying on the moors, Emily "studied the stars and listened for the voice of William Weightman" (311). There too, after her reunion with Nero, she is waiting in the heather when she hears Weightman's voice, a presence from beyond the grave that assures her they will have "*large time*" together (315, sic).

Just as it is impossible to articulate precisely the bond between Dillon and the mountains, between Carrie and the Homeplace, or between King Harry and Wales, exactly what the moors are to Emily does not lend itself to perfect analysis. Nevertheless, Emily's identity, the moors, and a state of being that transcends the limitations of mortality merge in a single complex.

Ethically Committed

The "clear understanding that good and evil exist" is one of the elements Giardina has repeatedly attributed to "Appalachian writing," even when the Appalachian writer is not writing about Appalachia.[36] Several critics, among them Laurie Lindberg and Sylvia Bailey Shurbutt,[37] have noted that the most powerful aspect of Giardina's work is its ethical commitment, what Shurbutt terms Giardina's "ethical imperative."[38] This imperative, a deep, personal mandate to ask foundational questions and do the right thing, is another characteristic of the Giardina hero. This does not mean the heroes always know the right thing to do, but they act with the faith that there is an ethical best, that seeking it matters, and that the seeking itself is a moral choice. In a world that seems to lack ethical guideposts, Giardina heroes feel their way forward, sometimes doubting the next step but sure that a destination exists. They refuse, ultimately, to rationalize evil. And when they fall short of their ideals (e.g., King Harry and Dietrich), their sins inevitably find them out. Such ethical convictions lead most obviously to deeply held positions concerning the equality of races, classes, and genders.

With the exception of some discussion of prejudice against the Irish, *Emily's Ghost* lacks the historical context to comment about race. Class, however, is central. From the beginning, Patrick Brontë is outspoken in his defense of the working class, and Weightman goes still further in his sacrificial ministry to the poor and through his participation with the Chartist movement. The oppression of the mill workers, their social and economic abuse by the mill owners, and the tendency of the latter to blame their victims is as constant a theme in *Emily's Ghost* as it is in the Appalachian novels. Emily's sympathies and actions throughout are completely in harmony with an egalitarian understanding of class.

Yet the most powerfully egalitarian call to justice for Emily and in the novel as a whole is the advocacy for gender equality. The Brontë family framework lends itself well to this theme. Emily's keen understanding of the injustice comes to the fore in reference to her beloved but ne'er-do-well brother Branwell: "it galls him, you see, that Charlotte and Anne and I possess more talent than he does. It should gall *us* that because we are women *we* are deemed unfit to make our way as portrait painters or authors. For us it is teaching or nothing. But Branwell has the advantage of his sex. It is not enough" (69). Emily feels the injustice sharply, as does her father, who "admired Emily's attributes" and "thought of her as a sort of son" (127). What makes Emily heroic in this regard is her persistent refusal to accept the shortcomings of her culture. Though in a practical way she has little alternative but to tolerate her lot, she refuses to concede her interior life to a cultural hegemony that devalues women. She does not let her thinking be perverted; in fact, her dissatisfaction and anger are often tied to this very refusal. Giardina's portrayal of Charlotte makes her Emily's foil in this regard. They have been reared in the same home, and they are equally gifted and ambitious. They even note many of the same gender injustices and commiserate about them. The difference is that in response to the hegemony, Charlotte accommodates by accepting, if bitterly, her place as a woman. Although she knows the situation is unjust, she also reasons that her clearest way forward is to comply, to follow the path more typical for women of her limited means.

Charlotte begrudgingly accepts, concerning gender and other social questions, the conventional ways of the world. She has neither the material wealth nor the good looks that would smooth her way, and "she felt the want" (59). So she pursues marriage with a clergyman as a way to work the system. The bitterness engendered by her accommodation is clear, particularly given the fact that she possesses a "contempt for the clergy, especially curates" (126), even as she remains alert for one to marry. Charlotte's accommodation is a sharp distinction between her and Emily, who chooses to maintain a righteous anger at the injustice over the bitterness that comes with accommodation. In contrast to her sister's persistent strategizing to catch a man, Emily does not think men "merit such heroic effort" (60). She will not, as she tells Weightman, "trim [her] sails for convention" (114), preferring to suffer the consequences.

Even Weightman, in many ways the perfect—or too perfect—Christian hero, fails in his understanding of gender. That such a deeply ethical man cannot see clearly regarding gender equality testifies to the dense, pervasive power of the hegemonic ideology. He loves Emily, and he admires her refusal to bend to convention. But even while he articulates progressive positions (128), he struggles to see beyond the culturally determined discrimination. Most disappointingly, when he is trying to devise a context in which he might marry such an unconventional woman, he still assumes that in their relationship Emily will be under his control. He reflects to Patrick, "But would [marriage to a clergyman] be so much loss of liberty? I would be indulgent" (265). Despite his enlightened views—"women are no more to be confined to a cage than is a merlin" (194)—and despite the fact that he is entranced by the kind of revolutionary woman Emily is, he cannot quite make the step toward gender equality. He never quite reaches the realization that she does not want to be controlled, no matter how *indulgently*. That Emily can love Weightman so passionately yet refuse to accept the advantages of marriage at the price of her own integrity speaks to the heroic strength of her ethical commitment.

CALLED TO ACTION

What ultimately keeps the two apart is Weightman's distinct call to be a pastor. Though discussed most extensively in relation to Dietrich Bonhoeffer, the concept of *call* pertains to all Giardina's other heroes as well. As Brian Cole has suggested, Giardina might well be defined not as an Appalachian writer but as a "'call' writer," so central is the concept to her fiction.[39] And none is more emphatically depicted than Weightman's call to pastor the poor. Emily, however, will not sacrifice her authenticity to conform to the conventions of the parsonage parlor, to society's expectations of a clergyman's wife. "You know as well as any the way I am seen in the village," she reminds Weightman. And she also has doubts about accepting the limitations of motherhood—unless she could ramble the moors "like an American Indian and her papoose" (214). But neither does she want Weightman to change. Emily takes *his* call as seriously as he does himself: "if he were to give up his calling for her, she would love him less. And if he found the strength to relinquish her, she would love him more. They were doomed, either way" (211). Death spares the couple this difficult choice.

So the question may arise: Does Emily fulfill the code of a Giardina hero without a call? That we have to ask that question points again toward the difficulty of being a talented woman in Victorian England. In Emily's portrayal,

Giardina is highlighting the restrictions that generations of gifted women have suffered. In a discussion with Weightman about his daughter's noble qualities, Patrick makes the point succinctly: "But society, as you know, does not countenance [courage] in a woman. Emily has no place to apply her gifts" (129). She is a woman who would be a hero, but there are no dragons for her to slay; or, more precisely, there is no road open for her to pursue them. She feeds the poor, she cares for her family, and she aids Weightman's work with the Chartists—all good things to do—but she apparently has no particular call in the sense we have been using the term.

If we consider the concept more broadly, however, her writing may be seen as a call. The creation of an interior world is the drive that has compelled Emily along throughout her life, from the Clergy Daughters' School to her deathbed. It is her way of making sense of the world—or of coping day by day in a world that does not make sense. Constructing her paracosm is the process at the center of her interior life, and not surprisingly, it is part of the same ideational complex as her passionate unity with the moors. As noted, her walks are a "precious" time for her "to escape into her fictional world of Gondal" (70). When early in their friendship Weightman tries to caution her about late-night wandering, she responds that "not even gratitude will allow you to encroach" (71). Her writing and her rambling are as sacrosanct as Weightman's more typical call to serve the Haworth poor. After their romantic passage through Ponden Kirk, when Weightman brings up the marriage question, Emily asks, "What clergyman could bear a wife who wandered the moors without detriment to his career? And what of my writing? How could I pursue it?" (213). This juxtaposition highlights the importance of her fiction and characterizes it as her vocation: each of the two lovers has a call, but the two calls are incompatible.

In desperation Emily asks Weightman, "Can I be other than I am?" (213). The rhetorical question form would suggest *no*, yet she could have been. Charlotte, as noted, bitterly adapts to convention. And many of Giardina's other heroes have tried, at least temporarily, to evade their call. Like Tom returning to Number Thirteen to evade Honduras or Dietrich fleeing Germany for Union Seminary, Emily is tempted to change, to let herself accept a more conventional life. At one point she even asks her father, "Why can't I be like everyone else?" (233). Along with her writing, then, it may finally be accurate to suggest that Emily's call is to persist in being the woman she is: in the face of a world that would change her, Emily's sacred, heroic call is to be Emily.

Given the deep Christian thought structures that inform Giardina's work, it is fitting that self-sacrificial—Christlike—action is the culmination of each call. As noted previously, the historical Bonhoeffer put this reality in the strongest terms: "When Christ calls a man, he bids him come and die."[40] And in fact, what we see in Giardina's heroes is a call that is usually consummated, directly or indirectly, is some variety of martyrdom. King Harry's self-sacrifice is one of the less glorious: though he feels a call from God and works himself to death to fulfill it, he dies a disillusioned invalid with the bloody flux. *Storming Heaven's* Albion is the most overtly drawn Christ figure in the Appalachian novels. He is directly motivated by his Christian faith to work for justice, and he fulfills many of the typical Christ motifs right down to prophesying his own death and striving to gaze on his murderers with love.

Dillon gives Giardina's clearest statement of the self-sacrifice that comes with following one's call, and it is all the more applicable because while it is true to Giardina's deep Christian thought, it reaches beyond Christian convention. Though quoted in chapter 4, the passage is worth reading again:

> You never thought of me as religious, and I aint in the church-going way. But I believe in God, and I believe they's a fire running through everything that lives. When the Bible starts throwing rules at me, I laugh, but when it tells how sin burns and says turn the other cheek and when God gets hung on that cross, buddy I'm right there. I chose me and that's sin. I aint no better than a goddamn Nazi. That's what they do, choose themselves. And the rich people that keep what they got, they do the same. It's sin and the only way you burn it out is to die. Only it don't work if you just die for yourself, it's got to be for somebody else.[41]

These words contain a key element of Giardina's heroic code: "it's got to be for somebody else." How Emily fulfills the sacrificial aspect of her call is ambiguous, if present at all. Of course any thematic deficit that might create in the novel is compensated by Weightman, who, like Albion, is drawn as an obvious Christ figure. His devotion to his particular call is repeated throughout, and fulfilling it means that he must choose, on behalf of his Haworth parishioners, to die. It may be more true to the text to conclude that while Emily's call gives her a kind of vision, she does not fulfill the sacrificial aspect of Giardina's code. But it might be at least suggested that Emily does sacrifice her life or that she sacrifices a conventional life for one devoted to greater things—to her art, to her understanding of gender, to her vision of a larger, more mysterious world—even though it means living a life largely misunderstood. If Weightman's call is to die, possibly Emily's call is to live authentically her own life, sacrificing the life that might have been.

PASSIONATE COURAGE

The intertextual world of Giardina's novels is not one where, in the words of William Butler Yeats, "The best lack all conviction, while the worst / Are full of passionate intensity."[42] In Giardina's fiction, the best are full of passions and convictions that define their lives. All her heroes are motivated by a call to battle systemic injustice, what Carrie in *Storming Heaven* calls the "forces in this world, principalities and powers, that wrench away the things that are loved, people and land, and return only exile."[43] Confronting such forces demands passionate courage. We see this exemplified, for example, when Harry, determined to unite Christendom, leads his starving, ragtag army against the flower of French chivalry. We see it when Albion surreptitiously unionizes coal miners under the surveillance of Baldwin-Felts gun thugs, and when Carrie and Rondal help lead the march up Blair Mountain against overwhelming odds. We see it again when Dillon and Sim Gore engage the corrupt unions and energy conglomerates; when Dietrich Bonhoeffer and his fellow conspirators work against the Nazis; even when Noah Fallam risks playing Robin Hood beneath the oppressive thumb of Cromwell's governors, fully aware that a gruesome execution will likely consummate his devotion.

Such passionate courage characterizes the heroes of *Emily's Ghost* as well. Weightman falls squarely into this category of underdog as he works on behalf of the poor of Haworth. Not only does he work for systemic reform by conspiring with the Chartists, but he ministers to the workers day by day, helping them meet their daily needs and finally easing their deaths, acting upon his deep conviction that while those afflicted with cholera may be forced to die without a doctor, "they need not die without a minister" (281). In a more homely yet equally idealistic way, Emily, too, battles against the force of convention to realize spiritual wholeness, confronting a patriarchal hegemony in which a woman of her passions and temperament is left, in her father's words, "no place to apply her gifts."

Passionate courage is throughout the text Emily's defining attribute. As Charlotte tells Weightman, "Emily . . . is not afraid of anything. Not on earth or in Heaven or Hell" (54). To his credit, he too recognizes—and loves her for—her courage, as reflected in his Valentine tribute that begins, "Brave soul, / You fear nothing, that I see / Of all things that is clear to me" (120). It is, again in the words of Charlotte, "almost as if he were writing to a man." The extent of Weightman's growing admiration is further demonstrated using a version of one of Giardina's favored devices, the play-within-a-play. Just as she characterizes *Saints and Villains'* Dietrich through a dramatic reading of T. S. Eliot's *Murder in the Cathedral*, she offers insight into Emily's passionate courage through Weightman's lecture on Sophocles's *Antigone*, the dramatic heroine who defies King Creon's decree in order to give her brother a respectful burial. Like Giardina's heroes, Antigone chooses to follow divine law, not the laws of kings. As Weightman offers his lecture, including dramatic readings of Antigone's exchanges with Creon, it is clear that he has Emily in mind. When asked if he has ever met a woman "who would speak so to a man in authority," "Weightman's eyes met Emily's." And he responds, "Yes. I have known fine women capable of this" (144). Charlotte misses his intention, but Anne quickly squeezes Emily's arm.

Emily's passionate nature is clear, too, in her longing to join Weightman in hearing Beethoven's Ninth Symphony (another of the frequent musical motifs in Giardina's fiction). Frustrated by her father's refusal to let her make the twelve-mile trip unaccompanied, Emily chops off her hair, dresses as a man, and confronts Weightman in his office (231–2). This scene alludes to the commonplace in the Anglo-American broadside tradition of brave women who cross-dress to accompany their lovers to war or to sea. Most important here is the passion that drives Emily to try such measures. Her reason would have told her that such a ruse would never gain her father's consent, but that does not stop her from taking up the scissors—an action that is more a protest against injustice than a serious strategy. Her frustration with convention is deep and here results in one of the book's most poignant lines: "Oh, I hate being a woman" (232). She does not, we suspect, any more than does Carrie Bishop or Lydde Falcone, but she loathes gender conventions that limit her. Like Antigone, and in keeping with her deep Christianity, Emily seeks to live by the "ancient moralities," a deeper and more intuitive set of truths (143). But the world is not yet ready for her. It is worth noting, however, that while studying in France, Emily gains a young disciple who under Emily's influence "had taken scissors to her petticoat" and "showed no sign of losing her old friends because of her unconventionality" (263–4). Readers may take this as a sign of hope.

This passionate courage plays a part in one other key characteristic aspect of Giardina's heroic code: her heroes consistently do the right thing while knowing failure is all but inevitable. Faithful action does not necessarily, or even usually, end with the desired result. As she told *Sojourners* interviewer Jason Howard, "We're not guaranteed success. In fact, what happened to Jesus suggests we should expect just the opposite. Go figure. For whatever reason, it seems doing the right thing is destined to lose."[44] Commenting on Dillon's words to Jackie, that "a loser knows things about the world that a winner will never know and is better for it,"[45] Giardina observes, "This seems to be a very

Christian attitude. Christianity seems to be based on losing, a religion that grows out of a loser who lost everything. He preached that 'the first shall be last and the last shall be first.' I think I've always kind of resonated with that attitude."[46] Certainly her heroes, including Emily, do as well.

OPEN TO MYSTERY

Though Giardina's work generally assumes a typically realistic view of the world, at the same time, it persistently offers the possibility that things can be known that cannot be articulated, that phenomena can be experienced that cannot be explained. Another characteristic of her heroes, then, is their willingness to remain open to mystery: they possess an epistemological humility that refuses to exclude or belittle experiences that seem to circumvent reason. The ideational space this worldview creates can be uncomfortable for the secular, scientific mind; yet it can be equally unsettling for religionists.

Giardina has been candid about her Christian faith, but she has also been intentional about distinguishing her conception of Christianity from those most prevalent in the contemporary cultural marketplace. This distinction has often been intended to distance her from the dominant faction of Christian fundamentalism that has merged with right-wing politics. But she also needs the nuance to distinguish her thinking from any worldview, secular or religious, that reduces *what is* to *what is known*. "For me," she states, "that word *mystery* is a very important word."[47] She is especially troubled by those tendencies of contemporary religions that are

> squeezing the life out of spirituality and mystery. . . . For them, it's got to be proven, and if it's not set in concrete, then there's nothing to it. That attitude, I think, is the opposite of what religion and spirituality should be and have been through the centuries. . . . One of the things I'm interested in doing is exploring again, pushing the boundaries out into mystery.[48]

Her pushing is judicious, more often a suggestive rhetorical tacking than storming the gates of the citadel. But mystery is always present.

As we have noted, Giardina's understanding of place, while fully appreciating and celebrating the natural world, consistently suggests something mysterious. The bond that her heroes feel to their particular places moves beyond the rational to the metaphorical, then mysteriously beyond metaphor. The

Homeplace of *Storming Heaven* is not simply a farmstead in Kentucky; it is also a metaphorical suggestion of heaven, then something that transcends the material world and the metaphor. And Emily Brontë's moors are not simply an expanse of heather, grand as that is. They suggest a world of perfect freedom and spiritual fullness where things happen that cannot quite be explained. In these cases and many others, realities are implied that finally demand some openness to the unknown.

This mysterious approach to place expands toward and merges with Giardina's understanding of time. This concept is most overt in the fantastical *Fallam's Secret*, but something similar is communicated in the realistic fiction. It is helpful to hold in mind that in Christian theology, the word *eternal* means more than an endless expanse of time, though that is part of the definition. *Eternal* also suggests a numinous quality of existence that may be experienced in the present. Such an understanding was suggested in our discussion of Fallam's sermon, when he asserts that the "Kingdom of God" is "like another dimension present with us always," another instantiation of reality of which humans may occasionally have an intimation "in sublime moments of beauty, of truth, of peace."[49] Rondal, for example, pushes toward this idea when he and Carrie, walking up Blair Mountain, talk about the nature of heaven. "Heaven is this here," Rondal proposes. "Hit's all these men together, and you, and knowing this here is the way we was meant to do. But it only lasts a minute. Then hit's gone."[50] Though these passages may often be read more simply as winsome figures of speech, such mysterious suggestions surface in all the novels and cannot be dismissed. They suggest an alternate way of understanding reality.

Another way of edging toward this expanded understanding of time incorporates the more typical Christian language of an afterlife. Various kinds of *heaven* or *afterlife* language are used in all the novels, and Giardina has affirmed belief in something like an afterlife in the conventional Christian sense. She does not believe that the physical body "simply disintegrates and dies." "Everything that I've encountered and experienced and that I hear other people encountering and experiencing . . ." she states, "suggests that there's more to life than that. . . . I really see death, for example, as the first stage on a trip. We've got more places to go."[51] Such thinking finds its way into several of her heroes. Dillon, for example, tells Rachel at the moment of her death, "Go on now. Wherever you're going, I'll come after. I swear I'll find you."[52] More mysterious yet is the message Dietrich Bonhoeffer, who certainly does not lack theological sophistication, sends to George Bell as he is climbing on a truck that will carry him to his execution: "Tell him 'For me it is the beginning.' Can you remember that?"[53] Precisely what Giardina means by such statements is finally less important than their suggestive resonance: something lies beyond.

This is particularly true in *Emily's Ghost*. When Emily first hears the disembodied voice of Weightman, she is in Brussels attending a performance of Beethoven's Ninth Symphony, not knowing he has died two days before. His voice prompts her to pay special attention to the words the chorus is about to sing: "*Here is the best part*" (298). After Emily learns of Weightman's death, she turns to Schiller's lyric again for solace. And though in the symphony these lines refer to God, she reads them as a promise about Weightman: "*Seek him above the canopy of stars. Surely he lives above the stars*" (304). Contemplating those lines, "Emily knew she must walk upon the moors beneath those stars before she would hear his voice again" (304). And as we know, she does hear his voice again on the moors—a voice promising her that although they would have had a short time on earth, they will have "*large time here*" (315).

As Giardina once told interviewer W. Dale Brown, "My approach in writing about religion is to ask questions rather than to answer them,"[54] and this pertains not only to theological nuances but to the grander questions of space and time. She offers her readers permission to explore the mysterious unknown.

UNIVERSAL SALVATION

A final attribute that characterizes many of Giardina's heroes is their belief in universal salvation. From a conventional Western Christian perspective, it may be the most heterodox—or even heretical—theological concept she offers, and she offers it repeatedly. In our *Storming Heaven* chapter, the idea was discussed extensively in relation to Albion Freeman, the "no-heller" hero, but it occurs at least obliquely in all the novels.[55] In *Emily's Ghost* its importance is ratcheted up still further: here, the belief in universal salvation has become a litmus test. It functions as "a secret code as the [Brontë] sisters sorted out the good clergy, in their view, from the bad" (148). In the passage below, they use it to test the Reverend Dury:

> "What do you think, " Anne asked, "of the possibility of universal salvation?"
> "Universal—what? Universal salvation? You mean that everyone would go to Heaven?"
> "Yes," Anne said.

> "Preposterous!" Dury cried. "Why bother to be a good Christian?"
>
> "Is that the reason one is a good Christian?" asked Emily. "To get to heaven? But is that not selfish?"
>
> Dury continued as if he hadn't heard her. "Murderers and lechers and pagans in Heaven? I think not. I have my doubts if Catholics shall be there!"
>
> "Heaven would be too crowded," Charlotte said.
>
> Dury missed the mockery in her voice. "Precisely," he said. "And how would it be Heaven if one were cheek to jowl with riffraff?"
>
> Charlotte coughed, said "How indeed?" and added Dury to her list of ridiculous curates. (148)

Giardina casts few specific theological doctrines so forcefully and frequently, and it is worth our while to explore why she insists on driving this point in such absolute terms. The importance of the idea goes beyond holding or not holding a particular Christian belief.

A brief return to how the concept is introduced in *Fallam's Secret* will clarify this broader significance. As a student, Fallam had written a tract that supported several revolutionary egalitarian ideas, among them democratic government, the education of all people, redistribution of wealth, and better treatment of indigenous peoples; in short, it argued on behalf of all forms of social justice. And most problematically, according to his father, the tract "proclaims universal salvation."[56] When the last is mentioned, the entire family "sat in silence for a time, considering the enormity of such an idea, the very threat to the security of *this* world in the notion that all would gain entrance to the next."[57] While their reaction might seem like comic irony to contemporary readers, in fact the family understands something about the concept that most readers miss. And their reaction suggests why universal salvation is necessarily included along with Fallam's other just causes.

The conventional orthodox idea of exclusive salvation affirms that some souls are destined for an eternity with God (heaven) and others for an eternity of torment or annihilation (hell). It is, not surprisingly, one of the most difficult doctrines of Christian belief to understand, let alone defend. But considered as a culture-informing metaphor, exclusive salvation has still greater implications for life in the present: if God makes an apparently inscrutable yet infinitely consequential choice, choosing some and effectively rejecting others, why would humans do otherwise? Humans—or at least humans in positions of power—may consciously or unconsciously adopt that concept as a divine justification, even as a divine model, for their own most egregious acts of discrimination. If the divinely appointed order is that some are saved and some damned—for reasons humans cannot comprehend—it is a short step to generalize the concept: it may also be the divinely appointed order that some are rich and some poor, some slave and some free, some educated and some ignorant, and so on. Understood in this light, exclusive salvation becomes a divinely sanctioned foundation for the creation of the Other, indeed, for all forms of alterity. The notion that God would choose some over others thus creates a precedent for all kinds of discrimination and marginalization, whether based on ethnicity, nationality, social standing, economic class, gender, or any other category in which the creation of an Other enables and maintains systems of (divinely appointed) power.

In radical contrast, the universalism of Giardina and her heroes is the proclamation that such Otherness, such inequality, is not a part of God's will. It is consistent, then, that since Giardina's heroes are depicted as egalitarian opponents of nationalism, racism, classism, and sexism, they would be portrayed as universalists as well. Universal salvation functions not only as a theological proposition but as a master metaphor for the final breaking down of all discriminatory distinctions between classes of people: it is the ultimate denial of alterity. It is egalitarian justice of the most radical sort. Little wonder Noah Fallam's aristocratic family—and parsons like the Reverend Dury—find it so unsettling. It is.

Such a revolutionary egalitarianism, such a pervasive call for equality, is the central message in *Emily's Ghost*, just as it has been central to Giardina's work throughout her career. Whether portraying a king who values the lives of Welsh archers equally with those of his chivalrous peers, the wealthy son of a capitalist who opts to suffer cholera with his parishioners instead of enjoying his father's largesse, or union miners who refuse fatalism and choose instead a deadly struggle for a fair wage, she has told the stories of flawed people working hard for justice.

As this chapter has attempted to demonstrate, Giardina has, in developing a broadly variegated cast of heroes, effectively created a heroic code. And whether her heroes are succeeding or failing in their attempts to abide by its principles, the code reflects the values at work in her fictional world and, I believe, in the heart of the author: a deep spirituality, articulate in its commitments but open to mystery; a grounding in place that demands and nurtures ethical commitment; and, most dramatically, a passionate courage that drives each hero to heed the call to action. That a common code would evolve from such a diverse set of historical contexts confirms that Giardina has, indeed, returned to the same handful of issues in each book: what we owe ourselves, our communities, our world, and, however we understand the concept, our God. At last, those themes may even reduce to a single ethical query: What does it mean to do the right thing in this world? The question remains the same, whether the hero pondering it is a king or a coal miner, a patriot or pastor, or a young woman who cherishes the right to walk alone on the moors at night, thinking her own thoughts.

CHAPTER 8

Conclusion: Facing the Questions, Living with Mystery

In a 2006 panel discussion published in the *Iron Mountain Review*, Fred Chappell laments the tendency in Appalachian fiction to portray in religious characters a too-simple faith. He decries the apparent dearth of characters who wrestle with religious doubt in carefully articulated theological ways, a complaint that culminates in his query, "Can anyone here recall any work in which religious questions are earnestly pursued in an Appalachian setting and in which those questions are central to the drama of the text?"[1]

As I have returned to that transcript while completing this study, Chappell's question has troubled me for several reasons but, most perplexingly, because Denise Giardina was the next speaker on the panel. What must she have been thinking about his question? And what might she have been thinking when she began her own comments with this transition: "Fred's remarks are really quite challenging and have given me a lot to think about"? Challenging indeed. I can imagine her having a lot to think about as she determined how best to respond after that question—a question for which, I believe, she had written the affirmative answers.

One of Giardina's most significant achievements—despite Chappell's oversight—has been her successful delineation of the complexity of religious faith in an Appalachian context. As our study has tried to demonstrate, her work brings to the careful reader a recognition that the forces shaping theological thought in the academy, in the pews, and around the world were also at work in the coalfields. This is no small accomplishment: without compromising the verisimilitude of her fiction or burdening her work with alienating terminology, she has demonstrated that many of the most significant strains of twentieth-century theological thought—the social gospel of Reinhold Niebuhr, the radical discipleship of Dietrich Bonhoeffer, the liberation theology of Gustavo Gutiérrez, and more—were at work in the Appalachians, both in the historical dialectic and in the questioning hearts of individuals. Intricately developed characters—such as Albion Freeman, Tom Kolwiecki, and to a degree several others—struggle with their belief and with putting their belief into action, as surely as any I can recall in contemporary fiction.

If that had been Giardina's only achievement, she would be a significant regionalist. But of course there are other, more obvious reasons and, some would argue, more important reasons, that she has earned her place as an Appalachian novelist of the first rank. Her portrayal of the intricate historical fabric that culminated in the Battle of Blair Mountain is destined to shape the understanding of that piece of history for future generations; in fact, regarding that battle, Wess Harris notes that *Storming Heaven* "provides a better understanding of events than most 'non-fiction' accounts."[2] And Giardina's continuing portrayal of the struggle in the coalfields, even up through the early twenty-first century, seems likely to influence the thinking of future generations.

To be clear, I am not suggesting that Chappell intended to slight Giardina's work. Quite the contrary, he had earlier written a glowing review of *Storming Heaven* in the *Los Angeles Times*, an essay that placed the book alongside the work of John Yount and James Still as one of the three great Appalachian coal-mining novels. So how is it that as erudite a writer and sympathetic a critic as Chappell might overlook Giardina's carefully nuanced theological portrayals? Maybe this: I believe the tendency to find in a novel what one looks for is, on some level, as true of the expert as it is of the general reader. And Giardina's novels are rich enough to respond meaningfully to many different and pertinent sets of questions, some of which inevitably overshadow others.

In chapter 1, I noted that Giardina may rightly be considered an Appalachian novelist, a political novelist, and a theological novelist; and it seems to me that the order of that list may suggest the sequence of claims her work makes on the attentive critical sensibility. As accomplished as *Good King Harry* is, it was not until the success of the coalfield novels that Giardina commanded significant popular and academic attention. Critics with a professional interest in Appalachian studies were the first to be engaged by a new, serious writer of literary fiction who wrote with commanding authority of life in the coalfields and the history that brought that way of life about. Commentators with interest and expertise in the region were naturally the first to take her work seriously and recognize its importance. *Appalachianness* was her first claim on their attention.

Giardina's achievement as a political novelist comes necessarily alongside her achievement in portraying the region. Any exploration of Appalachian history immediately births a plethora of political questions: to write realistically about West Virginia, especially about the coal economy, demands a rare depth of political understanding and a breadth of very particular historical knowledge. Good scholarship, regardless the discipline but certainly literary criticism, must inevitably maintain a political interest and attention. And

Giardina's broader reputation as an activist would further attract critical attention to the political concerns that inform and enrich her work.

So it is to be expected that an appreciation of Giardina's fiction should begin with a regional focus and continue through a political lens. It would be lamentable, however, if that were where critical consideration should end. Possibly those of us deeply invested in the value of Appalachian literature are ourselves prone to construct a de facto Appalachian literary ghetto, contenting ourselves with the regional and political themes and failing to attend adequately to the universal. By doing so, we limit the broader significance of the writers who have spoken most deeply to our condition. My hope is that while Giardina was initially studied for her regional and political importance, future criticism will explore with equal rigor the universal motivations that shape her characters and drive her plots.

The title *regionalist* will necessarily be laid aside as Giardina's work engages the critical discussion it deserves. Though she is deeply grounded in the coal country of West Virginia, more significant than the Appalachian particulars are the Appalachian *sensibilities* she has demonstrated broadly, from fourteenth-century London to the Weimar Republic to the New River Gorge, and finally to the wuthering heights of Haworth: the lack of pretense, the clear-eyed reason coupled with passion, and, most importantly, the conviction that not only do right and wrong exist but that it is worth our time and blood to determine which is which. The questions that keep recurring, the deep thematic strains, are not Appalachian questions but human questions. And for Giardina, the most deeply human questions are cast inevitably in a theological framework.

Like most readers, I began my reading relationship with Giardina through *Storming Heaven*, and I read it because of my interest in Appalachian literature and culture. But what I found most compelling about the book was her expertise in dealing both expertly and empathetically with theological questions. As I read and studied the rest of her novels, I found that her spot-on portrayal of Albion's faith had been no accident. Many years later, I am more impressed with each new reading, and I have even come to believe that we may understand Giardina's Appalachian texts more fully when they are informed by readings of her non-Appalachian books.

When we read *Good King Harry*, we are confronted head-on with the deepest questions of church and state. When we read *Saints and Villains*, we are confronted with the questions of how personal religious belief must respond to the responsibilities of a citizen to the government—and when, if ever, laws must be broken for a higher law to be followed. In *Fallam's Secret*, the religious undergirding of human responsibility to the planet we call home is expressed in deeply spiritual terms. And in *Emily's Ghost*, the questions of poverty and social class and gender are drawn still closer to the center. Through Giardina's use of the theological metaphor of universal salvation, we are confronted with the human tendency to create the Other, whether by gender, by race, by class, or by sect.

Returning to the Appalachian novels, we may bring our new attentiveness, our new questions, back to our readings of the texts. In doing so we find that all the major thematic strains have been there from the beginning. As Giardina has often noted—and as she stated in the aforementioned panel with Chappell, "It's not so much any one specific place that I keep being drawn back to, but it's the same questions over and over again and the people who are exploring those questions of existence and the meaning of existence, which seems to me a central mystery of life."[3] Close readers of Giardina's work must face those questions and contemplate those mysteries. In our world of perpetual war, she has asked the great questions of war and peace. In a world that questions the legitimacy of governmental actions, she has asked the perplexing questions of personal responsibility. Questions of gender roles, of the meaning of sexual intimacy, even of gender orientation, have all found their place in her work, often with an intricate level of nuance and a subtle sophistication that seem now to have been prescient. And the questions of class, of the relationship among the rich, the poor, and the poorer, have never been slighted in her work; indeed, they have often taken center stage.

Each of her novels is situated in the context of a major social crisis; each centers on a particular set of historical and political questions. And in each, those questions are at work dialectically with a clear set of theological and ethical questions. Even as we look with care at the most intimate details of the stories, we see that in each case even the romantic element is shaped—often in clear and definite ways—by the political tension and the theological concerns of the characters. While that may seem a rather broad claim, we need only reflect on the intimate relationships of King Harry and Merryn; of Albion and Carrie or of Carrie and Rondal; of Dillon and Rachel or of Jackie and Tom; of Dietrich and Elisabeth or Dietrich and Maria; of Fallam and Lydde; or of Emily and Weightman, to see just how essentially the political, the theological, and the personal are tied: "it's the same questions over and over again."

Giardina never lets her lovers, her protagonists, or, for that matter, her readers, escape their place in the community, whether the community of neighbors or the community of nations. Early in *Storming Heaven* when Albion must leave Carrie's Homeplace to travel with his peddler father, a mature narrative voice frames her loss in the words of Saint Paul: "I loved him, but it was not enough to hold him. I first began to understand what I have learned since, that there are forces in this world, *principalities and powers*, that wrench away the things that are loved, people and land, and return only exile."[4] In Giardina's work the phrase "principalities and powers" should not be trivialized into the "angels and demons" language of media-driven pop religion. These principalities and powers are biblical language for systemic evil, those forces of death that inhabit institutions, from town councils to national governments, from international energy conglomerates to the political networks that do their bidding, and these forces that stand behind institutions impact the course of individual lives. As theologian Walter Wink has noted, "What people in the world of the Bible experienced as and called 'principalities and powers' was in fact the actual spirituality at the center of the political, economic, and cultural institutions of their day."[5] When the forces of these "institutions, structures, and systems" fail to serve the common good, Wink reasons, they are *fallen*.[6] And it is in that fallen state that we find "unjust economic relations, oppressive political relations, biased race relations, patriarchal gender relations, hierarchical power relations, and the use of violence to maintain them all."[7]

In short, we find the world of Giardina's novels. The struggles of her characters, both personal and political, are most thoroughly understood in just such a theological framework. Maybe it is because of this consistently embodied worldview that Giardina has, indeed, persistently returned to the same handful of questions. For the same reason, proper attention reveals that there is nothing uniquely Appalachian about the greater problems she portrays. In every plot, in every historical context, Giardina has situated her protagonists in worlds distorted by deep systemic injustice and set them to a task. And always their actions are informed and guided by the ethical grounding that comes with a deep faith, whether implicit or explicit.

To her credit, although the books offer a consistent and pervasive theological acuity, Giardina never confuses the novel for the pulpit. Her ability to delineate the particularities of theology without talking (too much) *about* theology attests to the quality of her craft: it demands a great deal of sophistication to write so plainly. As she told interviewer Thomas Oder, she intends that *her stories themselves* "carry the depth, rather than the density of the language."[8] This choice sets her apart from many other literary novelists in an era in which serious fiction is often characterized by formal complexity, but she has apparently thought the risk worth taking. The faith she portrays with such clarity and care finds a fuller expression in practice than in creed, making the fairly traditional novel a perfect medium for her ministry.

And it is a ministry. Giardina's fiction is her art, to be sure, but it is also, by her own confession, her call: her way of serving the needs of a suffering world by working hard for a better one. As surely in her fiction as in her overt political activism, she embodies that most essential prophetic stance: she resists principalities and powers by speaking the truth. One of Giardina's heroes, Martin Luther King Jr., once defined "nonviolent resistance" as "nothing more and nothing less than Christianity in action."[9] We see Giardina's faith in action in her characters, and we perceive it in her own act of writing. In the same article, King echoed the phrasing of another Christian minister, the nineteenth-century reformer Theodore Parker, for a concept that has become one of King's most quoted: "the arc of the moral universe is long, but it bends toward justice."[10] Denise Giardina's work presents readers with models of women and men who keep their eyes on justice and who work courageously to hasten that bending of the arc.

Notes

CHAPTER 1

1. Giardina, "Coalfield Ancestors," 5.
2. Giardina, "Appalachian Images," 161–63.
3. House and Howard, *Something's Rising*, 53.
4. Giardina, "Coalfield Ancestors," 5.
5. House and Howard, *Something's Rising*, 54.
6. Wells, "Innerviews."
7. Giardina et al., "The Perils of Regionalism," 27.
8. Wells, "Innerviews."
9. Giardina, "About Denise Giardina."
10. Giardina, *Thunder on the Mountain*, xv.
11. Giardina, *Thunder on the Mountain*, xvi.
12. Giardina, "No Scapin the Booger Man," 129.
13. House and Howard, *Something's Rising*, 52.
14. Giardina, interview by Douglass, *Appalachian Journal*, 391.
15. Carlson, "Mountain Woman."
16. Giardina, *Thunder on the Mountain*, xv–xvi.
17. Giardina, interview by Douglass, *Appalachian Journal*, 389.
18. Giardina, interview by Douglass, *Appalachian Journal*, 389.
19. Wells, "Innerviews."
20. Wells, "Innerviews."
21. Giardina, interview by Douglass, *Appalachian Journal*, 389.
22. Giardina, interview by Douglass, *Appalachian Journal*, 389.
23. Oder, "Mining History," 69.
24. Howard, "Beauty in Battered Places."
25. Wells, "Innerviews."
26. House and Howard, *Something's Rising*, 58.
27. Giardina was ordained as noted but later renounced her vows; in 2007 she was reinstated as an ordained deacon. See "About Denise Giardina."
28. Howard, "Beauty in Battered Places."
29. Carlson, "Mountain Woman."
30. Oder, "Mining History," 69.
31. Wells, "Innerviews."
32. Oder, "Mining History," 69.
33. Giardina et al., "Perils of Regionalism," 27.
34. Wells, "Innerviews."
35. Wells, "Innerviews."
36. Oder, "Mining History," 70.
37. House and Howard, *Something's Rising*, 56.
38. Wells, "Innerviews."
39. Oder, "Mining History," 70.

40. House and Howard, *Something's Rising*, 56.
41. Wells, "Innerviews."
42. House and Howard, *Something's Rising*, 55.
43. House and Howard, *Something's Rising*, 57.
44. Howard, "Beauty in Battered Places."
45. Wells, "Innerviews."
46. House and Howard, *Something's Rising*, 51.
47. House and Howard, *Something's Rising*, 51.
48. Giardina et al., "Perils of Regionalism," 28.
49. Rash, "The Importance of Place."
50. Brown, *Fiction and Faith*, 147.
51. Giardina, interview in *Still: The Journal*.
52. Boudreau, "Fighting Back," 10.
53. Giardina et al., "Perils of Regionalism," 30.
54. Nichols, "Novelist Runs for Governor."
55. Giardina, interview by Douglass, *Appalachian Journal*, 390.
56. Conway, "Slashing the Homemade Quilt," 138–55.
57. Easton, "Class and Identity," 297.
58. Lindberg, "Challenging the Bullies of Appalachia," 21.
59. Boudreau, "Fighting Back," 10.
60. Thoreau, "Civil Disobedience."
61. Brown, *Fiction and Faith*, 149.
62. Giardina, "Appalachian Images," 164.
63. Giardina, "Appalachian Images," 168.
64. Giardina, "Appalachian Images," 168.
65. Giardina, "Allegiances," 63.
66. Howard, "Beauty in Battered Places."
67. Giardina, interview in *Still: The Journal*.
68. House and Howard, *Something's Rising*, 59.
69. Byer et al., "Religion, the Sacred," 42.
70. Brown, *Fiction and Faith*, 149.
71. Douglass and Giardina, "Resurrecting the Dead," 37.
72. Byer et al., "Religion, the Sacred," 45.
73. Byer et al., "Religion, the Sacred," 42.

CHAPTER 2

1. Burruel, review of *Good King Harry*, 732.
2. Dirlam, "Great Figures, Grand Figments."
3. Tritel, review of *Good King Harry*.
4. Brown, *Fiction and Faith*, 147.
5. Ballard and Hudson, *Listen Here*, 231.
6. Giardina, "Reader's Guide," in *Good King Harry*.
7. Giardina, "Reader's Guide," in *Good King Harry*.
8. Giardina, "Reader's Guide," in *Good King Harry*.
9. Review of *Good King Harry*, *Kirkus Reviews*.
10. Tritel, review of *Good King Harry*.
11. Buckley, *Season of Youth*, 18.

12. Hirsch, "Novel of Formation," 296–98.
13. Hirsch, "Novel of Formation," 297.
14. Hirsch, "Novel of Formation," 298.
15. Hirsch, "Novel of Formation," 298.
16. Hirsch, "Novel of Formation," 298.
17. Giardina, *Good King Harry*, 1. In the rest of the chapter, quotations from this book are cited parenthetically.
18. Buckley, *Season*, 19.
19. Buckley, *Season*, 17.
20. Burruel, review of *Good King Harry*, 732.
21. Dyson, *Aquinas: Political Writings*, xxvi–xxvii.
22. Brown, *Fiction and Faith*, 158.
23. For a contemporary statement, see the Vatican website, *Catechism of the Catholic Church*, accessed July 16, 2018, http://www.vatican.va/archive/ENG0015/__P81.HTM.
24. John 15:13 (King James Version).
25. Matthew 26:33–35, 73–75 (KJV).
26. Niebuhr, "Christian Church," 102–3.
27. Niebuhr, "Christian Church," 119.
28. 2 Corinthians 12:7 (KJV).
29. 2 Corinthians 12:9 (KJV).
30. Hirsch, *Novel of Formation*, 298.

CHAPTER 3

1. Giardina et al., "Perils of Regionalism," 27.
2. Wells, "Innerviews."
3. Chappell, review of *Storming Heaven*.
4. Review of *Storming Heaven*, *Publishers Weekly*.
5. Quigley, "Fiction Recreates Miners' Plight." *Tennessean*.
6. Kilpatrick, review of *Storming Heaven*, 94.
7. Giardina, "Reader's Guide," in *Saints and Villains*.
8. Boudreau, "Fighting Back," 9.
9. Brown, "True Stories: A Conversation," 42–43.
10. Giardina took her research for this novel very seriously indeed. In addition to those mentioned above, the acknowledgments page lists several other books that were particularly important, along with many people who contributed to the writing, among them Bill Blizzard, whose father was a leader at the Battle of Blair Mountain.
11. Corbin, "The Mine Wars."
12. Corbin, *Life, Work, and Rebellion*, 218–22.
13. Boudreau, "Fighting Back," 12.
14. For several foundational early essays on the colonization of Appalachia, see Lewis, Johnson, and Askins's *Colonialism in Modern America: The Appalachian Case*. Of particular relevance are "The Colonialism Model: The Appalachian Case" by Lewis and Knipe and "Industrialization and Social Change in Appalachia, 1880–1930" by Eller.
15. For a thorough discussion, see Eller's "A Magnificent Field for Capitalists," chapter 2 of *Miners, Millhands, and Mountaineers*, 39–85.

16. Eller, *Miners, Millhands, and Mountaineers*, 85.
17. Giardina, *Storming Heaven*, 104–5. In the rest of the chapter, quotations from this book are cited parenthetically.
18. Eller, "Industrialization and Social Change," 35.
19. For the decline in agricultural productivity during this period, see Eller, *Miners, Millhands, and Mountaineers*, xix–xx.
20. Brown, *Fiction and Faith*, 156.
21. Mooney, "Beyond Measure," 13.
22. Conway, "Slashing the Homemade Quilt," 139.
23. Conway, "Slashing the Homemade Quilt," 140.
24. Conway, "Slashing the Homemade Quilt," 150.
25. Mooney, "Beyond Measure," 13–14.
26. Wilson, "Exchange of the Feminine," 69.
27. Easton, "Class and Identity," 298.
28. Easton, "Class and Identity," 298.
29. When Rondal visits the Homeplace to get Carrie for the march on Blair, he entertains Flora and Ben's children with the story of an organizer who escapes company thugs by telling them he is going to organize them. Though Rondal relates the incident as a personal adventure (238–40), the story itself is historical, at least as told by Myles Horton, cofounder of the Highlander School, which Giardina often visited. See Moyers and Horton, "The Adventures of a Radical Hillbilly," 265–66. Horton's telling is also available in a video interview with Bill Moyers: *Myles Horton, Radical Hillbilly: A Wisdom Teacher for Activism and Civic Engagement*, https://www.youtube.com/watch?v=qSwW0zc-QBQ&t=3017s. The story begins at the 53:00 mark.
30. Eads, "Industrialization's Threat," 65.
31. Giardina, "Coalfield Ancestors," 5.
32. Ruberto, *Gramsci, Migration*, 20.
33. Helen Barolini notes that "Italian women who came to this country did so as part of a family—as daughter, wife, sister—or 'on consignment,' chosen, sometimes by picture or sometimes by hearsay from an immigrant's hometown to be his wife. But always in the context of a family situation" (*Dream Book*, 9). Clearly Rosa's situation was not unique.
34. Barolini, *Dream Book*, 4.
35. Barolini, *Dream Book*, 19.
36. Giunta, *Writing with an Accent*, 64–65.
37. Barolini, *Dream Book*, 22.
38. Douglass and Giardina, "Resurrecting the Dead," 33.
39. Conway discusses the mountain values demonstrated in *Storming Heaven* as resistance to competitive colonizing forces. She quotes Boudreau's interview in which Giardina reflects on those values, including Giardina's statement that "the culture has a theological [or spiritual] base" (139). The bracketed phrase "or spiritual" was apparently inserted by Conway. She then notes values in the text that may be defined as spiritual. But *theological* does not mean *spiritual*. Albion is noted as a tradition-bearer of stories and ballads, but the religious faith of Albion's adulthood is not mentioned. Easton's "Class and Identity" rightly notes that colonizing forces did much to shift local ways of thinking—"the development of specific kinds of schools, churches, and recreational activities"—and refers to

outside forces—including missionaries—that pressured the mountaineers "to shed their local habits and customs"; but he does not mention Albion or the religion he represents (298–99). Shurbutt's "Words, Actions, and 'Resurrecting Home'" examines the ethical emphasis of Giardina's work. She quotes Giardina as saying, "I am also interested in writing that includes the political and spiritual dimensions of life and am not much interested in fiction that pretends these areas do not exist" (110–11), but Shurbutt does not pursue the significance of the spiritual dimensions. Similarly, Mooney praises Giardina's moral vision, noting "her novels are refreshing and spirit-enriching" (13); and he notes "Albion Freeman's careful articulation of No Heller Baptist" theology, but he does not examine how the two are related (14). Lindberg's "An Ethical Inquiry" expertly points us toward the values Giardina's characters offer us—"justice, individual freedom, love—and the fight to guarantee all of these liberties" (667). But she does not mention the religious foundation of the text, nor does she refer to Albion.

40. Corbin, *Life, Work, and Rebellion*, 149.
41. Conway, "Slashing the Homemade Quilt," 146.
42. Corbin, *Life, Work, and Rebellion*, 158ff.
43. Mooney, "Beyond Measure," 10.
44. Howard, "Conversation with Denise Giardina."
45. Matthew 25:40 (KJV).
46. Conn, "Liberation Theology," 389.
47. For a fuller comparison of the Sojourners and liberation theology, see Taylor's "Authority in Ethics."
48. Sanks, "Liberation Theology and the Social Gospel."
49. House and Howard, *Something's Rising*, 53.
50. Though largely ignored in the earlier published scholarship, Albion has received attention in more recent studies. See Creasman's "Denise Giardina's *Storming Heaven*" in *Writing West Virginia*, 73ff. A useful study of Albion's theology appears in Sanders's "Mimetic Transformations of Sacred Symbols." See especially his comparison of the life and theology of Albion and Dietrich Bonhoeffer (16–27).
51. Eads follows a different but very insightful understanding of the notion of call that augments and complements our work here. See "Industrialization's Threat."
52. Corbin, *Life, Work, and Rebellion*, 158.
53. Corbin, *Life, Work, and Rebellion*, 148.
54. Corbin, *Life, Work, and Rebellion*, 154.
55. Taylor, "Authority in Ethics," 147.
56. Niebuhr, "Christian Church Is Not Pacifist," 102–3.
57. King, "I've Been to the Mountaintop."
58. Byer et al., "Religion, the Sacred," 42.
59. The essential study of this sect is Dorgan's *In the Hands of a Happy God: The "No-Hellers" of Central Appalachia*.
60. The importance of Christian universalism in Giardina's work will be evident throughout this book. See also my "Wide Reach of Salvation," 93–114.
61. Dorgan, *Happy God*, 5.
62. Douglass and Giardina, "Resurrecting the Dead," 33.
63. Savage, *Thunder in the Mountains*, 164.
64. Gillespie, "*Storming Heaven* in the Decade of Greed," 109.

CHAPTER 4

1. Kimble, review of *The Unquiet Earth*.
2. Bell, "When People Seek to Subdue the Land."
3. See, "No Happy Endings."
4. Review of *The Unquiet Earth*, *Publishers Weekly*.
5. Robinson, "Coal Miners' Daughter," 816–18.
6. Duke, "Two Appalachians," 62.
7. Giardina, *Unquiet Earth*, 116. In the rest of the chapter, quotations from this book are cited parenthetically.
8. Boudreau, "Fighting Back," 10.
9. Mooney, "Beyond Measure," 13.
10. Eliot, *Waste Land*, lines 115–16.
11. Eliot, *Waste Land*, lines 43, 55.
12. Mooney, "Beyond Measure," 9–10.
13. Giardina, "Appalachian Mirror."
14. Hickman, "What to Throw Away," 180–82.
15. Hickman, "What to Throw Away," 208.
16. For a fuller discussion of Dillon's formation, including this scene, see my "Individuation of Dillon Freeman."
17. Berry, Giardina, and Pancake. "The Role of Fiction in Activism."
18. Buell, *The Environmental Imagination*, 7–8.
19. Hickman, "What to Throw Away," 171–72.
20. John 15:13 (KJV).
21. The surname *Angelelli* will be familiar to readers of *Storming Heaven*. As Rachel notes, Tony's father and uncles were all killed in the Number Six explosion, and his psychotic grandmother stayed with his family until she was committed to the state asylum (25). He is, then, Rosa Angelelli's grandson. While *The Unquiet Earth* makes sense without this information, it does suggest, intertextually, why Carrie may be so correct in discerning that he is damaged. Even aside from the trauma of loss, readers will recall the brutal violence with which Tony's grandfather Mario treated his sons. It may not be too much to surmise that Tony, too, may have been treated in crippling ways. Finally, given the prejudice that comes so readily to mind in Flora, we may assume that being the object of racism is part of his wounding as well.
22. Douglass and Giardina, "Resurrecting the Dead," 32.
23. Locklear, *Negotiating a Perilous Empowerment*, 143.
24. Giardina told the *Washington Post*'s Elizabeth Kastor that the scene is based on a *48 Hours* segment hosted by Dan Rather in the 1990s.
25. For a perceptive discussion on the notion of *free space* in Giardina's coalfield novels, see Hickman, "What to Throw Away," 182ff.
26. Wilson, "Exchange of the Feminine," 99.
27. Mark 2:16 (KJV).
28. This concept is the focus of Bonhoeffer's most famous work, *The Cost of Discipleship*.
29. Jonah 1:10 (KJV).
30. Eads, "Industrialization's Threat," 69.
31. Mooney, "Beyond Measure," 9.
32. Eliot, "J. Alfred Prufrock," in *Complete Poems and Plays*, 7.

33. Genesis 6:6–7 (KJV).
34. Hickman, "What to Throw Away," 172.

CHAPTER 5

I thank the Faculty Development Committee of George Fox University for a course release that made possible the drafting of this chapter.
1. Giardina et al., "Perils of Regionalism," 26.
2. Brown, *Fiction and Faith*, 149.
3. Brown, *Fiction and Faith*, 156.
4. Giardina, "Reader's Guide," in *Saints and Villains*.
5. Shurbutt, "Words, Actions," 112.
6. Johnston, review of *Saints and Villains*.
7. Simon, "Moral Thriller."
8. Review of *Saints and Villains*, *Kirkus Reviews*.
9. Review of *Saints and Villains*, *Publishers Weekly*.
10. Slane, review of *Saints and Villains*.
11. Osborn, "Morality, Theology, and the Holocaust."
12. Hallsworth, review of *Saints and Villains*.
13. Carter, "Factual Fictions."
14. Baumann, "Executioner's Song."
15. Langer, "Martyred by the Nazis."
16. Review of *Saints and Villains*, *Publishers Weekly*, 37.
17. Carter, "Factual Fictions"; and Finn, "Fiction's Lens Enhances Dramatic True Story."
18. Giardina, "Afterword," in *Saints and Villains*, 485.
19. Congdon, "The Cost of Discipleship."
20. Brown, *Fiction and Faith*, 153.
21. Giardina, "Reader's Guide," in *Saints and Villains*.
22. Douglass and Giardina, "Resurrecting the Dead," 35.
23. Simon, "Moral Thriller."
24. McCarty, review of *Saints and Villains*.
25. Eads, "Industrialization's Threat," 56.
26. Giardina, *Saints and Villains*, 481. In the rest of the chapter, quotations from this book are cited parenthetically.
27. Review of *Saints and Villains*, *Publishers Weekly*, 37.
28. Langer, "Martyred by the Nazis."
29. For a different but complementary study of *call* in *Saints and Villains* and the earlier novels, see the two-part article by Pauline Cheek and Brian Cole, "The Call of Place in Denise Giardina's *Saints and Villains*," 22–30.
30. Bonhoeffer, *Cost of Discipleship*, 47.
31. Bonhoeffer, *Cost of Discipleship*, 99.
32. Eads, "Industrialization's Threat," 69.
33. Cole, "Bonhoeffer Today," 30.
34. Cole, "Bonhoeffer Today," 28.
35. Matthew 6:24 (KJV).
36. Giardina et al, "Perils of Regionalism," 30; Giardina, interview in *Still: The Journal*; House and Howard, *Something's Rising*, 53; and elsewhere.

37. Giardina, interview in *Still: The Journal*.
38. Giardina, *Storming Heaven*, 193.
39. Matthew 10:28–29 (KJV).

CHAPTER 6

1. Reid, review of *Fallam's Secret*, 230.
2. Friedman, "From Time to Time."
3. Zaleski, review of *Fallam's Secret*.
4. Friedman, "From Time to Time."
5. Bilton, review of *Fallam's Secret*, 116.
6. Review of *Fallam's Secret*, *Kirkus Reviews*.
7. Kubisz, review of *Fallam's Secret*, 1047.
8. Anderson, "Finding Fun."
9. Zaleski, review of *Fallam's Secret*.
10. Reid, review of *Fallam's Secret*, 228.
11. Eads, "Raising the Dead," 76.
12. Reid, review of *Fallam's Secret*, 228.
13. Giardina, *Fallam's Secret*, 270. In the rest of the chapter, quotations from this book are cited parenthetically.
14. Luke 4:16–30 (KJV).
15. Burke, *Counter-Statement*, 124.
16. Anderson, "Finding Fun."
17. Reid, review of *Fallam's Secret*, 229.
18. Newell, *Listening for the Heartbeat of God*, 13.
19. Eliade, *Sacred and Profane*, 20.
20. Eliade, *Sacred and Profane*, 11.
21. Weiner, "Heaven and Earth."
22. Newell, *Listening for the Heartbeat of God*, 24.
23. Newell, *Listening for the Heartbeat of God*, 66.
24. Wright, *Surprised by Hope*, 190.
25. Wright, *Paul: In Fresh Perspective*, 54.
26. Giardina, "Let Us Be Clear."

CHAPTER 7

1. Giardina, interview in *Still: The Journal*.
2. Quinn, review of *Emily's Ghost*, 18.
3. Piehl, review of *Emily's Ghost*.
4. Wyatt, "After 'The End': Fresh Takes."
5. Review of *Emily's Ghost*, *Publishers Weekly*.
6. Westmoore, "Brontës Go Gothic."
7. Holberg, "Chasing Emily."
8. Giardina and Holberg, "Chasing Emily Farther."
9. Holberg, "Chasing Emily."
10. Giardina and Holberg, "Chasing Emily Farther."
11. Holberg, "Chasing Emily."
12. Holberg, "Chasing Emily."

13. Giardina, "Reader's Guide," in *Saints and Villains*.
14. Giardina and Holberg, "Chasing Emily Farther."
15. Eads, "Raising the Dead," 76.
16. Eads, "Raising the Dead," 78.
17. Eads, "Raising the Dead," 75.
18. Giardina, *Emily's Ghost*, 23–24. In the rest of the chapter, all quotations from this book are cited parenthetically.
19. Holberg, "Chasing Emily."
20. Holberg, "Chasing Emily."
21. Giardina, *Good King Harry*, 323.
22. Giardina, *Storming Heaven*, 31.
23. Giardina, *Storming Heaven*, 133.
24. Giardina, *Saints and Villains*, 256.
25. Giardina, *Saints and Villains*, 256.
26. Giardina and Holberg, "Chasing Emily Farther."
27. Douglass and Giardina, "Resurrecting the Dead," 36.
28. House and Howard, *Something's Rising*, 47.
29. Giardina, "Allegiances," 63.
30. Woolman, "On the Keeping of Slaves."
31. Brown, *Fiction and Faith*, 153.
32. For a full discussion of this concept in Bonhoeffer's thinking, see Kelly, "'Unconscious Christianity' and the 'Anonymous Christian' in the Theology of Dietrich Bonhoeffer and Karl Rahner."
33. Giardina, *Unquiet Earth*, 114.
34. Giardina, *Unquiet Earth*, 127.
35. Giardina, "Allegiances," 63.
36. Giardina, interview in *Still: The Journal*.
37. Lindberg, "Challenging the Bullies" and "Ethical Inquiry"; and Shurbutt, "Words, Actions."
38. Shurbutt, "Words, Actions," 110 and throughout.
39. Cole, "Bonhoeffer Today," 30.
40. Bonhoeffer, *Cost of Discipleship*, 99.
41. Giardina, *Unquiet Earth*, 131.
42. Yeats, "The Second Coming," lines 7–8.
43. Giardina, *Storming Heaven*, 48.
44. Howard, "Beauty in Battered Places."
45. Giardina, *Unquiet Earth*, 84.
46. Douglass and Giardina, "Resurrecting the Dead," 33.
47. Byer et al., "Religion, the Sacred," 42.
48. Byer et al., "Religion, the Sacred," 42.
49. Giardina, *Fallam's Secret*, 318.
50. Giardina, *Storming Heaven*, 262.
51. Byer, et al., "Religion, the Sacred," 42.
52. Giardina, *Unquiet Earth*, 234.
53. Giardina, *Saints and Villains*, 480.
54. Brown, *Fiction and Faith*, 149.
55. For a full discussion of universal salvation in all Giardina's novels, see my "The Wide Reach of Salvation."

56. Giardina, *Fallam's Secret*, 228.
57. Giardina, *Fallam's Secret*, 228.

CHAPTER 8

1. Byer et al., "Religion, the Sacred," 41.
2. Harris, *When Miners March*, 402.
3. Byer et al., "Religion, the Sacred," 42.
4. Giardina, *Storming Heaven*, 48 (italics mine).
5. Wink, *Powers*, 24.
6. Wink, *Powers*, 24, 33.
7. Wink, *Powers*, 39.
8. Oder, "Mining History," 70.
9. King, "Long Night," 4.
10. King, "Long Night," 14.

Bibliography

Anderson, Belinda. "Denise Giardina: Finding Fun in a Time-Travel Romp." *BookPage* (March 2003). Accessed August 2, 2018. https://bookpage.com/interviews/8187-denise-giardina#.W2OelMknaYU.

Ballard, Sandra and Patricia Hudson. *Listen Here: Women Writing in Appalachia*. Lexington: University Press of Kentucky, 2003.

Barolini, Helen. *The Dream Book*. Rev. ed. Syracuse: Syracuse University Press, 2000.

Baumann, Paul. "Executioner's Song." Review of *Saints and Villains*, by Denise Giardina. *New York Times*, April 19, 1998. Accessed August 2, 2018. LexisNexis Academic.

Bell, Madison Smartt. "When People Seek to Subdue the Land." Review of *The Unquiet Earth*, by Denise Giardina. *Chicago Tribune*, May 10, 1992. Accessed August 2, 2018. http://articles.chicagotribune.com/1992-05-10/entertainment/9202110414_1_denise-giardina-miners-unquiet-earth.

Berry, Wendell, Denise Giardina, and Ann Pancake. "The Role of Fiction in Activism." Panel, Society of Environmental Journalists Annual Conference, Roanoke, VA, October 19, 2008. Accessed July 19, 2018. http://sej2008.typepad.com/files/SundayOpeningSession.mp3.

Bilton, Karen T. Review of *Fallam's Secret*. *Library Journal*, February 1, 2003.

Bonhoeffer, Dietrich. *The Cost of Discipleship*. Rev. ed. Translated by R. H. Fuller and Irmgard Booth. 1963. Reprint, New York: Macmillan, 1968.

Boudreau, Tim. "Fighting Back: Denise Giardina Talks about *Storming Heaven*." *Now and Then* 5, no. 1 (Spring 1988): 9–10.

Brown, W. Dale. "Denise Giardina: True Stories." In *Of Fiction and Faith: Twelve American Writers Talk about Their Vision and Work*, 147–58. Grand Rapids, MI: Eerdmans, 1997.

———. "True Stories: A Conversation with Denise Giardina." *Carolina Quarterly* 47, no. 1 (Fall 1994): 40–51.

Buckley, Jerome Hamilton. *Season of Youth: The Bildungsroman from Dickens to Golding*. Cambridge, MA: Harvard University Press, 1974.

Buell, Lawrence. *The Environmental Imagination: Thoreau, Nature Writing, and the Formation of American Culture*. Cambridge, MA: Belknap Press of Harvard University Press, 1995.

Burke, Kenneth. *Counter-Statement*. 2nd ed. Berkeley: University of California Press, 1968.

Burruel, Lydia. Review of *Good King Harry*, by Denise Giardina. *Library Journal*, April 1, 1984.

Byer, Kathryn Stripling, Fred Chappell, Denise Giardina, and Robert Morgan. "Religion, the Sacred, and the Appalachian Writer." *Iron Mountain Review* 23 (Spring 2007): 39–45.

Carlson, Peter. "Mountain Woman Is Out to Change Her World." *Washington Post*, October 25, 2000, final edition. Accessed August 1, 2018. LexisNexis Academic.

Carter, Betty Smartt. "Bonhoeffer: Factual Fictions." Review of *Saints and Villains*, by Denise Giardina. *Books and Culture*, September/October 1998. Accessed August 2, 2018. https://www.booksandculture.com/articles/1998/sepoct/8b5024.html.

Catechism of the Catholic Church. Accessed July 16, 2018. http://www.vatican.va/archive/ENG0015/__P81.HTM.

Chappell, Fred. Review of *Storming Heaven*, by Denise Giardina. *Los Angeles Times*, August 2, 1987. Accessed May 23, 2017. ProQuest Central.

Cheek, Pauline. "Whose Side Are You On?" *Iron Mountain Review* 15 (Spring 1999): 22–27.

Cheek, Pauline and Brian Cole. "The Call of Place in Denise Giardina's *Saints and Villains*." *Iron Mountain Review* 15 (Spring 1999): 22–30.

Cole, Brian. "Bonhoeffer Today." *Iron Mountain Review* 15 (Spring 1999): 28–30.

Congdon, Lee. "The Cost of Discipleship." *World and I* (June 1998). Accessed August 2, 2018. MasterFILE Premier.

Conn, H. M. "Liberation Theology." In *New Dictionary of Theology*, edited by Sinclair B. Ferguson and David F. Wright, 387–391. Downers Grove: InterVarsity Press, 1988.

Conway, Cecelia. "Slashing the Homemade Quilt in Denise Giardina's *Storming Heaven*." *NWSA Journal* 11, no. 3 (1999): 138–55.

Corbin, David Alan. *Life, Work, and Rebellion in the Coal Fields*. Urbana: University of Illinois Press, 1981.

———. "The Mine Wars." In *e-WV: West Virginia Encyclopedia*. West Virginia Humanities Council. Accessed August 1, 2018. https://www.wvencyclopedia.org/articles/1799.

Creasman, Boyd. "Denise Giardina's *Storming Heaven*." In *Writing West Virginia: Place, People, and Poverty in Contemporary Literature from the Mountain State*, 71–87. Knoxville: University of Tennessee Press, 2016.

Dirlam, Sharon. "Great Figures, Grand Figments." Review of *Good King Harry*, by Denise Giardina. *Los Angeles Times*, July 15, 1984.

Dorgan, Howard. *In the Hands of a Happy God: The "No-Hellers" of Central Appalachia*. Knoxville: University of Tennessee Press, 1997.

Douglass, Thomas and Denise Giardina. "Resurrecting the Dead, Recognizing the Human: A Conversation." *Iron Mountain Review* 15 (Spring 1999): 31–38.

Duke, David C. "Two Appalachians: Don West and Denise Giardina." In *Writers and Miners: Activism and Imagery in America*, 46–66. Lexington: University of Kentucky Press, 2002.

Dyson, R. W. "Introduction" to *Aquinas: Political Writings*, edited by R. W. Dyson, xvii–xxxvi. Cambridge Texts in the History of Political Thought. Cambridge: Cambridge University Press, 2002. EBSCO eBook. Adobe PDF.

Eads, Martha Greene. "Industrialization's Threat to Vocational Calling in Denise Giardina's *Storming Heaven*." *Appalachian Journal* 39, nos. 1–2 (Fall 2011 / Winter 2012): 56–70.

———. "Raising the Dead in Denise Giardina's Appalachian Fiction." *Christianity and Literature* 63, no. 1 (Autumn 2013): 75–87.

Easton, Terry. "Class and Identity in Denise Giardina's *Storming Heaven*." In *An American Vein: Critical Readings in Appalachian Literature*, edited by Danny L. Miller, Sharon Hatfield, and Gurney Norman, 296–305. Athens: Ohio University Press, 2005.

Eliade, Mircea. *The Sacred and the Profane: The Nature of Religion*. Translated by Willard R. Trask. San Diego: Harcourt Brace Jovanovich, 1959.

Eliot, T. S. *The Complete Poems and Plays, 1909–1950*. New York: Harcourt and World, 1952.
Eller, Ronald. "Industrialization and Social Change in Appalachia, 1880–1930." In *Colonialism in Modern America: The Appalachian Case*, edited by Helen Lewis, Linda Johnson, and Donald Askins, 35–45. Boone, NC: Appalachian Consortium Press, 1978.
Eller, Ronald D. *Miners, Millhands, and Mountaineers: Industrialization of the Appalachian South, 1880–1930*. Knoxville: University of Tennessee Press, 1982.
Finn, Robert. "Fiction's Lens Enhances Dramatic True Story." Review of *Saints and Villains*, by Denise Giardina. *Cleveland Plain Dealer*, April 19, 1998.
Friedman, Michael Shannon. "From Time to Time." Review of *Fallam's Secret*, by Denise Giardina. *Sunday Gazette* (Charleston), March 9, 2003. Accessed August 2, 2018. ProQuest Central.
Giardina, Denise. "About Denise Giardina." Internet Archives Wayback Machine. Accessed August 1, 2018. http://web.archive.org/web/20110709012722/denisegiardina.com/about.htm.
———. "Allegiances." *Iron Mountain Review* 23 (Spring 2007): 63.
———. "Appalachian Images: A Personal History." In *Back Talk from Appalachia: Confronting Stereotypes*, edited by Dwight B. Billings, Gurney Norman, and Katherine Ledford, 161–73. Lexington: University Press of Kentucky, 1999.
———. "Appalachian Mirror." *New York Times*, October 31, 1992. Accessed May 6, 2016. Academic OneFile.
———. "Coalfield Ancestors." *Iron Mountain Review* 15 (Spring 1999): 4–8.
———. *Emily's Ghost*. New York: W. W. Norton, 2009.
———. *Fallam's Secret*. New York: W. W. Norton, 2003.
———. Foreword to *Thunder on the Mountain*, by Peter A. Galuszka, xv–xxi. Morgantown: West Virginia University Press, 2014.
———. *Good King Harry*. 1984. Reprint, New York: Fawcett/Ballantine, 1999.
———. Interview by Thomas Douglass. *Appalachian Journal* 20, no. 4 (Summer 1993): 384–93.
———. Interview in *Still: The Journal* 15 (Summer 2014). Accessed May 6, 2016. http://www.stilljournal.net/interview-denisegiardina.php.
———. "Let Us Be Clear." *Charleston Gazette*, May 22, 2007. Accessed September 29, 2017. http://ohvec.org/links/news/archive/2007/fair_use/05_22.html.
———. "No Scapin the Booger Man." In *Bloodroot: Reflections on Place by Appalachian Women Writers*, edited by Joyce Dyer, 128–31. Lexington: University Press of Kentucky, 1998.
———, David Huddle, Sharyn McCrumb, Gurney Norman, and Lee Smith. "The Perils of Regionalism: Labels and Their Limitations." *Iron Mountain Review* 23 (Spring 2007): 25–31.
———. *Saints and Villains*. 1998. Reprint, New York: Fawcett Books, 1999.
———. *Storming Heaven*. 1987. Reprint, New York: Ivy/Ballantine, 1988.
———. *The Unquiet Earth*. 1992. Reprint, New York: Ivy/Ballantine, 1994.
Giardina, Denise and Jennifer Holberg. "Chasing Emily Farther: An Exchange between Denise Giardina and Jennifer Holberg." *Books and Culture Online*, September 2009. Accessed August 3, 2018. https://www.booksandculture.com/articles/webexclusives/2009/september/chasingemilyfarther.html.

Gillespie, Kim. "Storming Heaven in the Decade of Greed." *Journal of Appalachian Studies* 7 (1995): 101–110.
Giunta, Edvige. *Writing with an Accent: Contemporary Italian American Women Authors*. New York: Palgrave, 2002.
Gutiérrez, Gustavo. *Teología de la liberación: perspectivas*. Lima, Peru: CEP, 1971. Translated and edited by Sister Caridad Inda and John Eagleson as *A Theology of Liberation* (Maryknoll, NY: Orbis Books, 1973).
Hallsworth, Caroline M. Review of *Saints and Villains*, by Denise Giardina. *Library Journal*, March 1, 1998. Accessed September 26, 2016. Academic OneFile.
Harris, Wess. "Appendix 3: Relevant Literature Review." In *When Miners March*, by William C. Blizzard, 401–407. Oakland, CA: PM Press, 2010.
Hickman, Carolyn Neale. "What to Throw Away/What to Keep: Mobilizing Expressive Culture and Regional Reconstruction in Appalachia." PhD diss., University of North Carolina at Chapel Hill, 1998.
Hirsch, Marianne. "The Novel of Formation as Genre: Between Great Expectations and Lost Illusions." *Genre* 12 (Fall 1979): 293–311.
Holberg, Jennifer. "Chasing Emily: The Latest Entry in the Brontë Family Sweepstakes." *Books and Culture Online*, September 2009. Accessed August 3, 2018. https://www.booksandculture.com/articles/webexclusives/2009/september/chasingemily.html.
Horton, Myles. "The Adventures of a Radical Hillbilly." Interview by Bill Moyers. *Bill Moyers Journal*, PBS. June 5, 1981. Accessed May 23, 2019. https://www.youtube.com/watch?v=qSwW0zc-QBQ&t=3017s.
House, Silas and Jason Howard. *Something's Rising: Appalachians Fighting Mountaintop Removal*. Lexington: University Press of Kentucky, 2009.
Howard, Jason. "Beauty in Battered Places." *Sojourners Magazine*, June 2014. Accessed August 1, 2018. ProQuest Central.
———. "A Conversation with Denise Giardina." *Appalachian Heritage* 36, no. 4 (Fall 2016). Accessed May 23, 2017. http://appalachianheritage.net/2016/11/04/a-conversation-with-denise-giardina/.
Johnston, Bonnie. Review of *Saints and Villains*, by Denise Giardina. *Booklist*, February 15, 1998. Accessed September 23, 2016. Academic OneFile.
Jolliff, William. "The Individuation of Dillon Freeman: Images of Regeneration in Denise Giardina's *The Unquiet Earth*." *Literature and Belief* 33, no. 2 (2013): 77–97.
———. "The Wide Reach of Salvation: Christian Universalism in the Novels of Denise Giardina." *Renascence* 68, no. 2 (Spring 2016): 93–114.
Kastor, Elizabeth. "From the Heart of Appalachia." *Washington Post*, June 16, 1992. Accessed May 6, 2016. LexisNexis.
Kelly, Geffrey B. "'Unconscious Christianity' and the 'Anonymous Christian' in the Theology of Dietrich Bonhoeffer and Karl Rahner." *Philosophy and Theology* 9, no. 1/2 (1995): 117–49.
Kilpatrick, Thomas L. Review of *Storming Heaven*, by Denise Giardina. *Library Journal*, July 1987.
Kimble, Cary. Review of *The Unquiet Earth*, by Denise Giardina. *New York Times Book Review*, August 30, 1992.
King, Martin Luther, Jr. "I've Been to the Mountaintop." In *Martin Luther King, Jr. Encyclopedia*. Accessed August 2, 2018. https://kinginstitute.stanford.edu

/king-papers/documents/ive-been-mountaintop-address-delivered-bishop-charles-mason-temple.

———. "Out of the Long Night." *Gospel Messenger*, February 8, 1958. Accessed August 6, 2018. https://archive.org/details/gospelmessengerv107mors. PDF.

Kubisz, Carolyn. Review of *Fallam's Secret*, by Denise Giardina. *Booklist*, February 15, 2003.

Langer, Elinor. "Martyred by the Nazis." Review of *Saints and Villains*, by Denise Giardina. *Oregonian*, March 22, 1998.

Lewis, Helen and Edward E. Knipe. "The Colonialism Model: The Appalachian Case." In *Colonialism in Modern America: The Appalachian Case*, edited by Helen Lewis, Linda Johnson, and Donald Askins, 9–31. Boone, NC: Appalachian Consortium Press, 1978.

Lewis, Helen, Linda Johnson, and Donald Askins, eds. *Colonialism in Modern America: The Appalachian Case*. Boone, NC: Appalachian Consortium Press, 1978.

Lindberg, Laurie. "Denise Giardina: Challenging the Bullies of Appalachia." *Iron Mountain Review* 15 (Spring 1999): 15–21.

———. "An Ethical Inquiry into the Works of Denise Giardina." In *Culture and Custom*, edited by Robert J. Higgs, Ambrose N. Manning, and Jim Wayne Miller, 664–672. Vol. 2, *Appalachia Inside Out*. Knoxville: University of Tennessee Press, 1995.

Locklear, Erica Abrams. *Negotiating a Perilous Empowerment: Appalachian Women's Literacies*. Athens: Ohio University Press, 2011.

McCarty, Patty. Review of *Saints and Villains*, by Denise Giardina. *National Catholic Reporter*, May 22, 1998. Accessed September 26, 2016. Academic OneFile.

Mooney, Stephen. "'Beyond Measure': An Appreciation of Denise Giardina's *Storming Heaven* and *The Unquiet Earth*." *Iron Mountain Review* 15 (Spring 1999): 9–14.

Moyers, Bill and Myles Horton. "The Adventures of a Radical Hillbilly: An Interview with Myles Horton." *Appalachian Journal* 9, no. 4 (Summer 1982): 248–85. Accessed August 6, 2018. http://www.jstor.org/stable/40932454.

Newell, J. Philip. *Listening for the Heartbeat of God*. Mahwah, NJ: Paulist Press, 1997.

Nichols, John. "A Novelist Runs for Governor." *The Progressive*, November 2000. Accessed August 1, 2018. EBSCOhost.

Niebuhr, Reinhold. "Why the Christian Church Is Not Pacifist." In *The Essential Reinhold Niebuhr*, edited by Robert McAfee Brown, 102–19. New Haven: Yale University Press, 1986.

Oder, Norman. "Mining History in W.Va. and WWII." *Publishers Weekly*, February 9, 1998.

Osborn, Susan. "Morality, Theology, and the Holocaust." Review of *Saints and Villains*, by Denise Giardina. *Washington Post*, April 16, 1998. Accessed August 2, 2018. LexisNexis Academic.

Piehl, Kathy. Review of *Emily's Ghost*, by Denise Giardina. *Library Journal*, June 1, 2009. Accessed September 9, 2016. Academic OneFile.

Quigley, Linda. "Fiction Recreates Miners' Plight." Review of *Storming Heaven*, by Denise Giardina. *Tennessean*, August 16, 1987.

Quinn, Mary Ellen. Review of *Emily's Ghost*, by Denise Giardina. *Booklist*, May 15, 2009.

Rash, Ron. "The Importance of Place." Rusoff Agency. Accessed May 6, 2016. http://www.rusoffagency.com/authors/rash_r/ron_rash_onwriting.htm.

Reid, Robert L. Review of *Fallam's Secret*, by Denise Giardina. *Appalachian Journal* 30, no. 2/3 (Winter–Spring 2003): 228–30.

Review of *Emily's Ghost*, by Denise Giardina. *Publishers Weekly*, March 16, 2009. Accessed September 13, 2016. Academic OneFile.

Review of *Fallam's Secret*, by Denise Giardina. *Kirkus Reviews*. Accessed August 2, 2018. https://www.kirkusreviews.com/book-reviews/denise-giardina/fallams-secret/.

Review of *Good King Harry*, by Denise Giardina. *Kirkus Reviews*. Accessed August 1, 2018. https://www.kirkusreviews.com/book-reviews/denise-giardina-4/good-king-harry/.

Review of *Saints and Villains*, by Denise Giardina. *Kirkus Reviews*. Accessed July 30, 2018. https://www.kirkusreviews.com/book-reviews/denise-giardina/saints-and-villains/.

Review of *Saints and Villains*, by Denise Giardina. *Publishers Weekly*, December 22, 1997. Accessed September 26, 2016. Academic OneFile.

Review of *Storming Heaven*, by Denise Giardina. *Publishers Weekly*, August 4, 1987. Accessed August 3, 2018. https://www.publishersweekly.com/978-0-393-02440-1.

Review of *The Unquiet Earth*, by Denise Giardina. *Publishers Weekly*, March 16, 1992. Accessed August 2, 2018. http://link.galegroup.com/apps/doc/A12090021/PROF?u=newb64238&sid=PROF&xid=1397ae44.

Robinson, Lillian. "Coal Miners' Daughter." *Nation*, December 28, 1992.

Ruberto, Laura E. *Gramsci, Migration, and the Representation of Women's Work in Italy and the U.S.* Lanham, MD: Lexington Books, 2007.

Sanders, Adam. "Mimetic Transformations of Sacred Symbols: Christianity in Appalachian Literature." Master's thesis, East Tennessee State University, 2005.

Sanks, T. Howland. "Liberation Theology and the Social Gospel: Variations on a Theme." *Theological Studies* 41, no. 4 (1980): 668–82.

Savage, Lon. *Thunder in the Mountains*. Pittsburgh, PA: University of Pittsburgh Press, 1990.

See, Carolyn. "No Happy Endings in Coal Mining Tale." Review of *The Unquiet Earth*, by Denise Giardina. *Los Angeles Times*, June 29, 1992. Accessed August 2, 2018. ProQuest Central.

Shurbutt, Sylvia Bailey. "Words, Actions, and 'Resurrecting Home': The Fiction of Denise Giardina and the Ethical Imperative." *Journal of Kentucky Studies* 22 (2005): 110–15.

Simon, Clea. "*Saints* Is a Moral Thriller." Review of *Saints and Villains*, by Denise Giardina. *Boston Globe*, April 10, 1998. Accessed October 12, 2016. ProQuest.

Slane, Craig J. Review of *Saints and Villains*, by Denise Giardina. *Christian Century* 115, no. 20 (1998): 697. Accessed September 26, 2016. Academic OneFile.

Taylor, Bron. "Authority in Ethics: A Portrait of the Methodology of Sojourners Fellowship." *Encounter* 46, no. 2 (Spring 1985): 133–56.

Thoreau, Henry David. "Civil Disobedience." In *The Writings of Henry David Thoreau*, edited by H. G. O. Blake. Boston: Houghton-Mifflin, 1906. Accessed August 4, 2018. http://xroads.virginia.edu/~hyper2/thoreau/civil.html.

Tritel, Barbara. Review of *Good King Harry*, by Denise Giardina. *New York Times*, July 29, 1984. Accessed August 1, 2018, ProQuest Central.

Weiner, Eric. "Where Heaven and Earth Come Closer." *New York Times*, March 9,

2012. Accessed August 2, 2018. https://www.nytimes.com/2012/03/11/travel/thin-places-where-we-are-jolted-out-of-old-ways-of-seeing-the-world.html.

Wells, Sandy. "Innerviews: The Mountains Haunt Me." *Charleston Gazette*, February 3, 2014. Accessed August 1, 2018. Proquest Central.

Westmoore, Jean. "The Brontës Go Gothic in *Emily's Ghost*." Review of *Emily's Ghost*, by Denise Giardina. *Buffalo News*, July 21, 2009, central edition.

Wilson, David E. (Woody). "Exchange of the Feminine: Representations of Multiple Marginality in Contemporary West Virginia Fiction." PhD diss., West Virginia University, 2018.

Wink, Walter. *The Powers That Be: Theology for a New Millennium*. New York: Galilee Doubleday, 1998.

Woolman, John. "On the Keeping of Slaves." 1744. In *A Library of American Literature: An Anthology in Eleven Volumes*, vol. 3, *Literature of the Revolutionary Period, 1765-1787*, edited by E. C. Stedman and E. M. Hutchinson. New York: Charles L. Webster and Company, 1891. Accessed August 3, 2018. https://www.bartleby.com/400/prose/383.html.

Wright, N. T. *Paul: In Fresh Perspective*. Minneapolis: Fortress Press, 2009.

———. *Surprised by Hope*. New York: Harper One, 2008.

Wyatt, Neal. "After 'The End': Fresh Takes on Beloved Classics." *Library Journal*, May 5, 2011. Accessed September 13, 2016. Academic Search Premier.

Yeats, W. B. *W. B. Yeats: The Poems*. Edited by Richard J. Finneran. New York: Macmillan, 1983.

Zaleski, Jeff. Review of *Fallam's Secret*, by Denise Giardina. *Publishers Weekly*, February 17, 2003. Accessed August 2, 2018. EBSCOhost.

Index

afterlife, 180–81
  See also heaven
"Allegiances" (Giardina), 16
Anderson, Belinda, 140, 148
Anglican Church, 4, 14
anima/animus, 44, 151
Animal Farm (Orwell), 3
Antigone (Sophocles), 178
apocalypse, 110–11
Appalachia
  dialects, 55–56, 86–87
  Giardina as Appalachian novelist, 7–12, 112, 185–86
  Giardina as theological novelist, 15
  Giardina biography, 1, 2, 6, 7
  Giardina themes, 185–88
  resistance, 90
  stereotypes, 55, 91, 102–3
  in *Storming Heaven*, 50, 53–56, 59, 67, 71, 74–75
  in *The Unquiet Earth*, 86–87, 89, 95, 102, 103, 110–11
Appalachian fiction, 59, 71, 172, 185–88
Arnow, Harriette, 59

Ballard, Sandra, 21
Barolini, Helen, 68, 69, 194n33
Battle of Blair Mountain, 8, 51, 52–53, 83, 85, 186
Baumann, Paul, 114
Becket, Thomas, 120
Bell, Madison Smartt, 84
benevolent repression, 61, 105
Bethge, Eberhard, 117
Bible
  in *Fallam's Secret*, 141–42, 144
  Giardina childhood, 3
  Giardina themes, 189
  in *Good King Harry*, 39, 46
  in *Saints and Villains*, 132–34
  in *Storming Heaven*, 75, 76, 77
  in *Unquiet Earth, The*, 87, 92, 110

bildungsroman (novel of development), 23–33, 48
Bilton, Karen T., 140
Blair Mountain, Battle of, 8, 51, 52–53, 83, 85, 186
Blizzard, Bill, 193n10
bone imagery, 87–88
Bonhoeffer, Dietrich
  call to action, 174, 176
  Cost of Discipleship, The, 121, 122
  influence on Giardina, 169
  legacy, 114
  Letters and Papers from Prison, 115, 169
  radical discipleship, 108, 122, 185
  in *Saints and Villains*, 8, 17, 113–20, 121–29, 130–38, 162, 166
  in *The Unquiet Earth*, 108–9, 122
Boudreau, Tim, 12, 14, 52, 86, 194n39
Brontë, Emily
  in *Emily's Ghost*, 160–68, 170–79, 180–81
  Wuthering Heights, 60, 160, 163, 166
Brontë sisters, 9, 160
  in *Emily's Ghost*, 160–61, 166, 173, 177, 181–82
Brown, W. Dale, 10, 18, 21, 52, 112, 181
Bryner, Jeanne, 59
Buckley, Jerome Hamilton, 23, 24, 32
Buell, Lawrence, 94, 97
Buffalo Creek flood, 8, 85, 96
Burke, Kenneth, 145
Burruel, Lydia, 21, 32

call, the
  conceptions of call, 121–23
  in *Emily's Ghost*, 174–76
  fulfilling the call, 137–38
  Giardina themes, 190
  in *Good King Harry*, 34, 35
  heeding the call, 121–37
  questioning the call, 130–37
  in *Saints and Villains*, 121–38

call, the (continued)
  in *Storming Heaven*, 76
  in *The Unquiet Earth*, 109–10
Calvinism, 80
capitalism, 12, 13, 40–42, 53, 54, 66, 89
Carter, Betty Smartt, 114
Catholicism, 69, 73, 108, 109, 193n23
Celtic spirituality, 144, 152–58
Chappell, Fred, 50, 185, 186
cheap grace, 121–22
child narrators, 101
chivalry, 42
Christ, Jesus, 97, 126, 128, 137–38, 141–42, 144, 174–75, 178
Christianity
  American Christianity, 127, 128
  Celtic spirituality, 152–56
  Christian and theological writers, 18–19, 112–13
  Christian Universalism, 80–83, 195n60
  deep Christianity, 168–70
  in *Emily's Ghost*, 168–70, 178–81
  in *Fallam's Secret*, 141–44, 152–56
  fundamentalism, 15, 17, 71–72, 80–81, 106–7, 127–28
  Giardina as theological novelist, 14–20, 112–13, 185–89
  Giardina themes, 190
  in *Good King Harry*, 32–33, 35–40, 42–46
  liberation theology, 73–79, 81, 108–9, 195n47
  missionaries, 15
  in *Saints and Villains*, 121–22, 126–30, 138
  in *Storming Heaven*, 71–75, 83
  universal salvation, 181–83, 188, 199n55
  in *The Unquiet Earth*, 106, 107, 108
Church
  institutional Church, 35–38
  and nationalism, 126, 129
  oppositional Church, 38–40
  patriarchy, 153
  and state, 126, 127, 129, 187
Cincinnatus, 65
Clarke, Arthur C., 146
class concerns, 9, 172–73, 188
"Coalfield Ancestors" (Giardina), 67

coalfield novels, 5, 12, 51, 112, 186, 196n25
  See also Storming Heaven; Unquiet Earth, The
coal mining
  activism, 5, 6–7
  Giardina as Appalachian novelist, 7–8, 9
  Giardina as political novelist, 12, 13
  Giardina biography, 1, 2, 3
  Giardina themes, 185, 186
  in *Storming Heaven*, 50–55, 58–59, 62, 64–70, 71–83
  in *The Unquiet Earth*, 85–88, 89–106
Cole, Brian, 126, 174
colonization of the coalfields
  economic and ideological colonizers, 15
  in *Storming Heaven*, 53–55, 58–59, 62, 65–66, 73–75
  in *The Unquiet Earth*, 85, 89–106
Congdon, Lee, 115
Conn, H. M., 74
Conway, Cecelia, 12, 58, 59, 72, 194n39
Corbin, David, 52, 71, 72, 76, 77
costly grace, 121, 122, 130
Country of the Pointed Firs (Jewett), 11
Creasman, Boyd, 195n50
creation, 156

death, 162–63, 170, 172, 174, 180, 181
deep Christianity, 168–70
deep regionalism, 9, 10, 11
dialects, 55–56, 86–87
Dirlam, Sharon, 21
doppelgängers, 117–18, 137, 138
Dorgan, Howard, 81, 195n59
Douglass, Thomas, 3, 83
Dykeman, Wilma, 59
Dyson, R. W., 34

Eads, Martha Greene, 64, 109, 116, 163, 195n51
Easton, Terry, 13, 62, 194–95n39
egalitarianism, 12, 183
Eliade, Mircea, 155
Eliot, T. S.
  "Love Song of J. Alfred Prufrock, The," 110
  Murder in the Cathedral, 120, 177

in *Saints and Villains*, 120–21, 162
Waste Land, The, 87, 88, 89
Eller, Ronald, 54, 55
Emily's Ghost (Giardina), 160–84
  Giardina as Appalachian novelist, 8, 9
  Giardina as political novelist, 13
  Giardina as theological novelist, 188
  and Giardina hero, 167–84
  from history to fiction, 161–62
  mystery, 180, 181, 183
  overview, 160
  publication, 7
  reviews, 160, 161–62, 163
  understanding the voices, 162–67
environmental works, 94, 158–59
Episcopal Church, 4, 14, 71, 80
Eriugena, John Scotus, 155, 156
eschatology, inaugurated, 142, 144
eternal, the, 180
ethical questions, 13, 14, 172–74, 184
ethnic diversity, 67
exclusive salvation, 182–83

failure, 48–49, 178–79
Fall, the, 83
Fallam's Secret (Giardina), 139–59
  appearance and reality, 144–48
  Celtic spirituality, 152–58
  Fallam's sermon, 141–44
  gender questions, 148–52
  Giardina as Appalachian novelist, 8
  Giardina as political novelist, 13
  Giardina as theological novelist, 187–88
  and Giardina hero, 168, 180, 182
  Giardina's sermon, 158–59
  overview, 139–41
  publication, 7
  reviews, 139–40
Falwell, Jerry, 16, 128
female characters, 59–60, 167–68
  See also gender complexity; women's roles
fiction, and history
  Emily's Ghost, 161–62
  Good King Harry, 22–23
  Saints and Villains, 114–17
  Storming Heaven, 51–55
  Unquiet Earth, The, 85–86
Fisher, Frank, 116, 124

form, literary
  definition, 144–45
  Storming Heaven, 55–70
  Unquiet Earth, The, 86–89
free space, 196n25
Friedman, Michael Shannon, 140
fundamentalism, 15, 17, 71–72, 80–81, 106–7, 127–28

ganymedes, 147
Garrett, George, 5
Gaventa, John, 89
gender complexity
  in *Emily's Ghost*, 173–75, 177, 178
  in *Fallam's Secret*, 141, 147, 148–52, 153
  Giardina as theological novelist, 188
  in *Storming Heaven*, 60–61
Germany, 8, 116, 126, 129–30, 131, 132, 134
ghosts, 162–66
Giardina, Denise
  as Appalachian novelist, 7–12, 112, 185–86
  biographical overview, xii, 1–20
  birth, 1
  career, 4, 5–6
  childhood, 2–4, 100–101
  on Christianity, 178–79
  education, 3–4
  governor candidacy, 6–7, 158
  on landscape as character, 93
  major themes, 185–89
  on mountaintop removal, 159
  ordination, 4, 191n27
  political activism, 4, 6–7, 12–14, 158–59, 186–87, 190
  as political novelist, 12–14, 186–87
  regionalism, 112, 187
  on religion, 80, 178–79, 181
  religious background, 4–5
  as theological novelist, xi, 14–20, 112–13, 185–89
  view on writing, 34, 101
  See also "Allegiances"; "Coalfield Ancestors"; *Emily's Ghost*; *Fallam's Secret*; *Good King Harry*; *Saints and Villains*; *Storming Heaven*; *Unquiet Earth, The*

Giardina, Dennis (DG's father), 1, 3
Giardina, Leona (DG's mother), 1–2, 4
Giardina, Sam (DG's grandfather), 1
Giunta, Edvige, 68
Goldman, Laurel, 5
Good King Harry (Giardina), 21–49
   child narrator, 101
   coming to terms with failure, 48–49
   ghostly voices, 166
   Giardina as Appalachian novelist, 8, 9
   Giardina as political novelist, 13
   Giardina as theological novelist, 187
   and Giardina hero, 167, 176, 177
   from history to fiction, 22–23
   institutional Church, 35–38
   limitations of mortality, 46–48
   as novel of development, 23–33, 48
   as novel of ideas, 33–48
   oppositional Church, 38–40
   overview, 21
   radical Christian devotion, 42–46
   rise of capitalism, 40–42
   success of, 50
   writing of, 3, 5, 20
grace, 121–22
grief, 165–66
Gutiérrez, Gustavo, 73, 185

Hallsworth, Caroline M., 114
Harding, Warren G., 53
Harris, Wess, 186
Hawks Nest Tunnel disaster, 8, 115, 116–17, 125, 132, 146
Hawthorne, Nathaniel, 163, 166, 170
heaven, 80–81, 155, 158, 171, 180–82
hell, 80, 81, 182
Henry V (Shakespeare), 22, 147
hero figures, 167–84
   call to action, 174–76
   deep Christianity, 168–70
   ethical commitment, 172–74
   mystery, 179–81
   overview, 167–84
   passionate courage, 177–79
   relationship with place, 170–72
   universal salvation, 181–83
Hickman, Carolyn Neale, 91
Hirsch, Marianne, 23, 48

historical fiction, 5, 51, 139
history, and fiction
   Emily's Ghost, 161–62
   Good King Harry, 22–23
   Saints and Villains, 114–17
   Storming Heaven, 51–55
   Unquiet Earth, The, 85–86
Hitler, Adolf, 128, 129, 130–31, 132, 135, 136
Holberg, Jennifer L., 161–62, 163–64, 166
homosexuality, 105, 109
Horton, Myles, 116, 194n29
House, Silas, 168
Howard, Jason, 73, 168, 178
Hudson, Patricia, 21

idolatry, 129
immigration, 67–70, 194n33
inaugurated eschatology, 142, 144
incest, 91
inclusive communitarianism, 106
institutional Church, 35–38, 71
Iona Community, 154, 155
Ireland, 154, 155
Italian immigrants, 68–70, 194n33

James, Henry, *Turn of the Screw, The*, 163
Jefferson, Thomas, 65
Jesus. *See* Christ, Jesus
Jewett, Sarah Orne, 11, 56
Johnston, Bonnie, 113
Jones, Loyal, 15
Jubilee year, 142, 143
justice, 82, 83, 142, 183, 190
Just War theology, 36, 37, 43, 45

Kentuckians for the Commonwealth, 5
Kilpatrick, Thomas L., 50
Kimble, Cary, 84
King, Martin Luther, Jr., 16, 79, 109, 128, 190
Kingdom of God, 142–44, 155, 158, 159, 180
Kropotkin, Peter, 12, 58
Kubisz, Carolyn, 140

labyrinth motif, 157
landscape as character, 93–97, 170

Langer, Elinor, 114
language, and dialects, 22, 55–56, 86–87
Lewis, Rev. Jim, 4, 5
liberation theology, 73–79, 81, 108–9, 195n47
Lindberg, Laurie, 13, 172, 195n39
local color writing, 10, 11, 55–56, 80, 86
Lollards, 38–40
"Love Song of J. Alfred Prufrock, The" (Eliot), 110

MacLeod, George, 155
Marxism, 73, 74–75, 78
McCarty, Patty, 116
McDowell County, 1, 2, 3, 7, 10
Methodism, 3, 4, 14, 80
mining. *See* coal mining
missionaries, 15
Mooney, Stephen, 56, 59, 73, 87, 88–89, 110, 195n39
mortality, 46–48, 49, 172
Mountain Party, 6, 158
mountains
 importance of, 10, 93–97, 156, 157, 170
 mountaintop removal, 95, 156, 157, 158, 159
 mountain woman figure, 59
Mozart, Wolfgang Amadeus, 118–20, 137
multiple points of view, 57–70, 86
Murder in the Cathedral (Eliot), 120, 177
Murfree, Mary Noailles, 11
musical motifs, 118–20, 137, 178, 181
mutual aid, 58
mystery, 18–19, 95, 107, 148, 179–81, 188

Narrative of the Life of Frederick Douglass, 72
nationalism, 126–28, 129–30
Nazism, 116, 119, 128, 129, 130, 131
Newell, J. Philip, 153, 156
Niebuhr, Reinhold, 45–46, 79, 116, 124, 132, 185
Niemöller, Martin, 129, 130–31
No-Hellers, 80–81, 82, 181
nonviolence, 43, 78, 126, 131, 190
novel of development (bildungsroman), 23–33, 48
novel of formation, 23, 48
novel of ideas, 32, 33–48

O'Connor, Flannery, 11, 17
Oder, Thomas, 189
oppositional Church, 38–40
oppression, 73–75
original sin, 38, 48
Orwell, George, *Animal Farm*, 3
Osborn, Susan, 114
othering, 15, 55–57, 86, 102, 183, 188

pacifism, 46, 131, 132
Paint Creek–Cabin Creek strike, 51, 52, 76
Pancake, Ann, 59
panentheism, 155–56
pantheism, 96, 155
paradox, 19
Parker, Theodore, 190
patriotism, 127, 129, 130
Paul, Saint, 46, 49, 188
Pelagius, 153
Piehl, Kathy, 160
Piers Plowman, 25–26
Pittston Coal Company, 85, 96
place, importance of, 93–97, 170–72, 179–80
plays within plays, 120–21, 177
points of view, 57–70, 86
political activism, 4, 6–7, 12–14, 158–59, 186–87, 190
poverty
 Giardina as Appalachian novelist, 9
 Giardina biography, 3
 in *Good King Harry*, 32, 43
 in *Storming Heaven*, 68, 77
 in *The Unquiet Earth*, 86, 102, 103
power, 13, 14, 32, 34, 41, 43, 77
preternatural phenomena, 34, 122, 126, 146, 162–63, 165–67
principalities and powers, 189, 190

Quakerism, 1, 151, 153, 169
Quigley, Linda, 50
Quinn, Mary Ellen, 160

race issues, 66–67, 68, 116
radical Christian devotion, 42–46
Rash, Ron, 10
regionalism, 7, 8–11, 110, 112, 186, 187
Reid, Robert L., 139, 140

religion
    afterlife, 181
    Appalachian fiction, 185
    Christian Universalism, 80–83, 195n60
    in *Emily's Ghost*, 179, 181–83
    in *Fallam's Secret*, 141–44
    fundamentalism, 15, 17, 71–72, 80–81, 106–7, 127–28
    Giardina as Appalachian novelist, 9
    Giardina as theological novelist, 14–20, 112–13, 185–89
    Giardina childhood, 3, 4
    in *Good King Harry*, 29–30, 32–33, 35–40
    in *Storming Heaven*, 69, 70, 71–83
    universal salvation, 181–83, 188, 199n55
    in *The Unquiet Earth*, 106–10
    See also Christianity; spirituality; theology
religionless Christianity, 169
religious left, 75
religious right, 16, 106, 127, 128, 168, 179
rights, 66, 67
Robertson, Pat, 16, 106, 112, 128
Robinson, Lilian S., 84
romance, 148

sacred places, 155
Saints and Villains (Giardina), 112–38
    aspects of literary form, 117–21
    conceptions of call, 121–23
    doppelgängers, 117–18
    fulfilling the call, 137–38
    ghostly voices, 166
    Giardina as Appalachian novelist, 8
    Giardina as political novelist, 13
    Giardina as theological novelist, 17, 187
    and Giardina hero, 167, 177
    heeding the call, 121–37
    from history to fiction, 114–17
    Mozart's Mass in C Minor, 118–20
    overview, 112–14
    plays within plays, 120–21
    publication, 7
    reviews, 113–14, 116
salvation, 82, 181–83, 199n55
Sanders, Adam, 195n50

Sandino, Augusto Calderon, 109
Sanks, T. Howland, 75
Savage, Lon, 53, 83
See, Carolyn, 84
sexuality, 105, 149–50
Shakespeare, William
    As You Like It, 147
    and *Fallam's Secret*, 146, 147, 151
    and *Good King Harry*, 21, 22, 28, 40
    Henry V, 22, 147
    influence on Giardina, 3, 4, 87
Shurbutt, Sylvia Bailey, 113, 172, 195n39
Simon, Clea, 113, 116
sin, 38, 48, 77, 92, 158
Slane, Craig J., 113
slavery, 72
Smith, Lee, 12, 112
social class, 9, 172–73, 188
Social Gospel movement, 75
social justice, 142, 182
social realism, 14
Sojourners (magazine), 4, 178
Sojourners Fellowship, 4, 5, 15, 17, 75, 77, 78, 195n47
Sophocles, *Antigone*, 178
speech patterns, 55–56, 86–87
spirituality, 152–58, 179, 194–95n39
Still, James, 50, 56, 186
Still: The Journal, 11, 16, 160
Storming Heaven (Giardina), 50–83
    afterword and *The Unquiet Earth*, 83, 84, 89
    aspects of literary form, 55–70
    Battle of Blair Mountain, 52–53, 186
    challenge of the vernacular, 55–56
    child narrator, 101
    Christian Universalism, 80–83
    colonization of the coalfields, 53–55
    critical reputation, 21
    fundamentalism, 107
    ghostly voices, 166
    Giardina as Appalachian novelist, 7–8, 186
    Giardina as political novelist, 12, 13
    Giardina as theological novelist, 17
    and Giardina hero, 167–68, 176, 177, 180, 181
    Giardina themes, 187, 188–89

from history to fiction, 51–55
liberation theology, 73–79, 108
multiple points of view, 57–70, 86–87
overview, 50
reviews, 186
speaking truth to power, 83
theology in the coalfields, 71–83
writing of, 5
Stowe, Harriet Beecher, 56

theology
  Appalachian fiction and religion, 185, 186
  Celtic spirituality, 152–58
  Christian Universalism, 80–83, 195n60
  in *Fallam's Secret*, 141–44, 152–58
  Giardina as theological novelist, 14–20, 112–13, 185–89
  liberation theology, 73–79, 81, 108–9, 195n47
  in *Saints and Villains*, 123, 124, 125–26, 135
  and spirituality, 194–95n39
  in *Storming Heaven*, 71–83
  universal salvation, 181–83, 188, 195n60
  in *The Unquiet Earth*, 106–10
thin places, 154–55
Thomas Aquinas, 34
Thoreau, Henry David, 14, 94
time, 139, 140, 143–44, 180
Tritel, Barbara, 21, 22
Twain, Mark, 56

unconscious Christianity, 169
United Mine Workers, 12, 51, 52, 77
universalism, 80–83, 195n60
universal salvation, 181–83, 188, 199n55
Unquiet Earth, The (Giardina), 84–111
  Appalachian apocalypse, 110–11
  Appalachian resistance, 89–93
  aspects of literary form, 86–89
  child narrator, 101
  critical reputation, 21
  Giardina as Appalachian novelist, 8
  and Giardina hero, 167, 176
  from history to fiction, 85–86
  landscape as character, 93–97

overview, 84
responses to colonization, 89–106
and *Storming Heaven* afterword, 83, 84, 89
theology, 106–10
vernacular dialect, 56
writing of, 5

vengeance, 81–82, 83
vernacular dialect, 55–56, 86–87
violence, 43, 45, 78
Virginia Theological Seminary, 4, 14, 75
voices
  in *Emily's Ghost*, 162–67
  in *Storming Heaven*, 57–70

Wales, 9, 23, 28–29, 36, 45, 95
Wallis, Jim, 75
war, 36–37, 41, 45–48, 126, 188
Waste Land, The (Eliot), 87, 88, 89
water imagery, 88, 96
Weiner, Eric, 155
Wesley, John, 4
Westmoore, Jean, 160
West Virginia, 1, 6–8, 51–52, 93, 159, 186–87
West Virginia Mine Wars, 51, 52
West Virginia State College, 6, 7
Wilson, David E., 61, 105
Wink, Walter, 189
women's roles
  in *Emily's Ghost*, 167–68, 173–75, 178
  in *Fallam's Secret*, 141, 143, 148–52, 153
  and Giardina hero, 167–68, 173–75, 177–78
  in *Storming Heaven*, 59–60, 67–70
Woolman, John, 169
Wright, N. T., 158
Wuthering Heights (Brontë), 60, 160, 163, 166
Wyatt, Neil, 160
Wycliffe, John, 39

Yeats, William Butler, 177
Yount, John, 50, 56, 186

Zaleski, Jeff, 140

www.ingramcontent.com/pod-product-compliance
Lightning Source LLC
Chambersburg PA
CBHW030650230426
43665CB00011B/1032